SUBJECTIVITY, OBJECTIVITY, & INTERSUBJECTIVITY

SUBJECTIVITY, OBJECTIVITY, & INTERSUBJECTIVITY

A NEW PARADIGM FOR RELIGION AND SCIENCE

JOSEPH A. BRACKEN, SJ

With a Foreword by William R. Stoeger, SJ

TEMPLETON FOUNDATION PRESS
West Conshohocken, Pennsylvania

Templeton Foundation Press
300 Conshohocken State Road, Suite 550
West Conshohocken, PA 19428
www.templetonpress.org

Designed and typeset by Kachergis Book Design

*Templeton Foundation Press helps intellectual leaders and others learn
about science research on aspects of realities, invisible and intangible.
Spiritual realities include unlimited love, accelerating creativity, wor-
ship, and the benefits of purpose in persons and in the cosmos.*

Library of Congress Cataloging-in-Publication Data
Bracken, Joseph A.
 Subjectivity, objectivity, and intersubjectivity : a new paradigm for
religion and science / Joseph A. Bracken.
 p. cm.
 Includes bibliographical references (p.   ) and index.
 ISBN-13: 978-1-59947-152-5 (alk. paper)
 ISBN-10: 1-59947-152-3 (alk. paper)
 1. Religion and science.   2. Subjectivity.   3. Objectivity.
4. Intersubjectivity.   I. Title.
BL240.3.B695 2009
215—dc22

                          2008031300

Printed in the United States of America

09   10   11   12   13   14   10   9   8   7   6   5   4   3   2   1

To the many students, colleagues, and friends who have shared with me the fun of thinking out of the box this book is affectionately dedicated.

CONTENTS

FOREWORD

The knowledge and understanding of reality deriving from the natural sciences dominates our contemporary culture and strongly influences all its other components, including ethics and religion. That is simply because it has been and promises to continue being so incredibly perceptive and successful—in revealing the amazing dimensions and intricacies of nature and the universe and in applying them technologically. It even tends to displace all other forms of inquiry and belief—frequently inducing us to consider it to be without limits. Fortunately, in recent decades there have been a contingent of scholars representing the sciences themselves, philosophy, theology, and related disciplines who have begun to contextualize and relate this rapidly expanding scientific understanding of our universe and of ourselves to these other realms of knowledge and understanding in more profound and enlightened ways. The most challenging and important areas where this common quest seeks consonance and compatibility is with philosophy and theology. Though significant progress has been achieved, a great deal remains to be done—particularly in crafting a more adequate philosophical infrastructure for relating scientific and theological understandings.

In this book, Joseph Bracken has provided an outstanding contribution to this crucial long-range project. With extraordinary care and critical acumen, he opens an avenue toward fashioning a more adequate metaphysics for a dynamic richly emergent reality uniting the subject and object in an overarching intersubjectivity, inspired by and consistent with an expansive, radically incarnational Trinitarian theology—and potentially with theologies of several other non-Christian religions. This is a metaphysics partially based also on Whitehead's process thought, but with a number of crucial modifications which attune it to contemporary scientific understandings, as well as to the very best in Christian systematic theology and spirituality.

Focusing on the perennial central philosophical enigma of the One and Many and its diverse implications—including the universal and the particular, subject and object, reality and our perception of it—Bracken critically engages and sifts through the principal insights and approaches of Western philosophy to its present resolution. In the course of his search, he draws strongly on the most compelling landmark paradigms of recent scientific advances—including those of quantum theory, relativity, evolutionary biology, systems theory, and the physics of complex systems—as well as on the insights of Trinitarian theology.

From these insights he gradually distills the beginnings of a process metaphysics which is based on relatively autonomous agency at every level within a enveloping field of enabling creativity—within which the emergence of completely novel "societies" or systems, each with its own unique collective agency, is encouraged. Such a universe is radically intersubjective and accommodates the prolific interplay of both bottom-up and top-down causality. As Bracken himself mentions, in a sense it might be called "an emergent non-duality" approach to metaphysics. There is the enveloping dynamic field of creativity—the nature or dynamic principle of the Creator-God if you wish—which is both transcendent towards and profoundly immanent in all that it enables. What emerges, nevertheless, possesses its own individuality and freedom of action.

In envisioning and sketching this approach, Bracken provides a very attractive and carefully constructed set of philosophical hypotheses or models—which is by no means final or complete. Much remains to be done. Refinement and modification through further critical philosophical reflection and discussion, and through further detailed confrontation with, and interpretative application to, both scientific and theological understandings must continue. However, in this book he has provided us with secure beginnings and a profound and clear vision for constructing a metaphysics adequate to our burgeoning scientific, theological, and spiritual understanding.

WILLIAM R. STOEGER, SJ
Vatican Observatory Group
The University of Arizona
Tucson, Arizona
October 9, 2008

ACKNOWLEDGMENTS

My thanks to Templeton Foundation Press and Laura G. Barrett, its associate publisher, for agreeing to publish this book that is partly an intellectual autobiography and partly an argument for a new metaphysics based on the notion of universal intersubjectivity. Creative projects such as this do not always find a warm welcome from editors understandably preoccupied with the "bottom line" in their publishing ventures. Likewise, my special thanks to Natalie Lyons Silver who, as managing editor of the Press, worked with me to make the manuscript more coherent and reader-friendly. Likewise, I am grateful for the editorial policy of two religion and science journals, *Theology and Science* and *Zygon*, which allowed me to use revised versions of articles published in these journals as chapters 10 and 11 in this book ("Of Particles and Fields," *Theology and Science* 5 [2007]: 47–56, and "Space and Time from a Neo-Whiteheadian Perspective," *Zygon* 42 [2007]: 41–48). A condensed version of chapter 9 of this book is available on the website of the Metanexus Institute as an electronic transcript of a talk given at the ninth International Metanexus Conference in Madrid in July 2008. My thanks to Elizabeth Kenny of the Metanexus Institute and to Templeton Foundation Press for approving this dual publication. Still another reworking of chapter 9 will be included in a book of essays, *Applied Process Thought—II* edited by Marc Dibben and Rebecca Newton, to be published by Ontos Verlag in 2009.

SUBJECTIVITY, OBJECTIVITY,
& INTERSUBJECTIVITY

INTRODUCTION

In recent decades a great many books and articles have been published dealing with the relationship between religion and science, some by Christian theologians and proponents of the other world religions, others by scientists newly interested in the religious implications of their discipline. Yet, reviewing the history of Western civilization, one realizes that dialogue between representatives of religion and science has always been present and in some sense a focus of interest among educated people. The difference between the present and the past within this ongoing discussion, however, is quite important. Whereas in the ancient world and above all in medieval times, before the natural sciences as we now know them took shape, religiously and scientifically oriented people shared a common worldview or philosophy: the metaphysics of Plato and Aristotle as adapted to one's antecedent understanding of the Bible and the teaching of the church. At the present time, however, for a variety of reasons there is no such philosophical common ground. In the early modern era, for example, natural scientists like Galileo and Newton set forth a new, empirically based methodology for their research and writing that seemed to dispense with metaphysical speculation. Theologians, on the contrary, for the most part still held fast to the basic principles of Plato and Aristotle in their defense of the Christian faith. So the gap between proponents of religion and science grew larger over the centuries, with each side insisting on its necessary autonomy and independence of the truth claims of the other side.

What holds promise for the future is that both sides now seem to recognize the need for a new worldview or underlying philosophical conceptuality. Recent advances in physics, chemistry, and biology (see below, chaps. 9 and 10) have led many natural scientists to question whether the mechanistic approach to physical reality espoused by Galileo and Newton is still adequate to explain all the empirical data within their disciplines. Likewise, philosophers and theologians in increasing numbers have begun to reevaluate the classical metaphysical attributes of God (e.g., immutability, omniscience, omnipotence) in the light of an evolutionary understanding of reality (see chap. 11). As yet, of course, there is no agreement on the basic principles or theoretical presuppositions of such a new worldview other than the commonly shared conviction that it must somehow be based on dialogue or the willingness to listen to one another from a variety of different perspectives. Truth is thus more and more commonly seen as an ideal or long-term goal for all to work at together rather than as the secure possession of one group over all the others.

The aim of this book is to set forth for this sustained dialogue between experts in the humanities and the sciences a new paradigm that is based on a new understanding of subjectivity, objectivity, and intersubjectivity. These terms, however, are to be understood within a cosmic rather than a strictly interpersonal context. In other words, subjectivity, objectivity, and intersubjectivity must likewise be at work in the operation of Nature as well as in human discourse. Thus understood, what I am proposing is a new understanding of the relationship between the One and the Many on all the different levels of existence and activity within this world. The Many are the virtually infinite number of individual subjects of experience that exist at any given moment. The One is invariably some objective form of coherence and order produced from moment to moment through the ongoing dynamic interrelation of these multiple subjects of experience. Intersubjectivity, accordingly, is the common denominator in our human understanding of the world around us, both the starting point and the goal for resolving the tension between subjectivity and objectivity, the Many and the One, at all the different levels of existence and activity within Nature as well as within the world of human discourse and action.

To make this clear, however, it will be necessary first to review the differing solutions to the problem of the One and the Many, objectivity and subjectivity, proposed by some of the great philosophical minds of the Western world over the centuries and then by degrees to introduce my own process-oriented approach to reality, which is based on the philosophy of Alfred North Whitehead but at key points notably departs from it. In brief, I argue that Whitehead had a revolutionary insight into what is meant by the Many, the reality of concrete particulars, when he proposed in his masterwork *Process and Reality* that "the final real things of which the world is made up" are actual entities or actual occasions, that is, momentary self-constituting subjects of experience.[1] True individuals are then always self-constituting subjects of experience; they make themselves to be what they are by their own conscious (or more often unconscious) decision.

Yet, given this new understanding of the Many, Whitehead in my judgment failed to come up with a corresponding new metaphysical analysis of the nature of the One. As a result, his metaphysical scheme remained committed to philosophical atomism. As he himself says, "The ultimate metaphysical truth is atomism. The creatures are atomic."[2] Yet if physical reality is ultimately atomic in character, then the One can logically never be anything but an aggregate or collection of discrete individuals. Some aggregates, to be sure, are more tightly organized than others. But an aggregate by definition is an implicit denial of the distinctive reality of the One as something different from and other than the Many, its component parts or members.

Whitehead's insight into the reality of the Many as momentary self-constituting subjects of experience, to be sure, still allows one to evaluate and critique the work of many of his predecessors in the history of Western philosophy, each of whom sought in his own way to solve the problem of the One and the Many, universality and particularity. But, even with this new insight, the job is only half done. Atomism, whether it be material atomism or in Whitehead's case spiritual atomism, is an implicit admission of failure in dealing with this distinctive reality of the One. Moreover, the consequences of simply acquiescing in a doctrine of philosophical atomism are far-reaching. In one form or another it has been a dominant factor in the alleged conflict between religion and science since the beginning of the modern era.

Many religiously oriented people, for example, are deeply suspicious of the notion of evolution because it seems to call into question their traditional understanding of the God-world relationship. If Nature on its own can over time produce higher forms of organization and complexity, what is the role of a Creator God, if any at all, in this cosmic process?[3] Isn't God needed to bring the many things of this world into an overarching unity or providential plan of action? For their part, many natural scientists find themselves puzzling over how an empirical effect can be greater than its antecedent natural cause (or causes). Thus they, too, are consciously or unconsciously wrestling with the problem of the One and the Many. Can the One emerge out of the ongoing interplay of the Many and represent something genuinely new and different from its component parts? If not, then nothing really new ever happens. Nature is then equivalently a cosmic machine with everything explainable in terms of predictable interactions between subatomic particles. No reference to God as Creator or Architect of the cosmic process is needed.

Accordingly, a rethinking of the metaphysical scheme of Alfred North Whitehead in terms of a new worldview based on subjectivity, objectivity, and intersubjectivity might be what is needed if experts in the humanities and the sciences are to ever find common ground. Yet one cannot simply say to the reader, "This is the way it is; take it or leave it." So in the early chapters of this book I offer a cursory review of the history of Western philosophy in the light of the problem of the One and the Many insofar as it comes to focus in terms of what is meant by objectivity and subjectivity, universality and particularity. Admittedly, in undertaking such an overview of Western philosophy, one has to pick and choose among the philosophers to be considered. My choice was dictated in large part by my own intellectual history. I chose to concentrate on those thinkers who notably influenced me in my own intellectual journey toward the position that I hold today.

Yet for that same reason I do not attend in this overview to the work of many North American philosophers who flourished at the beginning of the twentieth century (e.g., William James, Charles Sanders Peirce, John Dewey et al.). My own training years ago for the master's degree in philosophy focused on Plato and Aristotle in the ancient world, Thomas Aquinas and other scholastic thinkers in the medieval period, and early modern European thinkers up to the time of David Hume and Immanuel Kant. Then for my doctoral work in philosophy I did further work in Kant and the German Idealists as the basis for a dissertation on freedom and de-terminism in the writings of F. W. J. Schelling. As a side interest, I became quite interested in the writings of Martin Heidegger, whose influence at the University of Freiburg in Breisgau during my stu-dent years there in the 1960s was still very strong. To be sure, one major American philosopher, Josiah Royce with his late work *The Problem of Christianity*, prompted me in my postgraduate years to undertake a deeper study of the nature of community and the pos-sibility of a new social ontology based on Royce's argument that communities are higher-order, specifically socially organized reali-ties distinct from the human beings that compose them.[4] But even then contemporary European thinkers on the subject of commu-nity (e.g., Martin Buber, Emmanuel Levinas, and others) remained the focus of my research until I was introduced in the 1970s to the philosophy of the Anglo-American philosopher Alfred North Whitehead and the tradition of process philosophy and theology in the United States.

I was eventually disappointed by Whitehead's failure (in my judgment) to think through more carefully what he meant by the notion of "society" in distinction from "actual occasion." But by this time I had begun to realize that working out my own metaphysics of universal intersubjectivity with its emphasis on Whiteheadian "societies" as other than and different from their constituent actual occasions would be my own contribution both to the process tradition and to the broader history of Western philosophy. I leave to the reader the judgment of whether this was in the end a worthwhile project.

I

THE INDIVIDUAL IN A WORLD
OF UNIVERSALS

The Swiss philosopher Karl Jaspers suggested many years ago in *The Origin and Goal of History* that humankind went through an "axial period" from 800 BCE to 200 BCE during which time human beings began to free themselves from a tribal mentality, in which the interests of the individual were routinely subordinated to the survival needs of the group, to a new sense of individual self-awareness and personal liberty.[1] Among those "axial" thinkers were Socrates and his disciple/scribe Plato. Certainly the analogy of the cave in Book VII of Plato's *Republic* has had an enduring influence (for better or for worse) on the subsequent history of Western philosophy.[2] The dualism between appearance and reality—that is, shadows on the wall of the cave representing ever-changing sense experience versus the universal forms of things seen in the light of the sun (human reason)—has been both enthusiastically embraced and strongly resisted over the intervening centuries. Idealists and materialists have argued ever since about what's really real and the ultimate source of human knowledge. Scientists, for example, have tended to be implicit materialists because of their insistence on empirical verification of abstract theories. Humanists, on the contrary, in their ongoing search for meaning and value in human life, have tended to be outspoken idealists.

In this chapter I indicate the historical roots of this contemporary clash of cultures within the philosophy of Plato and Aristotle in the ancient world and in the heated debates among medieval thinkers about the status of universals. Plato was understandably fascinated by the newly discovered power of the human mind to penetrate beyond appearances to the form or essence of the thing in question and then to use that elusive definition to put order and coherence into one's personal and community life. Aristotle, being by temperament more empirically oriented, converted the Forms that for Plato existed apart from material reality into substantial forms, the inner principle of existence and activity for individual things. But the substantial form still invariably represented what the individual thing had in common with other similarly constituted things and not how it was genuinely different from those other things. For example, if one seeks to determine what makes human beings different from one another, the alleged substantial form (humanity) is of little value. All the distinguishing physical characteristics of a given individual (e.g., being tall or short, fat or thin, with black, brown, white, or yellow skin) are in Aristotelian terms "accidents," contingent properties that apply to many other human beings. The particular "thisness" of that individual, that which makes him or her as an individual different from other human beings, somehow remains beyond rational comprehension.[3] Hence, even though he was much more aware of the importance of individual things than Plato, Aristotle too lived in a mental world dominated by the search for universals in the world around him.

Still another reason that Aristotle was preoccupied with the issue of universals, of course, was his interest in explaining the reality of change in the world of nature in terms of universal causal principles. W. T. Jones comments as follows:

Aristotle believed that in order to understand any individual thing we must know four aspects of it, each of which operates to determine its nature. We must know (1) the material out of which it is composed (the material cause); (2) the motion or action that began it (efficient cause); (3) the function or purpose for which it exists (the final cause); and (4) the form it actualizes and by which it fulfils its purpose (the formal cause).[4]

While Aristotle certainly wanted to explain the reality of individual things in terms of these causal principles, he found himself once again dealing with the individual existent in very general terms. Admittedly, to see something in terms of its relation to everything around it is a great help in understanding what it is in itself or in its particularity. But its individual "thisness" still remains elusive to full rational comprehension, given its explanation in terms of causal principles applicable to everything else that comes to be and ceases to be.

Why is this the case? Does it represent an inevitable limitation in human knowledge, or is something else at work here? Here I introduce a key component in my overall thesis for this book, namely, the distinction between objects of thought and subjects of experience. Objects of thought are invariably universal in scope since they abstract from the full reality of an individual existent and focus on some attribute or property that the individual shares in common with others of the same class. You and I as objects of thought for one another are both human beings; being human is what we have in common on the level of abstract thought. But as individual subjects of experience, you and I are quite different; we each have our individual approach to being human as manifest in our words and actions. Moreover, I cannot fully understand you in your particularity without becoming you and thereby losing my own personal identity. The same, of course, is true for you in your efforts to understand and deal with me.

By "subject of experience," of course, I do not mean a grammatical subject of predication in a sentence but an existential subject that is both active and passive in its relations with the world around it. That is, it is first receptive to its environment and then has an impact upon that environment by reason of its response to that initial stimulus. Unlike an object of thought, therefore, which has a determinate reality in the mind of the observer, an existential subject or subject of experience is indeterminate since it never stays precisely the same from moment to moment. Its identity keeps changing as it receives new environmental influences and responds to them in ever new ways. Each time that it responds, of course, it becomes for the moment determinate and can be an object of perception or reflection for other subjects and even for itself if it possesses self-awareness. But proper to the notion of subject of experience is potentiality, the power to be other than what it is right now. By way of contrast, proper to the notion of object of thought is de facto actuality, determinate reality lacking in potentiality or the power to change.

But is this not an unnecessary dichotomy? Is not everything in this world necessarily both subject and object? Agreed, but which of the two enjoys ontological priority over the other? Depending upon one's choice here, a radically different worldview emerges. As I elaborate in later chapters, the Anglo-American philosopher Alfred North Whitehead clearly gave priority to subjects over objects. That is, in his major work *Process and Reality*, he claimed that "the final real things of which the world is made up" are actual entities, momentary self-constituting subjects of experience.[5] Each such subject of experience has an objective component, its reality as a "superject" once its process of self-constitution is completed.[6] But, says Whitehead, once it is self-constituted and becomes a superject, it ceases to exist as a subject and a new subject of experience must take its place in order for the cosmic process as a whole to continue.

All this is explained in greater detail in subsequent chapters of this book. For now, it is only important to note that, while Plato and Aristotle were surely aware of their own individual subjectivity, their own reality as ongoing subjects of experience, unlike Whitehead they evidently gave ontological priority to objectivity and actuality in the world around them rather than subjectivity and potentiality. Both, to be sure, recognized the fact of change in the world of nature and tried to deal with it in different ways. Plato relegated change to the world of appearances, in sharp contrast to reality as represented by the mental world of the Forms. Aristotle, as noted above, was more empirically oriented and thus more accepting of the inevitability of change and becoming in this world. But in virtue of his causal scheme sketched above, Aristotle focused on the goal or final end for all changes, a state of permanent being or rest in which the entity in question would finally achieve full actuality. Hence, Plato and Aristotle both gave ontological priority to objectivity over subjectivity in their respective worldviews and found themselves as a result unable philosophically to explain the reality of the individual existent in objective terms. They implicitly lived in a mental world of universals or intelligible forms, and the individual existent (e.g., themselves as individual human beings and other subjects of experience) could not be adequately defined and explained in terms of objective characteristics shared with other subjects of experience.

Presumably Plato and Aristotle felt no frustration on this point since their respective philosophical agendas lay in another direction. Plato was eager to escape the world of appearances so as better to contemplate the unchanging world of intelligible forms. Aristotle was interested in the individual things of this world but only insofar as their coming and going (generation and corruption) could be explained in terms of his causal scheme. Yet causal explanations are always formulated in terms of laws or universal principles. The individual existent is only important as an instance of the empirical verification or falsification of some universal principle. That is, if the causal principle seems to explain the existence and activity of an individual existent a sufficient number of times, then the principle is considered empirically verified and treated as a law. If anomalies occur in which the causal principle seems not to be operative, then the causal principle is totally abandoned or at least significantly modified. In both cases, however, the individual existent in its particularity is ignored. In a thought-world dominated by the working of causal principles, its unique particularity is a distraction. In order to rise to the level of a causal explanation, one has to ignore individuating characteristics of the individual existent and focus on what the individual existent has in common with other individual existents under similar circumstances. Attention to the unique particularity of the individual existent is best left to artists of various kinds rather than to philosopher-scientists in search of universal principles.

Moving now to the thought-world of medieval thinkers, one can say that one of the major issues in that era was clearly the reality of universals, with realists and nominalists taking radically different positions on the matter. As W. T. Jones points out in his history of Western philosophy, however, early medieval thinkers were not well versed in the writings of Plato and Aristotle. In late antiquity Boethius had translated *Introduction to Aristotle's Categories*, written by a disciple of Plotinus, Porphyry, together with a modest number of Aristotle's own works on logic, and it was largely Porphyry's text that became the starting point for early medieval speculation on the nature of universals.[7] Boethius himself distinguished between "composition" and "abstraction" in the formation of new ideas from sense experience: "Composition (as in the composition of horse and man to form the centaur) produces a false idea, whereas abstraction produces an idea which is true [e.g., the idea of a straight line], even though the thing conceived does not exist extra-mentally in a state of abstraction or separation."[8] Boethius thus prepared the way for an Aristotelian approach to the doctrine of universals, namely, that universals are real but do not exist outside the mind in the same way that they exist in the mind. Ironically his initial successors in early medieval times were nearly all Platonists, holding to a doctrine of ultra-realism in this matter. Humanity, for example, in their view must exist outside the mind in the same way that it exists within the mind, namely, as the unchanging reality of which human beings are the changing and imperfect representations.

John Scotus Erigena, for example, and other Christian Platonists seem to have held this opinion even though logically this implies a form of monism. In the end, only one universal human being exists, with all individual men and women as its partial embodiments. For that matter, if God is identified with Being, then only God exists.[9] Inevitably, there arose among other medieval thinkers a reaction in the form of conceptualism (universals exist only in the mind) or even pure nominalism (universals are words used to organize experience of individual entities).[10] Frequently cited as a nominalist is

Roscelin (c. 1050–1120) although, as Frederick Copleston notes,[11] it is hard to know what Roscelin really held about the reality of universals, given that his views are only known through the writings of his opponents, for example, Anselm of Canterbury, John of Salisbury, and Peter Abelard.

Peter Abelard (1079–1142) in his student years listened to the lectures of both Roscelin and William of Champeaux, an ultra-realist, and sought to find a middle ground between them. Although accused by Bernard of Clairvaux of being a covert nominalist, Abelard clearly wanted to distinguish between words as physical sounds and words as symbols—that is, as logical referents to something real apart from the mind of the individual human being. Through a process of abstraction, "The nature [humanity] is set free, as it were, from all individuality and is considered in such a way that it bears no special relation to any particular individual but can be predicated of all individual men."[12] Ultra-realism in the treatment of universal ideas is thereby refuted since the word has an objective reference to something real that exists one way within the human mind and quite another way in things outside the mind. Within the mind it is an intelligible form applicable to many individuals; in sensible things it serves as a principle of existence and activity for individual entities in their particularity.

Two other moderate realists of the twelfth century were Gilbert of Porrée and John of Salisbury, both of whom agreed with Abelard that universals exist one way in the human mind and another way in sensible things apart from the mind. But in terms of the basic issue of this chapter—namely, the reality of the individual existent in a world of universals—Gilbert is more interesting, for he distinguished between logical universals devoid of all individuating characteristics and concrete universals, universal forms that have become individuated within particular entities. There is the form of humanity in general and the form of humanity in the person of Socrates.[13] Pushed to its logical extreme, of course, this distinction between logical and concrete universals results in conceptualism, the belief that only particular individuals exist and that universals have no objective referent outside the mind of the observer. Yet, in my judgment, better than others Gilbert realized that the full intelligibility of the individual entity eludes explanation in terms of universal concepts applicable in principle to all the members of a given class. As Copleston comments, Gilbert's doctrine of universals was heavily criticized, but on theological, not strictly philosophical, grounds. In distinguishing between God (*Deus*) and divinity (*Divinitas*), he seemed to introduce a fourth reality, a semi-independent divine nature over and above the divine persons, into the traditional doctrine of the Trinity.[14]

With his customary precision and attention to detail, Thomas Aquinas mediated in his *Commentary on the Sentences* of Peter Lombard between the ultra-realist and the conceptualist position on the nature of universals.[15] There is, in the first place, the universal prior to instantiation in individual creatures (*universale ante rem*). In this sense, the universal is an idea in the mind of God, one of the multiple ways in which the unitary reality of God is revealed in creation. Then there is, second, the universal as the essence or principle of operation of individual entities in this world (*universale in re*). Third, there is the universal as an abstract concept in the mind of the human observer (*universale post rem*). As Copleston comments, the foundation for Thomas' understanding of the doctrine of universals is the universal as existing in individual entities.[16] Given this presupposition, one can derive by a process of abstraction the universal concept existing in the mind of the human observer and one can infer the prior existence of the universal as a possible created imitation of the divine essence in the mind of God.

What is still missing in Thomas' account of universals, of course, is Gilbert's distinction between logical and concrete universals in sensible things (*in re*). Thomas is content to claim that the essence (e.g., humanity) is the same in all entities of a given class (human beings) but numerically different. But is it only a numerical difference, or is something more involved? After all, human beings differ from one another not only numerically but also in terms of various physical characteristics (size, weight, skin color, etc.). Likewise, there are still more subtle differences between human beings on a psychological level, which constitute their true individuality and difference from one another. Given that each human being has a personal history and grows to maturity in an environment peculiarly its own, Thomas' reference to simply numerical differences between individual entities belonging to the same class seems somewhat simplistic when applied to human beings and other higher-order animal species where psychological differences play such a prominent role in individuation. Thomas, in other words, is not mistaken in claiming that all entities sharing a common essence differ numerically, but it is only the starting point for an explanation of what it means to be an individual member of a given species.

Here one might object that this is simply a caricature of Thomas' full position on the reality of universals. Thomas, for example, likewise claims that universal ideas are not the goal of human cognition but only a means to human knowledge of the individual existent. As Copleston notes, "The mind has the power of reflecting on its own modifications and so can turn the concept into an object; but it is only secondarily an object of knowledge, primarily it is the instrument of knowledge."[17] That is, through the senses the mind perceives an individual corporeal entity and forms a phantasm or mental image of that sensible reality. Then, in virtue of its agent intellect, it abstracts the intelligible species or universal concept from the phantasm and imprints it upon the passive intellect. Finally, in the act of knowing the mind returns to the phantasm and knows the individual corporeal entity in and through the intelligible species or universal concept.[18]

Human knowledge, therefore, is of individual entities, albeit through universal concepts. Abstraction of the universal concept from the phantasm or mental image of the corporeal entity is necessary not because it is singular but because it is corporeal,[19] for the human mind is incapable of knowing material things in their materiality or full particularity. In principle, it could know a singular immaterial reality (e.g., the mind or soul) directly through its immaterial intelligible form. But even here Thomas concedes that the human mind does not know itself except in and through its act of intellection, for only what is in act is knowable.[20] The human mind simply as a potency apart from the act of knowing is unknowable.

One can only admire the subtlety of Thomas' explanation of human cognition in terms of the Aristotelian doctrine of act and potency. But the basic problem of knowing individual entities in and through their universal forms still remains. If materiality is the obstacle here, why cannot the human mind directly know itself as an immaterial principle of existence and activity? Aquinas claims that only what is in act is knowable; the mind is only a potency, not an actuality, and thus cannot be known as an object of perception or thought. But don't we know ourselves, the inner workings of our minds and hearts, even though we cannot in this way reduce ourselves to an object of perception and thought? Do we not also intuitively know other people, their ways of thinking and acting, without being able to give an abstract definition of who they are in distinction from other people?

What may well be at stake here is the distinction between subjects of experience and objects of thought which was presented earlier in this chapter. Subjects of experience and objects of thought obviously both possess some degree of actuality, but only subjects of experience likewise have the power to become other than what they are here and now. In this sense, subjectivity eludes full objectification as a fixed object of perception or thought. Yet we still have a reasonably reliable understanding of ourselves and other human beings as subjects of ongoing experience. There are, thus, evidently many different ways to grow in knowledge of the people and things in our lives, and Aquinas' focus on the knowledge of people and things through abstraction of their universal form or essence is only one of them.

Before bringing this chapter to a close, I review here the thought of two other medieval thinkers on the status of universals and the problem of individuation. The first is John Duns Scotus, born shortly before Thomas Aquinas died, and likewise a monastic but a member of the Franciscan rather than the Dominican order. This difference in their intellectual training plus a more critical attitude in general toward the philosophy of Aristotle in the late thirteenth century may well have influenced Duns Scotus' critique of Aquinas on the nature of human knowing.[21] While Scotus and Aquinas both agreed with Aristotle that metaphysics is based on the abstraction of universal forms or essences from material things, Scotus differed from Aquinas in maintaining that the human mind nevertheless has an intuitive intellectual knowledge of the individual existent as an existing reality.[22] The individual existent is, accordingly, intelligible in itself, and the current human need for abstraction to obtain its essence or universal form is limited to life in this world.[23] For, once in heaven, human beings will know God and one another directly as individuals, just as even now God and the angels know each of us as individual existents. Unlike Aquinas, therefore, Scotus maintained that the proper object of human knowledge is not in the first place the universal form or essence but the individual existent in its particularity or individual way of being, albeit only in a confused manner.

Scotus, to be sure, then confused the issue by claiming that the particularity of the individual material existent is itself the effect of still another universal form, *haecceitas* or "thisness."[24] How can a universal, something applicable to many individuals, be at the same time the principle of individuation for any one individual, its difference from other individuals in the same class?[25] Scotus here reveals the preoccupation of medieval thinkers with the Platonic-Aristotelian belief that scientific knowledge must be grounded in essences or universal intelligible forms. But to Scotus' credit, better than Aquinas he realized that objective knowledge of the physical world has to take account of the de facto individuality of material existents and not simply of their a priori relationship to one another in terms of universal forms or essences.

Still another way in which Scotus differed from Aquinas and thereby unconsciously set the stage for subsequent developments in the history of Western philosophy was his insistence on the primacy of the will over the intellect (love over knowledge) in the human psyche. Whereas for Aquinas the human will was considered to be the rational appetite that necessarily chooses what is good but only subsequent upon the judgment of the intellect on the relation of any particular good to the Ultimate Good (beatitude),[26] for Scotus the will is a free potentiality (*libera potentia*) to choose between alternatives rather than a rational appetite dependent upon the final judgment of the intellect as to the good.[27] Thus, even though it still depends upon the mind for knowledge of what to choose, ultimately its decision is not based on reason—that is, the final practical judgment of the mind on the good in question—but on its own spontaneity or power to make a free choice. This is a significant departure from Aquinas' vision of a rationally ordered world in which everything acts according to its pre-given nature or essence.

Even more dramatic in this regard was Scotus' contention that the divine will holds priority over the divine mind. For, if the divine will rather than the divine mind is primary in God's providence for the world of creation, then most human acts have to be judged morally good or evil not in terms of reason or natural law but only insofar as God declares them to be morally good or evil. As Copleston points out, this is not to say that human morality is a matter of arbitrary choice on God's part.[28] Rather, says Scotus, God knows which actions are in conformity with human nature and which are not. But the moral obligation to do good and avoid evil derives from the divine will and not from the divine mind as revealed in the natures or essences of created things. Hence, under special circumstances God can dispense human beings from full observance of the secondary precepts of the biblical Decalogue or Ten Commandments (4–10), those pertaining to relations of human beings with one another rather than with God. Copleston concludes:

While, then, if we look at Scotus' philosophy by itself, we must allow that his moral doctrine is not that of arbitrary divine authoritarianism, we must also allow, if we look at the historical development of thought, that his moral doctrine helped to prepare the way for that of Ockham, in whose eyes, the moral law, including the whole decalogue, is the arbitrary creation of the divine will.[29]

It is easy to critique Scotus here for introducing a dangerous form of voluntarism or even irrationality into the medieval worldview. But this would be to overlook a possible link between Scotus' belief in intuitive knowledge of singular existents and his emphasis here on will rather than mind as the key factor in understanding the behavior of human beings and even of God. In both cases Scotus seems to be protesting against what he sees as the rationalism of the philosophy of Aristotle with its emphasis on the natural order and as a result the relative neglect of the divinely revealed supernatural order grounded in God's love for creatures and the creatures' love for God and one another. Love, in other words, is directed to the individual existent, not to its universal form of intelligibility or essence. Thus, Scotus' focus on the individual existent with its unique self-constitution, based at least in some cases on spontaneous free choice, may have been consciously or unconsciously a groping after a more adequate worldview grounded in the experience of individual subjectivity rather than in the strict logic of universal objectivity. Like all medieval thinkers, however, Scotus still lived in a thought-world dominated by universal forms of intelligibility; his employment of the concept of *haecceitas* as explanation for the problem of individuation bears witness to his continued trust in the power of universals to unlock the secrets of Nature.

Yet it is also obvious that he was more attentive than Aquinas to subtle differences between the requirements of pure logic and the details of concrete experience in human life. Distinguishing, for example, between real and rational distinctions, Scotus postulated what he called a formal distinction with respect to the thing (*distinctio formalis a parte rei*).[30] Any given empirical reality is inevitably multidimensional so that it cannot be fully grasped in terms of a single essence or rational form of intelligibility.[31] Further distinctions must be made that have a basis in concrete experience but which the mind intuits rather than objectively defines. Thus, to be intelligible it is sufficient for forms to be distinct from and yet related to one another rather than really different from one another as in Aquinas' notion of a real distinction. Essence and existence, for example, are interrelated dimensions of one and the same concrete reality in both God and creatures. But, whereas in God these two different dimensions of the divine being are necessarily related, in creatures they are contingently related, operative only in virtue of the antecedent divine choice to bring into existence a world of creatures.

Where Aquinas postulated a real distinction between essence and existence in creatures,[32] Scotus thus simply proposed a formal distinction with respect to the thing (*in re*) between essence and existence in creatures.[33] Once the creature is brought into existence by the divine will, essence and existence are just as inseparable within the creature as they are within God. For the same reason, concludes Scotus, not form but being is the proper object of the mind, whether that mind be divine, angelic, or human, for "being" is a univocal rather than an analogical concept, as in Aquinas' scheme.[34] In every being there is the same existential identity of essence and existence, though in formally different ways within God, angels, and humans.[35]

The second late medieval thinker (besides Scotus) whose views are important for the medieval understanding of the doctrine of universals and the problem of individuation is William of Ockham. As Jones notes in *The Medieval Mind*, Ockham "developed those tendencies in Scotism that were deviations from Thomism to a point at which the Thomistic compromise [between faith and reason] was destroyed."[36] With respect to the doctrine of universals, for example, Ockham held that all natural knowledge (knowledge derived from experience rather than divine revelation) is knowledge of individuals. But, since science aims at general knowledge, we invent universals or what he called terms of second intention (e.g., man) which stand for similarities among the individuals designated by terms of first intention (names of individuals—e.g., Plato, Socrates, etc.). Thus, a universal "is an immense convenience, a great time-saver, but it is only a term—a tool used in reasoning scientifically. It is not a thing, and not an object of thought except in logic, in which, of course, it is simply a term of second intention."[37] This, of course, is conceptualism, perhaps even nominalism. In any case, it is clearly opposed to the various forms of realism discussed earlier in this chapter (e.g., ultra-realism allegedly to be found in the thought of John Scotus Erigena, critical realism as represented in different ways by Aquinas and Scotus).

The medieval worldview was even further undermined by what has been called "Ockham's razor": what can be explained on fewer principles is explained needlessly by more; or, in simpler terms, do not multiply entities beyond necessity.[38] Ockham used this principle to deny any extra-mental status whatsoever to universals; these terms are simply the result of the act of thinking. Attention should be paid exclusively to the individual material entities to which the universal term refers. Yet, as Jones points out, Ockham was still very much a scholastic thinker in his method of argument. That is, even when he was questioning the empirical status of universals, he reasoned deductively from concepts, not inductively from observation of individual entities.[39] Much more important for the future of Western philosophy was his insistence that reason and revelation represent totally different spheres of mental activity, each with its own methodology or mode of operation. In his mind, revelation was superior to reason and, given belief in divine omnipotence, could even contradict the dictates of reason.[40] But, in thus setting human reason free from reliance on divine revelation in its own mode of operation, Ockham opened the door for a far more secular and results-oriented approach to the world of nature that became characteristic of the thinking of early modern natural philosophers like Descartes and Locke (as we shall see in the next chapter).

2

THE TURN TO THE SUBJECT

The early modern period in Western philosophy was heavily influenced by concurrent developments in the philosophy of nature, notably the adoption of a new methodology for doing work in astronomy and physics and its impact on one's understanding of the nature of physical reality. Accordingly, before dealing with René Descartes on the continent and John Locke in England on the problem of objectivity and subjectivity, I review first the thought of three pioneers of this period in setting forth that new methodology for scientific research, namely, Francis Bacon, Galileo Galilei, and Isaac Newton. As we shall see, they were not completely of one mind on the procedure to be followed in doing scientific work, but all three differed considerably from what had been customary in pursuing the philosophy of nature during the medieval period.

Francis Bacon (1561–1626) was in many ways a bridge figure between the thought-world of medieval Scholasticism and the world of Galileo and other seventeenth-century scientists in Western Europe. Bacon recognized the limitations of Scholastic deductive logic—that is, simply reasoning from premises to conclusions without reference to actual experience.[1] He saw the need for more careful observation of what actually happens within the world of Nature. But he remained within the world of Scholastic thought in continuing to look for the underlying natures of the things of this world through a process of induction whereby he could isolate what is essential as opposed to what is purely contingent in the behavior or operation of the thing in question. Heat, for example, is always associated with motion, so that when motion ceases, heat also dissipates. Hence, given that not all types of motion involve production of heat, motion must be the genus of which heat is a species.[2]

What escaped Bacon's attention, however, was that under close inspection Nature is seen to be far more dynamic than previously suspected. Physical entities are not governed by timeless intelligible forms with invariant essential properties. Rather, those same entities are subject to gradual modification and sometimes dramatic change as a result of contingent events taking place within them and around them. Hence, as W. T. Jones comments, the focus in the philosophy of nature should be on physical events and the relations between them that can be empirically measured rather than on intelligible forms and their logical properties.[3] But measurement allows one to introduce mathematics with its focus on numbers and the ratios or proportions between them. This new mathematical approach to Nature escaped the notice of Bacon with his concentration on carefully cataloging and analyzing entities in terms of their physical appearances, but it was clearly the focus of attention for Galileo from his earliest days as a medical student in Pisa. For example, he is said to have intuitively grasped the "law of the pendulum" by noting the swings of a sanctuary lamp suspended from the ceiling of the cathedral in Pisa after it had been accidentally set in motion by a sacristan.[4]

Yet Galileo's brilliance as a mathematician may have blinded him to the limitations of this discipline in investigating physical reality. In the words of Alfred North Whitehead in *Science and the Modern World*, Galileo (and others after him) may have been guilty of the "fallacy of misplaced concreteness."[5] That is, they may have ended up treating their mathematical formulae as more real than the physical entities whose interactions they were supposed to describe. It is well known, for example, that for Galileo God was seen as the Great Geometer: "When God produces the world, He produces a thoroughly mathematical structure that obeys the laws of number, geometrical figure, and quantitative function. Nature is an *embodied mathematical system*."[6] But to follow through on this assumption, Galileo had to distinguish between primary qualities that can be given a precise mathematical description (e.g., motion, rest, size, weight, position in space) and secondary qualities (e.g., tastes, odors, colors, heat, sounds). The latter were seen as illusory except insofar as they could be reduced to quantitative analysis. In this way, both for God as Creator and for human beings in the investigation of Nature, the physical world is simply a well-ordered machine, quite contrary to the testimony of the senses about Nature as full of spontaneous activity and behavior on the part of the entities within it.

In this sense, Isaac Newton was more cautious than Galileo in his approach to physical reality. "Mathematics is the mind's sovereign tool of universal demonstration, but it must be adapted to the conditions of a dynamics that is regulated at every stage by the sensory evidence of motions."[7] Thus Newton allowed for experimental corrections to his mathematical calculations in a way that Galileo would have regarded as unnecessary. For Galileo, experimental verification only confirmed what he was already reasonably sure of in virtue of his mathematical deductions. Newton accepted Galileo's distinction between primary and secondary qualities in Nature and focused exclusively on the quantitatively measurable aspects of physical entities. But, for him, a failure to verify empirically a mathematical calculation meant that the mathematics somehow had to be revised so as better to fit the data of sense experience. Furthermore, he did not regard his laws of motion as the genuine efficient causes of what happens in Nature. They only offer the mathematical measure of what takes place between two bodies in mutual interaction. His celebrated law of gravity, for example, does not specify what gravity as a force within Nature is or where it comes from, but only how it de facto works between two bodies in terms of their respective masses and the distance between them. The deeper philosophical reason for the very existence of gravity in the universe goes beyond what Newton felt that he could analyze and explain in virtue of his own mathematically based methodology.[8]

As W. T. Jones comments, the net result of this new scientific approach to Nature was a dualism between matter and spirit, that is, between the world of Nature as "matter in motion" and the immaterial or spiritual reality both of the human mind and of God as the Creator of the material world.[9] That is, most philosophers of the early modern era were reluctant to follow the ancient philosopher Democritus and their own contemporary Thomas Hobbes in proposing a materialistic monism wherein spirit is an illusion and everything that exists is a contingent result of matter in motion.[10] Hence, while in dealing with the world of Nature they valued measurable primary qualities of entities as genuinely real and regarded the nonmeasurable secondary qualities of those same entities as illusory, in the world of the spirit (the human mind and the mind of God) their value-order was subtly reversed. Here spontaneity and creativity rather than mechanical regularity were thought to be key factors in understanding the activity of the spirit. But this still left open the question of the proper relation between matter and spirit. What is to replace the medieval synthesis of matter and spirit as different but still necessarily interrelated realities?

This is not to claim, of course, that the medieval thinkers had it right and the early modern philosophers got it wrong. As we saw already in chapter 1, for the medieval scholastics the notion of subjectivity was virtually ignored within a purely objective worldview molded by the interplay of divine revelation and Aristotelian philosophy. Aquinas and others failed to see the importance of the individual existent in its unique subjectivity because they were looking for rational order in terms of universals, objective intelligible forms found first in the mind of God and then in different ways within the world of creation. Yet, given their postulated hierarchy of beings with God as Pure Spirit at the top and prime matter at the bottom of that same hierarchy, they had a clear sense of the distinction between matter and spirit and their necessary interrelation in the world of creation. In the early modern era, on the contrary, there was a new recognition of the value of individual subjectivity as the starting point for philosophical reflection. But, since the relation between matter and spirit was no longer evident, for Descartes, Locke, and their followers a new and unexpected problem surfaced, namely, the issue of logical certitude. How do I know that I am right in my personal judgments about the world of Nature all around me?

Subjectivity and Objectivity in Descartes

Like so many of his scientifically minded contemporaries, René Descartes (1596–1650) was intrigued by mathematics as a privileged way to obtain certitude in a world where traditional beliefs had been radically called into question by the Protestant Reformation and the voyages of discovery to other parts of the globe. If, in line with the principles of geometry, one could proceed from a few chosen axioms that are unquestionably true to a set of propositions that follow with logical rigor, then one would be in a position to set forth a scientific worldview that would command the attention and respect of all. The three axioms for him were the existence of the self, God, and the material world. But a certain order was required even among the axioms.

Descartes did not begin by proving the existence of God from his experience of causality in the world around him (as did Thomas Aquinas in his *Summa Theologiae*.)[11] He began by questioning the veracity of his own experience of himself as someone seeking the truth. Even if "God" proved to be a demon bent on deceiving him at every turn, Descartes could not doubt or call into question his own existence as someone here and now doubting everything else.[12] From this established fact of his own finite existence, Descartes moved to an affirmation of the existence of God as the necessary cause of his idea of God as infinite and thus as lacking nothing by way of perfection.[13] His assumption here was that if he already had

some awareness of the infinity of God in recognizing his own finitude and the contingency of the world of Nature around him, then
the idea of the infinity of God must be innate (communicated directly by God to him as a finite creature) rather than fictitious (simply a product of his imagination) or adventitious (coming by chance
from his experience of life in this world).[14] Finally, from this proof
of the existence of God as infinite and perfect Being who thus cannot deceive his creatures, Descartes was able to conclude that his
senses are not deceived and that the material world around him
really exists.[15] From these three indubitable truths as the axioms of
Descartes' metaphysical system, everything else logically flows.[16]

Several points are noteworthy here when one compares Descartes'
system with that of his medieval predecessors. First of all, he has
indeed made a "turn to the subject" that would be virtually incom-
prehensible to Aquinas and Scotus. In the medieval worldview, the
individual subject of experience is virtually ignored as one focuses on
the panorama of the objective God-world relationship. Everything
comes forth from God as its First Efficient Cause and returns or in
any case is ordered to God as its Ultimate Final Cause. The individual human being fits into an orderly scheme of causes and effects
constituting the world of creation, but the world of creation itself
has meaning and value only in virtue of its orientation to and total
dependence upon God its transcendent Creator. To begin a metaphysical scheme with reflection upon one's own subjective experience of self, God, and the world would be incongruous, given such a
totally objective worldview. At the same time, Descartes shared with
the medieval scholastics the conviction that the God-world relationship is real and rational. Hence, like most medieval philosophers he
was basically a realist who believed that universals (in his case, clear
and distinct ideas) truly represent the world as it really is.[17] In that
sense, Descartes' turn to the subject did not imply subjectivism or
metaphysical relativism—that is, the belief that truth is relative to
the subjectivity or particular perspective of the truth seeker.

Yet from another perspective Descartes was likewise a conceptualist in his thinking about universals. For, while Aquinas claimed that we know the things of this world in and through abstraction of their universal forms or essences, Descartes proposed that universal concepts are only representations of the things of this world, not their intelligible forms or essences as such. Hence, in the end all that the mind knows is its own ideas.[18] Naturally, Descartes could appeal to the veracity of God for confirmation that these universal ideas correspond to the mode of operation of the things of this world. But he thereby still opened up a gap between the human mind and the world around it which did not exist for Aquinas and other medieval thinkers who distinguished quite carefully, as already noted,[19] between the universal *ante rem* in the mind of God, the universal *in re* as the intelligible form or essence of the thing in question, and the universal *post rem* in the human mind as a result of a process of mental abstraction from individuating sense data. Descartes' notion of a clear and distinct idea, to be sure, likewise presupposed elimination of various contingent properties so as to focus on the purity of the concept itself (e.g., the concept of matter as extension, quite apart from other properties such as size, weight, position with respect to other material things, etc.). But in the final analysis, Descartes was working with ideas as the representations of things rather than with the things themselves in virtue of their intelligible forms or essences.

One further issue in working with concepts or essences instead of with things themselves, of course, is the problem of individuation. In dealing exclusively with concepts, one never has assured knowledge of things in their concrete particularity; with the concept one grasps at best simply a dimension or partial representation of the thing in question. As we saw already in chapter 1, this was likewise an issue for medieval thinkers. Aquinas proposed that matter individuates the substantial form but left unanswered how matter as basically passive with respect to form can nevertheless individuate or further specify its own active principle. Scotus sought an answer to this question in postulating a new form, *haecceitas*, to provide individuality for each concrete existent, but this leaves unanswered how what is the same in each individual entity is the deeper reason for their being different from one another.

Descartes' problem with individuation was even more acute because he had set up a logical gap between the separate worlds of mind and matter. How can mind as thinking substance accurately reflect the physical world around it when the foundational concept of matter is reduced to that of pure extension? That is, if knowledge of Nature is limited to analysis of the motion of material bodies in terms of various mathematical formulae, then, as Newton realized, a metaphysical understanding of why things work the way they do is beyond our comprehension. Descartes accordingly in his search for true and certain knowledge had no other recourse but to admit that in the end all we human beings know are our ideas and their logical connections with one another.[20]

Locke's Empirical Approach to Reality

John Locke (1632–1704) as a graduate student at Oxford studied the philosophy of Rene Descartes, admiring its clear rational approach to obscure philosophical issues. But, while Descartes was basically a mathematician-turned-philosopher, Locke studied medicine as a profession, with its necessary close attention to the medical history and current physical condition of the patient. It is no surprise then that when Locke began to write *An Essay Concerning Human Understanding*, his approach to human cognition was quite different from that of Descartes. He employed what he called the "historical, plain method" of introspection into the workings of his own mind as it reflected on and organized the data of experience.[21] At the same time, he was one with Descartes in thinking that what human beings know are not things in themselves but only ideas as mental representations of those things.[22] This made him like Descartes a conceptualist rather than a realist in terms of epistemology.

But it also inclined him to reductionism in his analysis and cataloging of ideas. That is, he took it for granted in line with current scientific method that the whole is nothing more than the sum of its parts; complex ideas are nothing more than the adroit combination of simple ideas directly derived from sense experience.[23] Moreover, in line with his commonsense approach to reality, he assumed that the mind works basically the same way in all normally intelligent human beings so that his phenomenological approach to cognition would have relevance to others than himself. What he thereby excluded from consideration, of course, was any metaphysical or even physiological explanation of why the human mind generally worked as it did in human beings. Finally, in distinction from Descartes' approach, he did not seek mathematical certitude in his conclusions but only empirically based probability.[24]

All these methodological issues were stated at the start of *An Essay Concerning Human Understanding*. Locke then initiated his own positive exposition with a rebuttal of Descartes' notion of innate ideas (or, as Locke phrased it, innate principles, both speculative and practical).[25] Singling out the principles of identity and contradiction, Locke denies that they are innate to the human mind "since they are not universally assented to; and the assent they so generally find, is no other, than what several Propositions, not allowed to be innate, equally partake in with them."[26] For Locke, all ideas and/or principles are derived from sense experience and reflection upon those same experiences.[27] There are simple ideas and complex ideas. Simple ideas can be derived from either (a) one sense or more than one sense, (b) reflection, or (c) a combination of sensation and reflection. Complex ideas are, as already noted, constructed by the mind in combining and contrasting with one another simple ideas so as to produce ideas of modes (properties), substances, and relations.[28] Yet, even though he claims that all we know are our own ideas, Locke also follows Descartes in distinguishing between primary and secondary qualities within physical bodies. Primary qualities of physical bodies directly produce the simple ideas of solidity, extension, figure, motion or rest, and number within our minds.

Secondary qualities of physical bodies are those that indirectly produce the ideas of colors, sounds, tastes, and so on. That is, whereas the ideas of primary qualities clearly resemble those same qualities as they actually exist in the body, the ideas of secondary qualities are due to powers of the body that we do not understand.[29]

Locke's commonsense approach to human cognition, however appealing it might be to the average reader, still has its drawbacks in that it leaves unanswered various key issues pertinent to objective knowledge of physical reality. As already noted, for example, the complex idea of a given substance (e.g., an apple) is derived from combining various simple ideas representing the primary and secondary qualities of that same substance (its size, shape, color, taste, etc.). But this is only what Locke called its nominal or humanly contrived essence, not its real essence existing independently of the mind in Nature. If what we customarily call essences were indeed "Nature's Workmanship, they could not be so various and different in several men, as experience tells us they are."[30] Human beings, after all, even differ in their understanding of what is closest to them, namely, their own human nature. Yet, if in this way particular substances are only perceived as collections of primary and secondary qualities, then the notion of substance as such is empty of meaning, standing for the unknown "substratum or support of those Ideas we do know."[31] As we shall see in the next chapter, this line of thought eventually led to David Hume's skepticism about human knowledge of any substances, whether physical or spiritual.

Likewise, there is considerable ambiguity in Locke's analysis of the notions of cause and effect. In principle, cause and effect should only govern the relations between two ideas: "Besides the *Ideas*, whether simple or complex, that the Mind has of Things, as they are in themselves, there are others it gets from their comparison one with another."[32] More specifically, "a *Cause* is that which makes any other thing, either simple *Idea*, Substance, or Mode, begin to be; and an *Effect* is that, which had its beginning from some other thing."[33] But does this mean that one idea displaces another in human consciousness or that one physical body somehow causes an effect in another physical body and that this objective change in the natural world is reflected in our subjective experience by way of a succession of ideas? Is it Heat or the simple idea of Heat which causes Wax or the idea of Wax to become fluid? Moreover, is fluidity itself an idea or a phenomenon of Nature? In fairness to Locke, he is presumably adhering here to Newton's caveat about not knowing the true nature of things even when we have determined the mathematical laws governing the way in which these physical bodies affect one another. But it still represents a strictly phenomenological approach to reality with no deeper insight into the way things really are apart from our observation of them.

Once again, this is not to argue that medieval thinkers like Aquinas and Scotus had it right with their focus on universal forms existing both in the mind and in things, albeit in different ways. For, as we saw earlier, knowledge of things through their essences or universal forms never reaches the specificity required for insight into the concrete reality of those same things. In that sense, Locke was correct in insisting on the priority of individual things over their general ideas in our experience of the world around us. As Aquinas and Scotus likewise in their own way recognized, universal ideas are tools for the understanding of physical reality, not ends in themselves. But the perduring temptation is to remain in the clarity of the world of ideas (or, in the case of Descartes, mathematical principles) and not probe deeper for a more satisfying explanation of why things in the world around us happen the way that they do. In that sense, Locke and the empirical tradition in England, just like Descartes and the rationalist tradition on the continent, remain guilty of what Alfred North Whitehead called the fallacy of misplaced concreteness, unconsciously mistaking mental abstractions for the reality that they are intended to explain.

The deeper weakness of Locke's "historical, plain method" for the analysis of human cognition, however, is most obvious in dealing with the issue of certitude and the possibility of science, namely, knowledge that remains true and certain with the passage of time and under different circumstances. In book 4, chapter 3 of the *Essay Concerning Human Understanding*, for example, Locke first notes that knowledge (as opposed to opinion) lies in the perception of the agreement or disagreement of any of our ideas.[34] This perception of agreement or disagreement among our ideas arises (1) through intuition or the here-and-now comparing of two ideas; (2) through demonstration, using intermediate ideas to conclude that two seemingly distant ideas are in fact compatible or incompatible; and finally (3) through sensation, when we are presently feeling the impact of some physical reality (e.g., the sun) on our senses.[35] In this way, says Locke, we can have intuitive knowledge of our own existence, knowledge of the existence of God by demonstration, and immediate sense knowledge of the existence of the world around us from moment to moment.

But this means, as Locke himself concedes, that the extent of our knowledge falls "not only short of the reality of Things but even of the extent of our own Ideas."[36] In particular, as Richard Aaron comments, there is as a result no way to claim scientific knowledge of the world of Nature. For all our knowledge of the external world is derived from the senses, and through the senses we can never know real essences but are constrained to formulate nominal essences that may or may not correspond to the real essences at work in physical bodies.[37] Furthermore, even the formulation of nominal essences presupposes what we cannot confirm simply from the examination of our ideas, namely, that nature is uniform so that information about a limited number of individuals likewise gives us reliable information about the species to which they presumably belong, and that the future will basically be like the past and thus not invalidate conclusions drawn from past data.

Hence, it is no surprise that at the end of book 4, chapter 3, Locke concludes that rational certitude is to be found only in the realm of abstract ideas (equivalently, eternal truths). For, one can only have certitude about what is happening in the world of Nature in virtue of immediate sense experience.[38] But, if truly scientific knowledge of Nature transcends immediate sense experience of what is happening here and now, then certitude apart from the realm of abstract ideas is logically impossible within Locke's epistemological scheme.

Here one might well object that contemporary natural science is likewise not based on a priori knowledge of essences and universally valid metaphysical principles but still makes claims to at least provisional truth and certitude. That is, while taking for granted the uniformity of Nature (barring empirical evidence to the contrary), scientists first look for patterns of recurrence among entities in dynamic interrelation, then formulate hypotheses to explain those same natural recurrences, and finally seek to confirm the hypotheses through further observation of and experimentation on the entities in question. If observation and experiment check out favorably with the hypothesis, then the hypothesis is considered valid and true, until and unless falsified by subsequent empirical findings or further experimentation. Locke's phenomenological approach to knowledge of Nature through so-called nominal essences thus seems to be more in accord with accepted procedures in contemporary natural science than the medieval philosophers' systematic inquiry into the alleged real essences of things in the light of a priori metaphysical principles. The medieval approach to natural science employing deductive logic has then irretrievably given way to the modern, more empirically oriented approach to reality based on statistical probabilities and a new logic of discovery.

While all this is unquestionably true, one should also bear in mind Newton's reservations, noted earlier, about the limits of scientific investigation using the tools of mathematics. One can certainly come to a better understanding of how things happen, but not why they happen. Newton was acutely aware of the fact that he really did not know where gravity comes from and what kind of force it is even though he was able to lay out in detail the mathematics of how it operates between bodies physically separate from one another. In similar fashion, contemporary natural scientists have to concede that there is much about the workings of Nature that they do not understand. As we shall see in later chapters, there is at present no general agreement on how Nature works at the quantum level or how it has seemingly progressed from nonlife to life to rational life in virtue of its own inbuilt principle of spontaneity or self-organization. Richard Aaron concludes his historical and systematic treatise on the classical doctrine of universals with the claim that universals are indeed grounded in observed recurrences within the world of Nature but then he adds:

What is the final explanation of the recurrences in nature? It might be said that this is the real problem of universals and that the one attempt to tackle it thus far is the attempt made by the advocates of the theory of Forms [the medieval scholastics]. Certainly, this is not the question which has concerned us in this book.[39]

Yet it will necessarily remain the primary focus of investigation in this book as we continue our overview of Western philosophy in the light of the problem of objectivity and subjectivity, namely, the relation of universal concepts or laws to the individual things that they are supposed to explain.

3

WHAT IS MATTER AND
WHAT IS SPIRIT?

In this chapter I review the efforts of philosophers on both sides of the English Channel to come to terms with the pioneering efforts of René Descartes and John Locke to address the problem of certitude. On the continent Descartes was succeeded by Spinoza and Leibniz in the so-called rationalist tradition. In the British Isles Locke was succeeded by Berkeley and Hume in the empiricist tradition. All four thinkers were in their own way probing into the reality of matter and its relation to mind or spirit. None of them came up with a totally satisfactory answer to that question, but each set forth insights into that relationship which will be helpful to us in our survey of Western philosophy in terms of the problem of subjectivity and objectivity (what we think we know versus the way things really are). I begin with Berkeley's critique of Locke's philosophy and his own formulation of a philosophy that denies the reality of matter as classically understood but which still affirms the possibility of scientific understanding of the world of Nature.

George Berkeley (1685–1753)

Berkeley is sometimes dismissed simply as a bridge figure between the two major thinkers of the British empiricist tradition, namely, John Locke and David Hume. Berkeley exposed various inconsistencies in the "historical, plain method" of Locke in analyzing human cognition and ended up denying the reality of matter as the necessary substrate for the primary and secondary qualities of material things. But Hume completed the critique of Locke's theory of cognition by casting doubt likewise on the substantiality of the spiritual self and questioning the classical understanding of the principle of causality. As a result, one may well believe in the existence of God, a permanent self, and the extra-mental world of Nature, but one cannot rationally prove (or, for that matter, disprove) any of these assertions simply from analysis of the data of human experience.

But in the light of subsequent efforts to understand the process of human cognition, Berkeley plays an important role, as I indicate below. First of all, he called attention to what Locke preferred to ignore, namely, that, if all we know are our own ideas, how do we know that they truly represent the physical reality all around us? There is no way to compare our ideas with an independently existing material reality.[1] Furthermore, if Locke maintains that secondary qualities (color, sound, heat, and cold) exist as such only in the mind and are the effect of unknown powers in Nature causing us to have these sensations, then how can he be sure that primary qualities (size, shape, motion, rest, solidity) are any different, that is, that they correspond to the actual characteristics of physical reality apart from the mind?[2] After all, they too are simply ideas, and their value as accurate representations of physical reality can never be verified, given the prior assumption that all we know are our own ideas.

Second, Berkeley's counterproposal was to bypass this logical impasse by stipulating that God as Infinite Mind imprints the ideas of primary and secondary qualities on human minds.[3] The world of Nature, accordingly, only exists as ideas first in the mind of God and then in the minds of human beings. Yet these ideas are objective since they are not actively produced by the human mind but passively received from God in the act of perception. Moreover, says Berkeley, human beings have basically the same ideas about physical reality, albeit with minor differences, because God is their source and inspiration.[4] Scientific knowledge of physical reality is still possible, therefore, provided we recognize that with the laws of Nature we are dealing with relationships between ideas and not with regularities within Nature as an independent reality. As W. T. Jones comments, for Berkeley a scientific law is "a generalization about what ideas coexist with or follow other ideas in our experience."[5] This eliminates the problematic gap between ideas of things and the things themselves within Locke's theory of cognition. Yet it also logically presupposes that God as Infinite Mind, the source of our ideas about the world of Nature, really exists and will not deceive us about the nature of reality.

But how can we be sure that God exists? Berkeley seems to engage here in a curious form of circular thinking, in the end presupposing what his system is designed to prove. Experience tells us that we are passive in the reception of simple ideas and active only in the formulation of complex ideas; hence, there must be an Infinite Mind that is purely active in the formation of ideas and which implants these divine ideas in our minds: "The cause of our experience, with all its marvelous order and regularity, must be something like the self, but much greater. It must be active; specifically, it must be a mind."[6] Yet where does Berkeley get knowledge of the human self as active? He has to distinguish here between ideas and "notions," namely, intellectual intuitions that somehow transcend the realm of ideas:

I own I have properly no idea, either of God or any other spirit; for these being active, cannot be represented by things perfectly inert, as our ideas are. I do nevertheless know that I, who am a spirit or thinking substance, exist as certainly as I know my ideas exist. Further, I know what I mean by the terms *I* and *myself*, and I know this immediately, or intuitively, though I do not perceive it as I perceive a triangle, a colour, or a sound.[7]

From this intellectual intuition of his own existence as finite spirit, Berkeley felt justified in inferring the existence of God as Infinite Spirit, the sole source of all our ideas about the world of Nature.

Hume and others, of course, were quick to point out that, if all we know are our own ideas, Berkeley has no logical basis for thus distinguishing between ideas and notions. Still another logical inconsistency in Berkeley's scheme, of course, was his claim that we can infer the existence of other human beings from the way in which they affect our senses: "We cannot know the existence of *other spirits* otherwise than by their operations, or the ideas by them excited in us."[8] Yet if all our ideas are supposed to come from God, how can ideas be received by us from other finite spirits as proof of their activity in our regard?[9] The only solution would seem to be that God as Infinite Mind mediates between finite minds by providing each human being with the ideas needed to recognize the activity of the other in his or her regard. As Berkeley comments, God "maintains that intercourse between spirits whereby they are able to perceive the existence of each other."[10]

So there are unquestionably logical inconsistencies in Berkeley's attempt to prove that matter as enduring substrate for our ideas about the world is an illusion and that all these ideas actually come from God as Infinite Mind or Spirit. But there are insights about the relation between spirit and matter within his scheme that deserve further consideration. For example, Berkeley insisted at the beginning of *The Principles of Human Knowledge* that to exist means either to perceive or to be perceived.[11] Hence, everything is either a mind or exists for a mind. Things have no reason to exist in themselves. What got Berkeley into trouble, of course, was his further claim that things only exist while they are being perceived. Hence, he had to postulate the existence of other finite minds and, above all, the existence of God as Infinite Mind to keep things in existence when individual human beings cease to perceive them.[12]

But the deeper insight in his statement is that in the end material things exist to facilitate communication between minds (or, perhaps more broadly, subjects of experience). In direct opposition to the materialist thesis that minds emerge as a result of the interplay of material entities or forces, Berkeley contends that things or, more precisely, the ideas of things come into being as a result of the interplay of minds with one another: that is, in the first place the mind of God in dealing with human beings, and then the minds of human beings responding to God and to one another. First Leibniz and then Alfred North Whitehead refine and systematize this insight, as we shall see below, so as to construct a more consistent cosmological scheme. But Berkeley's pioneering work should not be discounted despite its evident inconsistencies. In thinking through the complex relationship between matter and spirit, he insisted that matter is ultimately derivative from spirit and not vice versa, all appearances to the contrary notwithstanding.

Yet he was not thereby a pure idealist living in solitary splendor within his own mental world. He likewise insisted on the necessary dynamic interrelation of matter and spirit. Neither can exist without the other. Matter, above all in the form of words and ideas (self-representations), is the necessary medium of communication between minds or spirits and implicitly the principle of individuation or differentiation between minds or spirits. Without objective expressions of their thoughts and feelings toward one another, minds would be totally isolated from one another and nothing would happen; no common world would emerge as a result of their ongoing interchange. How minds (subjects of experience) through the sharing of ideas or self-representations can progressively construct a material world was, of course, beyond Berkeley's ability to understand and explain. But he did at least recognize the danger to the traditional spiritual values of humankind in the materialistic monism that was explicitly formulated by Hobbes and implicitly accepted in scientific circles within Western Europe as a practical consequence of the new scientific method.

David Hume (1711–1776)

Even though one could argue that Hume effectively undermined the theoretical foundations of Western natural science with his critique of the classical principle of causality, from another perspective he was actually applying to the study of human nature the methodology already employed by Newton and other early modern scientists. Much like a practicing natural scientist, a true philosopher of human nature "should draw his evidence from experience and observation, refer all his propositions to their sensory origin, be parsimonious in his causal explanations, and proceed gradually to a few general principles governing all mental phenomena."[13] A philosopher should not accordingly inquire into the essences of things or of the spiritual self but be content "to observe the uniformities within our experience, identify and demarcate the powers at work, and render our principles of explanation as general as possible within empirical bounds."[14]

In line with that methodology, Hume began *A Treatise on Human Nature* with the following statement: "All the perceptions of the human mind resolve themselves into two distinct kinds, which I shall call Impressions and Ideas. The difference betwixt these consists in the degrees of force and liveliness which they strike upon the mind, and make their way into our thought or consciousness."[15] Here he was clearly following in the tradition of Locke and Berkeley, albeit with slightly different terminology. Whereas Locke proposed that what we directly know are our simple ideas, Hume called them "impressions." But Hume agreed with Locke that we do not directly know external things in virtue of these mental images. From Berkeley, he took the conviction that ideas in the strict sense are copies or faint images of impressions, not, as Aquinas and other medieval thinkers proposed, the intelligible form or essence of the thing in question.[16] Finally, he followed Locke and Berkeley in assuming a doctrine of psychological atomism, namely, that perceptions (both impressions and ideas) are divided into simple and complex, the latter being a collection of the former in virtue of the power of the mind to link together and separate from one another simple impressions and ideas.[17]

Hume's own contribution to the empiricist understanding of human cognition lay in his appeal to imagination as the power of the mind to see the various kinds of relations between ideas. Universal ideas, for example, are not formed by abstracting an intelligible form from a concrete particular thing but by using the power of imagination to make one image (e.g., that of an isosceles triangle) representative of many other images (all other triangles, whether isosceles or not).[18] Likewise, Hume's understanding of causality in Nature is derived from perception of relations between ideas. He distinguishes, to be sure, between natural relations whereby "two ideas are connected together in the imagination, and the one naturally introduces the other,"[19] and philosophical relations where the union of two ideas in the imagination is more arbitrary but still conceivable. Cause-and-effect relations are both natural and philosophical, but in both cases they are dependent upon observation and experience, albeit in different ways.

In the first case, one simply notes the ongoing conjunction of images in one's experience and spontaneously infers a relation of cause and effect.[20] In the second case, one reflects on this experience of constantly conjoined images and comes up with the abstract principle of causation, which is itself not given in and through the experience of conjoined images: "From the mere repetition of any past impression, even to infinity, there never will arise any new original idea, such as that of a necessary connexion" or ontological principle of causality.[21] The source of the principle of causation, accordingly, is to be found in the power of imagination to conjoin separate ideas within the mind, not in any objective intelligibility within Nature as a whole or in the impressions themselves in their combined impact on the mind. The philosophical understanding of causality is in the first place derivative from the natural relation of cause and effect, that is, the constant conjunction of the same images in the mind. Then human imagination goes to work to make it a fixed habit of mind or custom; one no longer questions the necessary connection between these two impressions, one as the cause and the other as the effect.[22] Thus understood, however, perceived cause-and-effect relations never achieve the level of demonstrative or absolutely certain knowledge but are only more or less probably true, barring falsification as a result of concrete experience to the contrary. This is what Hume means by moral as opposed to demonstrative reasoning; as such it "can never yield more than a high degree of probability or moral certitude."[23]

In point of fact, this is the normal understanding of cause-and-effect relations within most scientific research to this day. Scientists generally do not look for essences or other ontological principles providing demonstrative knowledge of the entities in question, but rather for consistently recurring patterns within ongoing events and between successive events. On that basis they conceive possible cause-and-effect relations to explain these patterns or recurrences within Nature and then use further methods of observation and experiment to determine which scheme best fits the empirical data. But conclusions are always tentative, more or less probable, since either new data or new experiments on existing data may ultimately falsify or at least throw into doubt the hitherto accepted causal explanation.

So, in being faithful to the methodology of Newton and other natural scientists in his study of human cognition, Hume was providing a philosophical rationale for scientific method as then understood. But it is important to realize that this rationale was grounded in an early form of empirical psychology rather than in ontology or metaphysics as such. That is, like Locke and Berkeley, Hume professed not to know the powers at work in Nature that produce Locke's simple ideas or in his own case the impressions of things in the human mind; he was content to analyze and mentally organize the data of sense experience. But in distinction from Locke and Berkeley he questioned whether or not the same data of sense experience justify belief in the ongoing existence of a spiritual self to do the work of analysis and mental organization of these impressions and ideas. Given his purely psychological explanation of the principle of causality as a "custom" or habit of the mind induced by a constant conjunction of images within one's experience, he could not be sure that there is a permanent self likewise at work to unify and systematize those same perceptions.

The sense data, in other words, seem to yield a perception of the mind or self as "a heap or collection of different perceptions, united together by certain relations," but without any necessary reference to the self as a reality distinct from its individual perceptions.[24] For, given his antecedent belief in psychological atomism, as noted above, for Hume each perception is a reality unto itself and only contingently conjoined to the heap or collection of perceptions supposedly constituting the self. Elsewhere in *A Treatise of Human Nature* he writes, "The mind is a kind of theater, where several perceptions successively make their appearance; pass, re-pass, glide away, and mingle in an infinite variety of postures and situations."[25] Yet even this metaphor of the mind as a theater is misleading since it presupposes something permanent whereas all that we truly experience is an ongoing succession of perceptions.

Given that Hume has no room in his philosophy for either material substance in the world of Nature or spiritual substance in the sphere of mental activities, nothing is permanent; everything is in flux. But common sense suggests that we only recognize change when something else in our experience is unchanging or enduring. This line of thought led Immanuel Kant and the German Idealists to postulate the existence and activity of a transcendental (as opposed to an empirical) subject of experience as the unchanging source of the order and regularity both within the human mind and, for the German Idealists, throughout Nature as well. Then in the early twentieth century Alfred North Whitehead proposed that "societies" of actual occasions (momentary subjects of experience linked by a "common element of form" or conjoint pattern of existence and activity) should replace what was meant in classical metaphysics by substance, both spiritual and material. Both of these metaphysical alternatives to the classical notion of substance, as we shall see below, have significant drawbacks if one thinks through their logical consequences. But in their own way both of these approaches to the problem of subjectivity and objectivity go back to Hume's basic question: what is the self as a purely spiritual reality over and above its objects of perception or material forms of self-expression?

Benedict (Baruch) Spinoza (1632–1677)

Although many sources including Jewish mysticism (e.g., the Kabbalah) influenced Spinoza in formulating his theory of the God-world relationship,[26] what he evidently inherited from studying the philosophy of René Descartes was a passion for systematic thinking *ordine geometrico*, beginning with a set of definitions and axioms and then deducing the logical propositions that follow from these presuppositions. Moreover, since he claimed that "the order and connection of ideas is the same as the order and connection of things,"[27] he was able to equate empirical cause-and-effect relations with logical ground-consequent relations within his thought-system. Thus the ultimate physical cause of all that exists in Nature is at the same time the theoretical first principle of his logical thought-system, namely, God understood as Substance, "that which is in itself and conceived through itself."[28]

This Substance has two known essential Attributes, namely, Thought and Extension, and both general and particular modes or modifications of itself. The general modes are Intellect or Thinking with reference to the attribute of Thought, and Motion-and-Rest with reference to the attribute of Extension.[29] The particular modes are the finite things of this world, representing in each case a combination of thought and extension. That is, my body is a finite mode of the divine substance understood as extension; my mind is a finite mode of the divine substance understood as thought. As W. T. Jones comments, however, mind and body do not divide reality such that some finite modes are bodies and others are minds. Rather, "The whole of reality is body, the whole of reality is mind. . . . The mode that is your body is the mode that is your mind.[30] Finally, there is no contingency or creaturely activity apart God in Spinoza's system since "all things are determined by the necessity of the divine nature for existing and working in a certain way."[31] Therefore, "whatever is, is in God, and nothing can exist or be conceived without God."[32]

Such a pantheistic understanding of the God-world relationship would compare favorably with certain forms of Advaita Vedanta Hinduism wherein strong emphasis is laid on the unity of all things in Brahman. But to the more empirical and pragmatic Western mind-set, it is by and large much too mystical and otherworldly for broad acceptance. Yet Spinoza's thought still offers major insights into the problem of subjectivity and objectivity from an ontological and a psychological perspective. For example, Spinoza claims that a substance is cause of itself (*causa sui*).[33] For Spinoza, this meant that there is only one substance—namely, God—and that everything else is a modification of the one divine substance. But Whitehead later argues that every actual entity or actual occasion is ultimately cause of itself or self-constituting.[34] It is dependent, to be sure, on a divine "initial aim," past actual entities and the overall structure of the environment out of which it is emerging for the concrete data of its self-constitution.[35] But in the end it becomes itself, achieves its own identity, in and through an immanent self-constituting decision. Thus, whereas Spinoza proposed that "the power of God is the same as his essence,"[36] Whitehead extends this power of self-constitution to all actual entities as "the final real things of which the world is made up."[37] Subjectivity understood as the power of radical self-constitution thus lies at the base of physical reality, and the individuation of entities from one another is the result not of the conjunction of form and matter, as with medieval Scholastic thinkers like Thomas Aquinas, but in virtue of their innate power of self-constitution in responding to the established conditions of the environment in which they find themselves.

Along the same lines, Spinoza's claim that the two known essential attributes of God are thought and extension offer valuable insights into both the conventional understanding of the nature of God and the alleged interrelation of matter and spirit. How can the reality of God embrace such polar opposites unless in point of fact they are not polar opposites but different modes or manifestations of one and the same foundational activity?

Whereas in common speech, the word God ranks as a noun so that theologians will make Him the subject or object of quite ordinary predicates with astonishing facility, Spinoza thinks of God rather as a verb and of all existent things as modes of this activity. The world is not a collection of things but a conflagration of Act whose innumerable flames are but one fire.[28]

Thus, if God is indeed *Actus Purus*, unbounded activity, and if this activity manifests itself to us human beings both as spirit (thinking) and as matter (motion and rest), then there is no reason not to say that everything in this world is a combination of matter and spirit, albeit in differing proportions.

In terms of Spinoza's scheme, however, how does this work out to produce individual bodies and minds in some sort of graded hierarchy? In particular, what is the relation between the human mind and the human body? Collins offers a succinct overview:

[The human body] is composed of many kinds of subordinate bodily individuals, each of which is composed in turn of the most simple bodies. . . . The human mind or soul is nothing other than the formal reality of the idea of the human body. As such, it is posited in being by the actual presence of the human body. . . . The mind is thus the idea of *this* body, whereas the body is expressed mentally by *this* idea which is its mind or soul. Spinoza does not try to *solve* Descartes' problem of uniting two substances; he substitutes for it the more manageable problem of correlating an idea and its ideatum.[39]

What Spinoza has done therefore in his philosophical cosmology is first to postulate that physical organisms are nothing more than aggregates of still other invisible subordinate entities as their component parts and then to combine this principle of philosophical atomism with his own conviction that mind and matter are simply different dimensions of bodies wherever they are found. In this way he first comes up with the notion of the visible physical body as a composite of invisible subordinate bodies acting as a unitary reality or single agent.[40] Then, since the formal essence of these visible physical bodies in Nature corresponds to the objective or representational essence of those same bodies in the mind of God (and the mind of the philosopher),[41] one can juxtapose a hierarchy of ideas in the human mind with the hierarchy of physical bodies in Nature since only together are they the full self-expression of God who is both Thought and Extension.

In this way, as we shall see below, Spinoza anticipated Leibniz's hypothesis in the *Monadology* that immaterial entities in dynamic interrelation produce the material things of this world. In addition, via Leibniz's work in the *Monadology*, Spinoza anticipated the work of Whitehead in *Process and Reality* with his notion of actual occasions as momentary self-constituting subjects of experience and of societies as perceptible aggregates of actual occasions. So, even though Spinoza's understanding of the God-world relationship was essentially static, with everything viewed from the divine perspective or *sub specie aeternitatis*, he indirectly provided the inspiration for a much more dynamic, process-oriented approach to reality in later centuries.

G. W. Leibniz (1646–1716)

Like Descartes and Spinoza, Leibniz reflected deeply on the notion of physical substance as the foundational concept for a new metaphysics supporting contemporary natural science. But, while Descartes identified physical substance with extension and Spinoza made extension one of the two known attributes of God as Infinite Substance, Leibniz realized that extension was necessarily derivative from something more primitive in Nature, namely, the notion of force.[42] After all, if Nature is matter in motion, where does the motion come from? Descartes claimed that it came from God, who creates and conserves Nature. Leibniz proposed that motion came from within the individual physical substance as an immanent activity. A physical substance is an infinitely small unit of force that through constant reiteration and in conjunction with other such units of force produces the sensible effect of extension in space and time. This is the theoretical basis for Leibniz's *The Principles of Nature and Grace, Based on Reason* and a companion work *The Monadology*, both written and privately circulated in 1714 shortly before his death.

In these writings he, like Descartes and Spinoza, espoused philosophical atomism, the belief that complex physical substances (the persons and things of commonsense experience) are composed of simple substances or monads. But for him these monads are psychic centers of activity rather than conventional atoms (minute physical entities moved only by external forces). As he says in *Principles of Nature and Grace*, "Substance is a being capable of action" or self-initiated movement.[43] These internal movements are of two types: perceptions (representations of the compound substance to which it belongs) and appetitions (tendencies to move from one perception to another). Furthermore, as he notes in *The Monadology*, these monads "have no windows through which anything can enter or depart."[44] Accordingly, each monad is a unique mini-universe, a privileged perspective on the broader universe in which it finds itself. They are created by God and organized into compound substances or bodies and simple substances (entelechies, souls, spirits) as their life-principles.[45]

Thus in the divine plan there are various combinations of compound and simple substances.[46] In conjunction with inanimate bodies, there is an entelechy or a living but nonconscious monad. In conjunction with animal bodies, there is a soul monad or principle of sensation and memory. In conjunction with the human body there is a spirit monad that is capable of apperception or self-reflection. The compound substances made up of bodily monads thus need the simple substances as organizing principles, and the simple substances need the compound substances to clarify their perceptions. Every bodily monad, of course, is distinct not only from the simple substance (monad), which is the organizing principle of the body as a whole. It is also distinct from every other bodily monad within the same complex substance. Order instead of chaos prevails only because God as the Infinite Simple Substance or Spirit-Monad without a body of its own perceives all these interconnections and in virtue of its own appetition for the best possible world sets up among the finite monads, both corporeal and spiritual, a pre-established harmony.[47]

Leibniz offers both an a priori and an a posteriori proof for the existence of God. According to the a priori proof, God "must exist if he is possible. And, since nothing can hinder the possibility of that which possesses no limitations, no negation, and, consequently, no contradiction, this alone is sufficient to establish the existence of God *a priori*."[48] The a posteriori proof is based on the principle of sufficient reason: "The final reason of things must be found in a necessary substance, in which the detail of changes exists only eminently, as in their source; and this is what we call God."[49] Both of these proofs, of course, are heavily dependent for their validity on Leibniz's cosmological scheme as a whole. So skeptics like David Hume will inevitably point out that there is circular thinking going on here. Yet, in terms of what it means to be a functioning individual in a world composed of monads or mini-subjects of experience, Leibniz offers some interesting insights.

Since every monad is unique in its self-constitution, there is for Leibniz no problem of individuation in terms of simple substances or individual monads. But on the level of compound substances (the persons and things of commonsense experience), a major problem remains: how do all these individual substances function as a single substance? As Collins points out, a compound substance is "an operational union between a principal act and subordinate acts."[50] The principal act, that of the life-principle, soul, or spirit, coordinates the mass of bodily monads, each of which is already in act on its own; the subordinate bodily monads in turn provide the dominant monad (entelechy, soul, spirit) with its distinctive perspective in space and time, its place in the cosmic process as a whole. There is some affinity here with the Thomistic notion of matter as the principle of individuation for the substantial form, but there is also a significant difference. Within Leibniz's scheme, matter is active in its own right rather than passive (i.e., dependent upon its relation to a substantial form, as in classical Thomism). Every monad is alive and thus every monad contributes in its own way to the individuation of the compound substance. This is a far more dynamic understanding of the relation between mind and matter than in the philosophy of Aquinas and in the philosophy of Leibniz's immediate predecessors, Descartes and Spinoza. There is, to be sure, a timeless character to Leibniz's philosophy since changes only take place within monads, not between them. Furthermore, the relations between monads are fixed by God in terms of a preestablished harmony. But the seeds of an evolutionary approach to the God-world relationship are still present in Leibniz's philosophy with his stipulation that "all nature is full of life."[51]

With respect to our human knowledge of individuals, Leibniz likewise made an important point. Monads for him are infinitely small units of force; hence, they are immaterial since anything material can in principle be divided. Yet in combination they produce the effect of something extended in space and time. This is a reminder to us that the way we human beings customarily perceive the world is not necessarily the way the world is actually constituted. Our range of perception is quite limited so that things very small and very large can be imagined but never directly perceived. Individuals corresponding to our middle-level range of perception do indeed exist. But, as Leibniz argues, they are complex substances, not simple substances. They are individuals composed of even smaller imperceptible individuals with a dynamic pattern of interrelation. Likewise, says Leibniz, the universe is a *plenum*, a complex individual entity composed of innumerable smaller entities, all interconnected.[52] It too is therefore an individual entity that can only be imagined but never directly perceived. In urging us to think more creatively about what it means to be an individual entity, Leibniz was accordingly considerably in advance of the natural science and philosophy of his day.

4

KANT'S COPERNICAN REVOLUTION

In his early years, Immanuel Kant (1724–1804) was strongly influenced by the work of Christian Wolff, who was himself a follower of Leibniz.[1] Thus Kant was well acquainted with the rationalist tradition in early modern Europe, which focused on the employment of a priori or metaphysical concepts to explain the deeper structure of reality, the nature of the God-world relationship, and so on. But, as Georges Dicker comments, over time Kant began to question the presuppositions of the rationalist tradition.[2] How do metaphysical concepts yield verifiable knowledge of that which cannot be directly experienced (e.g., the self as source of its own mental operations, the world as a whole, God as Creator and Preserver of the world)? Furthermore, once he read David Hume's *A Treatise of Human Nature*, Kant's suspicions were further aroused about the applicability of these metaphysical concepts to the explanation of empirical reality. In particular, he was impressed by Hume's critique of the principle of causality. Is the principle of causality nothing more than a habit of mind or mental disposition arising out of observation of a particular pattern of sense "impressions" within consciousness, or is it rather a law of Nature recognized by the human mind in its efforts to organize and control the data of sense experience?

Realizing that the validity of Newtonian science depended upon how one resolved this dispute between the rationalists and the empiricists of his day, Kant set himself to answer the following question in his celebrated *Critique of Pure Reason*: are synthetic a priori judgments about physical reality possible, and, if so, how are they operative so as to account for objective human knowledge? For, if they are genuinely a priori, then they have a reality that goes beyond the experience of the moment. But, if they are likewise synthetic, they are not purely analytical. They do more than spell out the logical consequences of an idea; they provide certain knowledge about the nature of reality.

In order to achieve this middle ground between the empiricist and rationalist traditions, Kant had to rethink the classical relationship between the human mind and the world around it:

Hitherto it has been assumed that all our knowledge must conform to objects. But all attempts to extend our knowledge of objects by establishing something in regard to them *a priori*, by means of concepts, have, on this assumption, ended in failure. We must therefore make trial whether we may not have more success in the task of metaphysics, if we suppose that objects must conform to our knowledge. This would agree better with what is desired, namely, that it should be possible to have knowledge of objects *a priori*, determining something in regard to them prior to their being given [in experience].[3]

Kant, accordingly, was consciously using the approach to nature already being employed in the mathematics and natural science of his day. These scientists had already learned "that reason has insight only into that which it produces after a plan of its own," and so, in dealing with nature, that reason "must itself show the way with principles of judgment based upon fixed laws, constraining nature to give answers to questions of reason's own determining."[4]

In contradistinction to Hume, therefore, Kant argued that human experience is not grounded in a constant flow of sense impressions that can be ordered by human beings in different ways according to habit or custom. Human experience is ordered in the same way for everyone. But whence comes this order in experience? Does it come from an order already at work in physical reality and mediated to human beings through reflection on experience, or does it come from the ordering activity of the human mind in dealing with sense impressions? Here, in contradistinction to rationalists like Descartes, Spinoza, and Leibniz, Kant argued that the second alternative is correct. But, to make this claim logically, Kant had to limit genuine human knowledge (as opposed to pure speculation) to the data of sense experience. The human mind cannot order and control extramental reality, but only the physical data delivered to it by the senses. The question that I deal with in the rest of this chapter is whether Kant overplayed his hand here, that is, whether he claimed too much in saying that the mind alone is the ordering principle within human experience. Perhaps the mind partly conforms to an order already present in Nature even as it (re)constructs that order in consciousness through its own immanent activity. To explain this hypothesis further, however, will demand an overview of the *Critique of Pure Reason* with special attention to the "Analogies of Experience."

The Transcendental Aesthetic

In this preliminary subdivision of the *Critique of Pure Reason*, Kant asks how synthetic a priori judgments are possible in mathematics, specifically in arithmetic and geometry. As synthetic, these judgments must be grounded in sense experience, not pure logic; as a priori or transcendental, they have to do with the necessary conditions for making such judgments. Kant is here dealing with the role of space and time in human experience, and his argument is that they are not physical realities distinct from the self, but a priori principles or pure forms of intuition within the human mind. "Just as our minds order our experiences spatially, as being above or below, to the right or the left, of other experiences, so they order these experiences temporally, as being before, after, or simultaneous with other experiences."[5] Space thus is the form of outer sense, what appears to exist outside the self; time is the form of inner sense, what evidently exists within the self. Together, they provide the necessary context for all particular sense impressions. An example of such synthetic judgments in arithmetic would be $7 + 5 = 12$, or in geometry, the axiom that a straight line is the shortest distance between two points.[6] In Kant's mind, neither of these judgments is purely analytic; both presuppose underlying mental representations of space and time as the basis for empirical measurement.

What Kant has done here is to strike a balance between Newton and Leibniz on the nature of space and time. Whereas Newton had held that space and time are extra-mentally real and absolute, Leibniz held that space and time are ideal (mental representations) and relative to each monad in its relation to other monads.[7] Kant's compromise position was to claim that space and time are ideal but absolute (operative in the same way for all human beings in their sense experiences). As we shall see below, Kant might have been better advised to adhere closer to Leibniz than to Newton on this point. For, as W. T. Jones notes, non-Euclidean geometries that do not correspond to ordinary commonsense experience have been developed and empirically tested in the years since the publication of the *Critique*.[8] Likewise, Einstein's theory of special relativity makes the measurement of space and time relative to the inertial frame of reference of the observer, but this too could not have been anticipated by Kant.

But, even with these post-Kantian qualifications, Kant's understanding of space and time as pure forms of intuition operative within the human mind in terms of sense experience rather than things-in-themselves distinct from the self is a remarkable achievement. He thereby drew attention to the radical difference between the empirical self and what he called the transcendental self within human cognition. The empirical self is the normal "I think" or feeling-level awareness of sense data. The transcendental self, however, is operative within consciousness "behind the scenes" to make possible a unified human experience. But for that same reason, precisely as an a priori or transcendental activity, it can never be objectified or in any other way empirically represented within sense experience. In the next section we see how the transcendental self likewise functions to organize sense data and logical concepts within the natural sciences.

The Transcendental Analytic

In this part of the *Critique of Pure Reason*, Kant deals with his second overall question: whether there are synthetic a priori judgments operative in the natural sciences. His argument is as follows. If, as the Transcendental Aesthetic has shown, there are pure as well as empirically based intuitions of sense objects, then conceivably there are likewise pure as well as empirical concepts about those same objects of experience that would then qualify as synthetic a priori judgments, thus providing the theoretical basis for work in the natural sciences.[9] The further question, of course, is: what are these a priori judgments, and how do they function to unify the empirical data of the natural sciences?

A key point to keep in mind here, as Jones comments, is that judgments are the product of the act of judging.[10] Hence, in the end what one is looking for in this part of the *Critique* is not a set of fixed concepts or logical categories but a unifying activity, what Kant calls the "transcendental unity of apperception," still another name for the transcendental self referred to above. Whereas in the Transcendental Aesthetic, this unifying activity put together the pure intuitions of space and time with the objects of sense experience so as to provide an act of sense perception for the empirical self, in this part of the *Critique* the underlying activity puts together logical categories and empirical sense data so as to constitute a unified object of thought for the empirical self. In every object of thought, accordingly, there is always an a priori component that transcends the sense data of the moment as well as an a posteriori component that is grounded in that same sense data.

Kant offers both a metaphysical and a transcendental deduction of that unifying activity or transcendental unity of apperception. In the metaphysical deduction he assumes that all judgments "can be brought under four heads, each of which contains three [successive] moments."[11] These are Quantity with the movement in judgment from universal to particular to singular or unique statements,

Quality with a movement in judgment from affirmation to negation and then to nonlimitation or infinity in one's statements, Relation with its movement in judgment from categorical to hypothetical to disjunctive statements, and finally Modality with its movement in judgment from problematic to assertoric and then to apodeictic or necessary statements. These logical categories are linked with the Categories of Being of Aristotle as given in his *Metaphysics*.[12] Commentators and critics have argued about the "fit" between these logical categories and Aristotle's categories of Being.[13] But this is to ignore the fact that Kant simply needed a starting point for the more important work of the Transcendental Analytic, namely, to show that such categories are the necessary a priori conditions for any object of thought within human experience. Without the implicit functioning of these a priori categories, human experience both of the empirical self and of the world of Nature would be impossible.[14]

In the transcendental deduction of the categories, Kant first establishes the necessity of a transcendental unity of apperception:

It is that self-consciousness which, while generating the representation *"I think"* (a representation which must be capable of accompanying all other representations, and which in all consciousness is one and the same), cannot itself be accompanied by any further representation. The unity of this apperception I likewise entitle the *transcendental* unity of self-consciousness, in order to indicate the possibility of *a priori* knowledge arising from it.[15]

The transcendental self, accordingly, manifests itself in and through the ever-present "I think" in all human knowledge of objects. But it has still more work to do in applying the above-noted logical categories to the data of sense experience so as to produce a unified object of thought.

It has to use its faculty of imagination to make these a priori categories applicable to the sensible data: "Now, since all our intuition is sensible, the imagination, owing to the subjective condition under which alone it can give to the concepts of understanding a corresponding intuition, belongs to sensibility."[16] Such a transcendental function of the imagination, in other words, is intermediate between pure thought and intuition of sense data. As active rather than passive in its operation, it is a strictly transcendental or a priori reality. In its end product, however, it is part of what is passively given to consciousness.[17] This so-called schematism of the a priori concepts of the understanding is, says Kant, an exercise of productive imagination as opposed to the more conventional work of the reproductive imagination which organizes empirical data according to recognized rules or principles of association (as in Hume's philosophy) but which "contributes nothing to the explanation of the possibility of *a priori* knowledge."[18]

But what about self-awareness, the ongoing sense experience of myself as myself? How is that to be explained within Kant's scheme? Kant incisively notes: "The consciousness of self is . . . very far from being a knowledge of the self."[19] I am indeed constantly aware of myself but I cannot become a direct object of perception for myself. Hence, I cannot in Kant's terminology "know" myself as a physical entity or substance in the way that I can "know" external things within my experience in virtue of the application of the a priori categories of the understanding to the data of sense experience. I can only intuit myself as a subject accompanying my objective experience of other people and things.

Here we may make the transition to Kant's Analogies of Experience where he lays out the schemata for the all-important categories of substance, causality, and reciprocity. A schema, of course, is not simply a generalized image derived from experience of sensible things, but rather a "rule of synthesis" for the transcendental imagination whereby various sensible images of the object in question can be gathered into a single comprehensive representation suitable for integration with an a priori concept.[20] "The concept 'dog' signifies a rule according to which my imagination can delineate the figure of a four-footed animal in a general manner, without limitation to any single determinate figure such as experience, or any possible image that I can represent *in concreto*, actually presents."[21] The schema or rule of synthesis for the a priori categories dealing with quantity, for example, is number (extensive magnitude); the scheme for categories dealing with quality is degree or intensive magnitude.[22] Both of these schemata correspond to commonsense experiences of quantity and quality. But the schemata for the categories dealing with relation (i.e., substance, causality, and reciprocity) are somewhat more complicated and for that reason controversial.

The general principle for all three of these analogies of experience, as Kant calls them, is as follows: "experience is possible only through the representation of a necessary connection of perceptions."[23] Here is where the schema as a "rule of synthesis" plays its role. It orders contingent sense impressions according to a prescribed rule. The schema for recognizing an object of experience as substance, for example, is unchanging permanence in time.[24] This may seem to be tautological, for what else by definition is substance but that which endures unchanged in time? But Kant is not dealing here with things in themselves but with the experience of permanence in human experience. From one perspective, this sense of permanence is time itself as the form of inner sense: "the time in which all change of appearances has to be thought, remains and does not change. For it is that in which, and as determinations of which, succession or coexistence can alone be represented."[25] But, says Kant, it is also time as configured or represented by the schematism of the a priori category of substance: "the substratum of all that is real, that is, of all that belongs to existence of things is *substance*."[26]

Such remarks, if applied to things in themselves apart from experience, would imply a form of Spinozistic monism; only one substance exists and everything else is only a mode of existence of that one substance. But Kant is in the first place not talking about things in themselves or even about individual things as they appear in human experience. On a more fundamental level, he is talking about the necessary experience of permanence in human experience as the basis for change or alteration in sense representations. For that purpose, time as the inner sense when conjoined with the schematized a priori category of substance is all that is needed. Individual things as they appear in experience are judged to be substances only insofar as they conform to this a priori structure of the mind putting order into what could be otherwise a purely contingent succession of sense impressions.

Yet is this immanent structure of the mind in ordering experiences purely subjective or is it instead objective? Kant appears to argue that it is both subjective and objective at the same time. It is subjective because it takes place within the experience of a given individual. It is objective because it takes place in the experience of every human being in the same way and thus must somehow correspond to what is going on in the world of Nature. It is, however, not objective in the sense that it can be proven to correspond to an order inherent in the world apart from the self and merely represented in the order of sense impressions received by the self.[27] Thus, Kant is not making a claim about the coming into being or going out of existence of substances in the world of Nature apart from human experience, but only saying that human experience as a unified reality would be impossible without this experience of unchanging permanence in time made possible by the dynamic synthesis of time as the inner sense with the schematized a priori category of substance. Furthermore, this structure of the human mind is necessarily antecedent to any given succession of perceptions within consciousness.[28]

This is, of course, Kant's way of dealing with David Hume's skepticism about the possibility of objectivity in human knowledge without sacrificing the certitude in scientific knowledge sought after by the rationalists. Objective a priori knowledge of the workings of Nature exists, but it is to be found in the structure of the human mind, not in the data of sense experience. Even to the present day many, if not most, natural scientists still implicitly espouse this instrumentalist approach to knowledge within their respective disciplines. Accordingly, without venturing an opinion on what is really going on in Nature, they share their experimental findings with one another in the confident expectation that other scientists will come to the same conclusions as themselves about the pertinent data if they perform certain specified experiments in the same way. But is it enough for human beings thus to agree on their common experiences of the workings of Nature and then prescind from what presumably is going on in Nature independently of their own observations and experiments? Is not some further understanding of Nature necessary even to continue to do good science? These metaphysical issues will be even more urgent as we examine Kant's other two analogies of experience, namely, the experience of causality and reciprocity or coexistence among the phenomena of Nature.

These two analogies of experience logically follow upon the first analogy: "All appearances are in time; and in it alone, as substratum (as permanent form of inner intuition), can either co-existence or succession be represented."[29] With reference to causality or the succession of sense impressions in time according to a "rule of synthesis," for example, Kant initially notes that all such changes are merely alterations of an underlying substance that does not change.[30] The key point, however, for the understanding of causality is that there is a necessary connection between these appearances and that the connection "is not the work of mere sense and intuition, but rather the product of a synthetic faculty of imagination, which determines inner sense in respect of the time-relation."[31]

Thus the determination of the causal relation—namely, that the one sense impression necessarily follows the other and that they cannot be placed in the reverse relation—is not to be found in the perceptions themselves as a reflection of the order of Nature apart from the self but in the ordering activity of the transcendental unity of apperception through the schematized a priori category of causality. Kant, to be sure, recognizes that the sequential apprehension of sense impressions in consciousness is always successive. Hence, there must be a way to distinguish between one's own successive apprehensions of an existing state of affairs (e.g., a house from different angles or perspectives) and an event where one sense perception necessarily precedes and the other necessarily follows. Only in the latter cause is the schematized category of causality at work in consciousness. In successive perceptions of a ship moving downstream, for example, the perception of the ship upstream must precede the perception of the ship downstream.[32]

To resolve this issue, Kant introduces the notion of the phenomenal object as "*that* in the appearance which contains the condition of this necessary rule of apprehension," namely, causal connection.[33] So it is not an arbitrary choice on the part of the transcendental imagination to apply the rule of causal connection to some sense impressions and not to others. As Kant notes, "Truth consists in the agreement of knowledge with the object."[34] Yet, as Jones notes, there is then a clear ambiguity in Kant's employment of the notion of the phenomenal object: "Because phenomenal objects (Newtonian matter in motion) are spatially and temporally organized, they are, like the sense data, modes of appearance. But they are supposed, by both common sense and natural science, to be the *causes* of the ordered sense data."[35] Hence, at one and the same time, the phenomenal object is causing its own representations in consciousness and is determined to be such a cause by the activity of the transcendental imagination as it applies the a priori concept of causality to its successive sense representations.

Kant is in an awkward position here since he wants to affirm that the notion of causality is not derivative from contingent sense data but from the antecedent synthesizing activity of the transcendental unity of apperception in applying a priori categories to the sense data. At the same time, he has to be able to distinguish between successive apprehensions of an existing state of affairs in which the order of apprehension is purely subjective from the apprehension of an event in which the order of apprehension in terms of earlier and later is antecedently fixed and objective. Otherwise, there would be no difference in consciousness between the experience of an objective event as something happening sequentially and successive apprehensions of an existing state of affairs. Kant resolves this issue by focusing exclusively on the a priori conditions for the objective *experience* of an event, not on the event itself as something likewise happening outside of consciousness: "I render my subjective synthesis of apprehension objective only by reference to a rule in accordance with which the appearances in their succession, that is, as they happen, are determined by the preceding state. The experience of an event [i.e. of anything as *happening*] is itself possible only on this assumption."[36] Characteristic of the experience of an event, says Kant, is recognition of an objective cause-effect relationship. But such recognition does not come from the contingent sense data alone; it can only be derived from the sense data as shaped into an object of experience by the transcendental imagination as it applies the schematized a priori category of causality to the sense data.

H. J. Paton comments: "Because Kant is an empirical realist, he believes that an objective succession may be directly present to my successive apprehensions. Because he is a transcendental idealist, he believes that such an objective succession, though not confined to my apprehension, is nothing apart from a possible human experience."[37] Either Kant should be a more consistent empirical realist and find a way to legitimate the causal impact of things-in-themselves on human experience; or Kant should be a more consistent transcendental idealist and stipulate that the transcendental self not only structures its object of experience but in the end creates it. As we shall see in the next chapter, this is basically the path taken by Kant's successors, the German Idealists.

Turning now to the third category of relation, reciprocity or community, we have the opposite problematic to that in the second analogy. Since sense impressions follow one another in human consciousness successively whether one is perceiving an unchanging state of affairs or an event involving a causal sequence, there must be a rule-governed way objectively to determine that one is experiencing reciprocal interaction between and among the sense data:

The synthesis of imagination in apprehension would only reveal that the one perception is in the subject while the other is not there, and *vice versa*, but not that the objects are co-existent, that is, that if the one exists the other exists at the same time, and that it is only because they thus co-exist that the perceptions are able to follow one another reciprocally.[38]

Kant's solution to this problem is to postulate the schematized a priori concept of reciprocity or community linked with time as the pure form of sense intuition so as to claim that "the reciprocal sequence of the perceptions is grounded in the [phenomenal] object" and thus represents the coexistence as objective.[39] Once again, the pertinent issue here is whether the objective relation of coexistence among the objects of sense perception is due exclusively to the synthesizing activity of the transcendental imagination in conjunction with time as the inner sense or whether it is somehow also due to the workings of Nature apart from consciousness. Just as before in dealing with the notion of causality, however, Kant limits the scope of his inquiry to the a priori conditions for the *experience* of reciprocity in human consciousness and says nothing about the possible a priori conditions for the existence of reciprocity in the world of Nature apart from consciousness.

Yet Kant still occasionally seems to speak of reciprocity among "substances" as if they were things in themselves in dynamic interaction:

If this subjective community [of representations in experience] is to rest on an objective ground, or is to hold of appearances as substances, the perception of the one must as ground make possible the perception of the other, and reversewise—in order that the succession which is always found in the perceptions, as apprehensions, may not be ascribed to the objects, and in order that, on the contrary, these objects may be represented as coexisting. But this is a reciprocal influence, that is, a real community (*commercium*) of substances; without it the empirical relation of coexistence could not be met with in experience.[40]

Since Kant is consciously limiting himself to the a priori conditions for the experience of reciprocity in human consciousness, he can still claim that this experience of reciprocity is due to the synthesizing activity of the transcendental imagination in linking the a priori category of reciprocity with time as the inner sense so as to make possible reciprocity as an objective fact within sense experience. Yet it leaves unanswered the question of how reciprocity works within the broader world of Nature—that is, how things-in-themselves simultaneously influence one another and thus allow for our human experience of reciprocity or community. In other words, we have to treat the representations themselves as substances that can have a mutual impact upon one another if we are to verify coexistence or reciprocity as a determining factor in human experience.[41] Yet these "substances" are objects of experience, not things in themselves. The necessity of their reciprocal interaction arises solely from the synthesizing activity of the transcendental imagination working with the a priori concept of reciprocity or communion, not from the way the things in themselves relate to one another in the world of Nature.

The final set of three schematized a priori concepts for Kant are possibility, actuality, and necessity under the general heading of modality. As he notes, these categories "only express the relation of the object known to the faculty of knowledge," indicating whether the object so conceived is possible, actual, or even necessary in terms of Kant's system of explanation for achieving synthetic a priori knowledge of the world of experience.[42] Whatever agrees with the formal conditions of experience is possible; whatever agrees with the material conditions of experience, that is, whatever is given in sense data, is actual; and whatever agrees with both the formal and the material conditions of experience is necessary. The employment of these categories is, accordingly, strictly empirical and never transcendental. They cannot be used to prove the existence of God, of the self as an enduring reality, or of the world as an organic unity, since these alleged realities are not governed by the material and formal conditions of experience (sensation and a priori concepts) and thus cannot be affirmed as necessarily existing. This is not to say that they do not exist, but only that they cannot be proved to exist: "In the *mere concept* of a thing no mark of its existence is to be found."[43]

The Transcendental Dialectic

In a later part of the *Critique of Pure Reason*, namely, the "Transcendental Dialectic," Kant explains how use of the concepts of God, the self, and the world as pointing to transcendental realities inevitably involves one in useless speculation or even logical contradiction.[44] Hence, these concepts should be understood as regulating but not as constituting human experience.[45] In this heuristic as opposed to ostensive use of the concepts of God, self, and the world, human experience is given a systematic unity that it would not otherwise have even with the application of the a priori transcendental concepts to the data of sense experience. Hence, "It is a necessary maxim of reason to proceed always in accordance with such ideas."[46]

The idea of the transcendental self, for example, connects "all the appearances, all the actions and receptivity of our mind, *as if* the mind were a simple substance which persists with personal identity (in this life at least), while its states . . . are in continual change."[47] Similarly, the transcendental idea of the world allows us to investigate the workings of Nature in human experience "*as if* the series of appearances were in itself endless, without any first or supreme member."[48] Finally, the transcendental idea of God allows us to proceed "*as if* the sum of all appearances (the sensible world itself) had a single, highest and all-sufficient ground beyond itself, namely, a self-subsistent, original, creative reason."[49] Thus, only if these transcendental ideas are treated as objectively real and constitutive of human experience in different ways are they illusory and a hindrance to the advance of human knowledge.

Conclusions

Even if one questions Kant's basic assumption in the *Critique of Pure Reason* that human knowledge is limited to the data of sense experience as antecedently structured by a priori rational categories, his analysis of the necessary role of subjectivity in human cognition is truly remarkable. Whereas his predecessors in both the rationalist and empiricist tradition remained focused on sense impressions and ideas as the objects of human cognition and never really asked themselves how the human mind is able to collect sense data and draw inferences from the data in the elaboration of general ideas, Kant through careful introspection came to see the primacy of subjectivity over objectivity in human cognition. It is not what the human subject of experience receives from the outer world that is all-important but what it does with the data once it has been received into consciousness. Thus the unity of human experience is primarily the effect of the unconscious workings of the mind on the data rather than of the data on the mind. As I have indicated at several points above, Kant in my judgment overstated his basic insight here in making the synthesizing activity of the mind the sole agency in human cognition. He himself, to be sure, avoids the charge of material idealism (a "mind-only" approach to reality) by insisting that human experience is invariably a synthesis of subject and object, mind and matter.[50] But his successors, the German Idealists, will in varying degrees overrule him on this point and stipulate that the transcendental self not only structures its object of experience but ultimately creates it.

Still another precious insight of Kant into human subjectivity is that the subject is never a direct object of experience because it is manifest in consciousness only as a synthesizing activity. Yet, if the unity of human experience is largely, even if not exclusively, the work of this synthesizing activity, then the search for what counts as an individual existent in this world is dramatically changed. Whereas with all previous authors covered in this book, the focus was outward on what can be known about things in terms of sense perception and rational reflection on universal forms, Kant has opened the way for exploring what it means to be an individual existent through an inward process of introspection, analyzing how the subject of experience becomes a unified subject of experience or individual reality in synthesizing sense data received from the world around it. Subjects of experience, accordingly, rather than objects of sense perception or thought should be the proper focus for dealing with the individual existent as what is ultimately real in this world.

One might at this point counterargue that Kant makes regular reference in his philosophy to the Thing-in-itself (*Ding an sich*) and includes within that category the enduring self, the world, and God. That is, even though these alleged realities cannot be directly experienced, they are still treated as nonempirical "things." Here, as I see it, we encounter the limits of Kant's own approach to human knowledge. Instead of shifting to a radically new worldview constituted by subjects of experience who co-constitute the external world all around them through their ongoing dynamic interrelation, Kant still thought in terms of a world dominated by objects of thought rather than subjects of experience. Even though all that human beings can know about those things are their appearances in experience under a priori conditions set up by the human mind, in the end it is still objects or things in Kant's worldview that primarily exist with subjects of experience playing a necessary but still secondary role in that world of things rather than vice versa. The other option—namely, the primacy of subjects of experience over things within a different worldview—was indeed explored by Berkeley and Leibniz earlier in the eighteenth century, but as we shall see in a later chapter, was not picked up and further developed until Alfred North Whitehead adapted it to his own purposes in the twentieth century. In the meantime, the German Idealists carried forward Kant's legacy in thinking through the logical implications of the notion of transcendental subjectivity, as I try to make clear in the next chapter.

5

TRANSCENDENTAL IDEALISM AND
THE EMPIRICAL OTHER

David Hume in *A Treatise of Human Nature* presented a formidable challenge to the natural scientists of his day with his incisive critique of the principle of cause and effect and other hitherto unquestioned presuppositions of scientific method. Immanuel Kant met that challenge with his *Critique of Pure Reason, Critique of Practical Reason*, and *Critique of Judgment*. But all three *Critiques* presupposed a radical distinction between phenomena (the data of sense experience) and noumena (things in themselves apart from human experience). The movement called German Idealism represented by Fichte, Schelling, and Hegel was a concerted effort to overcome that dualism between reality and appearances in Kant's philosophy by way of a transcendental monism—that is, by elevating Kant's postulate of the transcendental unity of apperception operative within human experience into a subsistent metaphysical principle, the absolute ego, creative not only of the form but also of the content of its own experience. As such, the absolute ego could alternately be identified with God or with the human being in the latter's moments of intellectual intuition when it creates what it intuits. There is, of course, some affinity here with the notion of Atman/ Brahman within Advaita Vedanta Hinduism. But within the context of nineteenth-century European intellectual life, it rather represented a growing awareness of the intrinsic dynamism of divine and human subjectivity, likewise the preeminence of spirit over matter in and through the transcendental imagination with its awesome creative powers.

But the triumph of speculative thought thus set forth by the German Idealists, above all by Hegel with his system of absolute idealism, had its own limitations in dealing with the empirical Other, the non-ego, as a persistent factor in human experience. In the pages that follow, I indicate how Fichte, Schelling, and Hegel all dealt with this problem in their own way. I focus, however, primarily on Schelling because in my judgment he probed the depths of human subjectivity far better than the other two. In addition, in his "late" period he acknowledged the reality of the empirical Other as the necessary starting point for what he called "positive" philosophy, a move that implicitly challenged the presuppositions of German Idealism as a viable approach to reality. In other words, Hegel with his elaborately conceived and executed philosophical scheme was a far more consistent proponent of German Idealism than Schelling. But to his credit, Schelling saw the inevitable limits of this idealistic line of thought much better than Hegel, even though in point of fact his "positive" philosophy in the end was very little different in style and content from the "negative" philosophy that Schelling associated with Hegel and his own earlier philosophical works.

Johann Gottlieb Fichte (1762–1814)

There are, says Fichte, only two consistent philosophical positions: dogmatism represented by the reigning *Schulmetaphysik,* which Kant rejected as a result of reading the work of David Hume, and critical idealism, a continuation of Kant's project.[1] Fichte chose idealism because for him it was accompanied by a feeling of freedom, the freedom to order the world of one's experience in line with deeply felt feelings and desires. Dogmatism, on the contrary, inevitably gave rise for Fichte to a feeling of necessity and constraint through contact with that which lies outside one's experience.[2] At the same time, Fichte was convinced that a scientific approach to reality (*Wissenss-*

chaftslehre) must be grounded in a single metaphysical principle from which all other conclusions deductively follow.[3] Fichte had been a student of Spinoza in his early years and much admired Spinoza's deduction of a philosophical system *more geometrico*.[4]

Appealing to Kant's principle of the transcendental unity of apperception in *Critique of Pure Reason* and Kant's notion of the categorical imperative in *Critique of Practical Reason*, both of which point to the self-legislating character of the transcendental ego, Fichte postulated that the ultimate metaphysical principle of his system was not a fact (*Tatsache*) but an activity (*Tathandlung*).[5] This activity is grasped in an intellectual intuition,[6] but its structure or mode of proceeding is derived from reflection on the "Antinomies" in Kant's *Critique of Pure Reason*. The antinomies, said Fichte, can only be overcome through a three-stage movement of thought: thesis, antithesis, synthesis.[7] Moreover, an entire thought system can be elaborated by moving from thesis to antithesis to synthesis over and over again; each synthesis is in turn a new thesis, provoking a new antithesis and still another synthesis.

The first and most fundamental application of this dialectical method is found in the opening pages of *The Science of Knowledge* (*Wissensschaftslehre*). The original thesis is the ego as positing itself in its own being; this corresponds to the logical axiom of identity (A = A) and the ontological category of reality.[8] The antithesis is the "op-position" of the non-ego to the ego; this corresponds to the logical axiom of difference (non-A is not A) and the ontological category of negation.[9] It is important to realize, however, that in Fichte's view the non-ego does not exist in its own right and for its own sake but only as an instrument for the realization of self-consciousness within the ego. The ego posits itself in being unconsciously; it needs the resistance (*Anstoss*) of the non-ego to become conscious of itself. Then, once aware of the provisional reality of the non-ego, it has to overcome it by way of a primordial synthesis or "com-position." In effect, the absolute ego "op-posits" within itself both a finite ego and a finite non-ego that then mutually limit one another.[10] In this synthesis we have the logical axiom of sufficient reason and the ontological category of limitation or determination.[11]

On the basis of this triadic structure—the finite ego and the finite non-ego in opposition to one another and the absolute ego "opposed" to both of them as their originary source—Fichte derives not only the Kantian categories or a priori forms of understanding in their application to the data of sense experience but also the physical contents of the external world. He is able to accomplish this by mentally moving back and forth between two complementary schemes for the construction of consciousness. In the "theoretical" construction of consciousness he adopts the standpoint of the finite ego, which finds itself really opposed in the fulfillment of its wishes and desires by the presence and activity of the non-ego in consciousness. The finite ego thus finds itself in a situation of reciprocity with the non-ego, alternately acting upon and being acted upon by the non-ego. But in the "practical" construction of consciousness Fichte adopts the standpoint of the absolute ego which creates the non-ego as the instrument of resistance to the finite ego and to its own strivings as absolute ego for full self-realization or self-awareness.

The practical self [absolute ego] combines the independence and freedom of the original act of self-positing with the dependence of an intelligence [the finite ego] oriented toward real objects in the world of the non-self. Hence the theoretical self [the finite ego] and the theoretical construction of consciousness are subordinate to, and dependent upon, the more fundamental operations of the practical self [the absolute ego].[12]

Notable here is the emphasis on the act of self-positing by the absolute ego and the consequent primacy of practical reason based on will over speculative reason based on reflection. "The practical self regards the world as a task, and sensible things as so many materials of duty or visible occasions for specifying the moral struggle and securing at least partial triumphs for consciousness. This moral purpose is the ultimate justification for positing the real world or sphere of the non-ego."[13] The absolute ego realizes itself over time in the growth of a moral order to which the finite ego makes its contribution through its time-bound struggle to deal with the finite non-ego in a morally responsible way. Fichte was at one point in his career accused of atheism because he identified God not with a transcendent person but with an immanent moral order. But, given the fact that he conceived the absolute ego as an activity rather than an entity, an activity that gave rise to both the finite ego and the finite non-ego as instruments of its own self-realization within this world, it is not surprising that Fichte saw this self-realization achieved in terms of a moral order rather than a specific entity. Through religiously oriented meditation, however, "The moral order takes on the personal characteristics of a God, having intelligence, will, and providential power. Our infinite striving toward the absolute is now expressed more in terms of *love* than of duty, or rather, love is taken as the basis of duty."[14]

F. W. J. Schelling (1775–1854): The Early and Middle Period

Schelling was initially a student of Fichte but he deviated from the latter with his own emphasis on the presence and activity of the Absolute in nature as well as in human consciousness. Whereas Fichte's system might be called a subjective idealism, Schelling's should be called an objective idealism since he sought to unite within his thought system both nature and spirit. At one point early in his career, Schelling referred to the Absolute as the Indifference of nature and spirit in the sense of their common ground or source. This occasioned Hegel's sarcastic remark that the Absolute Indifference of nature and spirit in Schelling's thought is "the night, in which, as we say, all cows are black."[15] Schelling was deeply hurt by this comment from an erstwhile friend; in this way an antipathy was set up between the two former classmates at the university in Tübingen that lasted the rest of their lives. Yet, at the same time,

Hegel's remark prompted Schelling to think through his own project more carefully with the result that he eventually incorporated into his own scheme insights from the theosophical writings of the German mystic Jacob Boehme, and to a lesser extent from the works of his philosophical predecessors, Leibniz and Spinoza. Combining features of all three systems, he eventually worked out a metaphysics in which freedom rather than rationality was the key factor.[16] The Unconditioned Identity of nature and spirit was no longer Absolute Mind but a personal God exercising Perfect Freedom.

Schelling's earlier reflections on the presence and activity of spirit in nature and on the drive of spirit within nature to achieve self-awareness in and through human self-consciousness are very rich, even prophetic in light of the work of Pierre Teilhard de Chardin and other evolutionary thinkers in the twentieth century.[17] But the writings of Schelling's middle period, where the influence of Boehme was so prominent, are far more important. Initially in *Philosophy and Religion*, but above all in *Essay on Human Freedom*, published in 1809,[18] Schelling came up with some groundbreaking insights into the God-world relationship and into the inner workings of human and divine subjectivity. These insights were in fact so startling and unconventional that they paradoxically led to a sharp decline in Schelling's reputation as an original thinker and at the same time indirectly contributed to the ascendancy of Hegel as the most significant German philosopher of the day. Hegel was lauded as a supremely logical and rational thinker, whereas Schelling was held in suspicion as someone who had somehow become lost in idle, even irrational speculation.

The first of Schelling's major insights in *Essay on Human Freedom* was to rethink Spinoza's identification of ground and consequent within logic with cause and effect in extra-mental reality. That is, whereas Spinoza had simply taken for granted the identification of logic and ontology, thought and being, within his own deductive system, Schelling argued that within every entity (including God) there necessarily exists a vital source but for that same reason a nonrational ground for its existence and activity.[19] Not just in logic but in reality, therefore, this ground is the explanation for the existence of the entity, the deeper reason that it comes into being and stays in being. With this dramatic insight, Schelling changed what it meant to be a subject of existence/experience as opposed to an object of perception or thought.

Whereas in classical metaphysics one conventionally linked objects of perception or thought within various chains of cause and effect so as to explain their existence and activity, Schelling argued that a subject of existence/experience was in a sense its own cause (*Causa sui*). It existed in virtue of its own vital source or ground of being. That ground of being for creatures, of course, was ultimately one with the divine ground of being, the vital source of existence and activity for God as Creator of heaven and earth. But still the immediate cause of existence and activity for a creature was its own immanent ground of being, which as a vital or nonrational principle was spontaneous and not fully predictable.[20] Here, in Schelling's mind, was the philosophical explanation of creaturely (but, above all, human) freedom as a choice for good or evil.[21] Out of this nonrational ground of being proceed two dialectically related principles. The first, the will of the ground, represents pure spontaneity; the second, the rational will or the will of love, exists to restrain the will of the ground in its spontaneity, to give it rational form or pattern and thus to achieve a synthesis of the two wills (on the human level, personality).[22] In all creatures, these two wills must be somehow synthesized. If the will of the ground prevails over the will of reason, then the creature effectively chooses evil over good. If the will of reason prevails over the will of the ground, then the creature chooses what is good. This is in imitation of God, who likewise experiences the will of the ground and the will of reason within divine consciousness but always chooses what is good, the supremacy of the will of reason over the will of the ground.[23]

Little wonder that educated readers shook their heads in disbelief upon reading Schelling's *Essay on Human Freedom*. The image of

God provided therein was far too anthropomorphic for their taste, and even the image of human beings and other creatures as possessing spontaneous impulses that could easily become the source of evil in the world was alarming. Only later in the nineteenth century did Sigmund Freud basically confirm Schelling's hypothesis about human subjectivity with his studies of the hidden influence of the unconscious on human behavior. Likewise, Freud's student Carl Jung subsequently raised the issue of a "shadow side" to God, that God is not pure light (total rationality) but a mixture of light and darkness (rationality and spontaneity) wherein light ultimately prevails but only after a struggle both within God and within the world of creation.[24]

Still another insight into the God-world relationship coming from *Essay on Human Freedom* was Schelling's explanation of the freedom of God to create and the freedom of the original human being to sin and bring evil into the creative process for the first time. In both cases it is an intelligible deed outside of the space-time parameters of the cosmic process.[25] Likewise, it is free only in the sense that it is not constrained by external forces. As something emanating from the divine and human ground of being, it is necessitated since otherwise God would not be self-realized in and through the work of creation, and human beings in the person of the primordial human being would never experience the difference between good and evil and thus become fully human, achieving true personhood or personality.[26]

Years ago I argued in my doctoral dissertation that Schelling had to place these primordial free acts of God and the first human being outside of space and time (so to speak, as existing from all eternity) because, if located within the cosmic process, they would have to be logically explainable in terms of the dialectic governing that same process.[27] Schelling's adaptation of Fichte's dialectic (thesis-antithesis-synthesis), in other words, was a doctrine of potencies (*Potenzen*) with the same logical rigor as the dialectic of thesis-antithesis-synthesis within Fichte's scheme. Schelling's dialectic of potencies, of course, was operative within nature as well as within human consciousness as in Fichte's scheme. But, in either case, it effectively excluded the possibility of a genuinely free decision arising out of the cosmic process, even one explicitly designed to explain the free act of God in creation and the free choice of the primordial human being (and the free choices of all subsequent human beings) to choose evil over good.

After publication of *Essay on Human Freedom* in 1809, Schelling wrote several drafts of an even larger work entitled *Ages of the World* (*Weltalter*),[28] which he never published; in my dissertation I argued that this presumably happened because he could not explain the passage from the past to the present of the cosmic process in virtue of a free divine act. For that free divine act was itself governed by the dialectical scheme of the potencies as operative in the divine mind before the dawn of creation.[29] In any event, he remained stuck in composition of the first part of the work, entitled "The Past" (*Die Vergangenheit*).

As I see it, what all this says about divine and human subjectivity is that it is ultimately grounded not in reason but in will. Rationality is in the end subordinate to spontaneity on all the various levels of existence and activity within the cosmic process. While this might initially give cause for alarm among those anxious to preserve order or at least restrain disorder within their lives both as individuals and as members of different communities or environments, the basic priority of spontaneity over rationality should be acknowledged and cherished. Without spontaneity within Nature nothing new happens. Determinism in one form or another then reigns supreme. This was, after all, the temptation within scientific method at the start of the modern era—namely, to reduce the workings of nature and ultimately of human beings as part of nature to the image of a "cosmic machine" totally regulated by natural law. But it proved to be only a temporary victory. Romanticism (of which the intellectual movement of German Idealism was only a part) reacted strongly against the rigidity of the Enlightenment vision of reason as the ultimate court of appeal. In addition, as we shall see later, within the natural sciences in the twentieth century new discoveries were made in connection with the development of quantum theory and chaos theory that seemed to point to a principle of spontaneity within Nature that dramatically calls into question the image of the world as a cosmic machine.

C. G. W. F. Hegel (1770–1831)

Hegel is unquestionably the best-known and most widely read German Idealist, in part because of the rigor of his thought and the scope of his philosophical vision, but also in part because of the skillful way in which he combined insights from both Fichte and Schelling into his own metaphysical scheme. From Fichte, for example, he borrowed the idea that Absolute Spirit uses material reality for its own self-realization in human history. From Schelling he borrowed the idea that the material world must still be taken seriously for the way in which it manifests the presence and activity of Absolute Spirit on various levels of existence and activity. His own standpoint is perhaps best reflected in his insistence at the beginning of *Phenomenology of Mind* that truth is identical with the whole—that is, a system of interconnected partial truths.[30] Implicit in this claim is his justification for the priority of spirit over matter. Only spirit can grasp the reality of the whole as a dynamic system of interconnected parts or members. Organisms within Nature may reflect in their internal structure and external behavior this sense of the whole, but they cannot conceptually grasp it and make it their own after the manner of finite spirit, the individual human being, and in the political order the State. Yet, in the end only Absolute Spirit can itself be the whole; only Absolute Spirit can be understood as the "concrete universal" or the Absolute Idea, that which perfectly synthesizes subject and object, spirit and matter, within itself.[31]

Hegel, accordingly, is the systematic thinker par excellence. But, as we shall see below, perhaps his achievement was a triumph more of speculative reason than anything else. In subsuming the particulars of human sense experience under abstract universals and then organizing all these abstract universals into the dynamic unity of a system of truths or concrete universals, he was effectively claiming not only that reality is ultimately spiritual in character, but, more importantly, that reality is uniform. Everything that exists is ultimately a partial manifestation of a singular reality: the reality of Absolute Spirit. Put another way, since Absolute Spirit is in its operation governed by dialectical method, the movement in thought (and according to Hegel in material reality as well) from thesis to antithesis to synthesis, the content of the system is ultimately subordinate to its method or form. Method, in other words, does not arise out of the analysis of empirical data but subtly screens the data and effectively eliminates from consideration what cannot be reconciled with its own procedure.[32]

To illustrate what I have in mind, I present here a brief overview of Hegel's thought system. His first major work was *Phenomenology of Mind* published in 1807. Therein Hegel detailed how one could begin with common sense, in which the objects of knowledge were thought to be really distinct from oneself, and end with absolute knowledge, a strictly philosophical understanding of reality.[33] The key to the entire process is to learn to view external things as existing not for themselves but in and for consciousness. If, for example, I view something here and now as a tree some distance away from me, I can shift my position in space and time to view instead here and now a house. So "here" and "now" are really not pertinent to extra-mental entities but only to me as the observer of those entities. In effect, "the *here* and the *now* are universals, requiring the presence of reason and the constitutive activity of consciousness."[34] Hegel's conclusion is that "the Universal is therefore in point of fact the truth of sense-certainty, the true content of sense-experience."[35]

But what about the tree and the house as physical realities apart from me as the observer? Are they simply occasions for me to realize that the notions of *here* and *now* are relative to me and my position in space-time? Hegel's objective in *Phenomenology*, however, is not to answer that question but rather to describe the itinerary of the inquiring human mind as it seeks to find itself and its own distinctive way of proceeding in dealing with the world around it. The all-important factor in this dialectical approach to reality is the notion of negation. Whenever something is given to me in sense consciousness as here and now existing, it provokes in me reflection on its antithesis; that is, I come to see that it can only be properly understood by me in terms of its contrary: what it is not. But then this mental tension between what a thing is and what it is not must be resolved in terms of a synthesis, a fuller understanding of the thing, no longer as seen in isolation but in its proper context as including its antithesis. Yet this initial synthesis in turn calls for integration into a further synthesis through the self-same process of first negating what is given and then negating the negation so as to arrive at still another synthesis, a new sense of the totality of what can be known on the basis of what was originally perceived as simply an isolated thing or event. Only in this way is there "a juncture and perfect interpenetration between the natural, naive attitude and the reflective, scientific attitude, between things as they *appear* in finite perspective and as they *are* in the absolute totality."[36]

Here one could object that this dialectical approach to a deeper understanding of reality has no final goal. One can always negate whatever mental synthesis one achieves and thus keep the process going ad infinitum. Hegel's response is to stipulate that the phenomenology of mind must end in the affirmation of Absolute Spirit as Absolute Knowledge (*Wissen*) or ultimate reality.[37] Once achieving in reflection the level of Absolute Spirit, a human being finally realizes that he or she is spirit in full possession of itself. Equivalently, it has become Aristotle's Unmoved Mover, thought thinking itself, and therefore in no need of anything apart from itself for its own existence.

But for the same reason one can further question whether this elaborate itinerary of the human mind in search of itself was already settled from the beginning. That is, while the individual human being has to travel through various mental stages in order to reach the level of Absolute Spirit, Absolute Spirit itself already exists as a reality that undergoes no change at all but is eternally the same. The individual human being at the end of its intellectual journey is then absorbed into Absolute Spirit or the concrete universal, whether the concrete universal be conceived as God, the world soul, or simply the higher self as in Advaita Vedanta Hinduism or some versions of Buddhism. In this sense, even though Hegel laid heavy stress on human self-realization through a process of reflection on the deliverances of consciousness, he was in the end a thoroughly classical thinker. Becoming in his mind was always ordered to Being, a final state of rest or consummation in which Becoming would be at an end.

Phenomenology of Mind is, of course, only an introduction or propaideutic to Hegel's exposition of his thought system as a whole. The latter is composed of three parts: the Logic, Philosophy of Nature, and Philosophy of Concrete Spirit. The Logic lays down not only the laws of thought but the laws of Being. Equivalently, the categories of the Logic are viewed as the self-determinations of Absolute Spirit in abstraction from the world of Nature and finite spirit; for that same reason they constitute the logical structure of Nature and finite spirit as stages on the way to the full self-realization of Absolute Spirit in the cosmic process and in human history.[38] The first three categories of Hegel's Logic, for example, are Being, Nothing, and Becoming. Being is initially pure thought stripped of all further determination.[39] Being as such gives rise to its antithesis, Nothing, as likewise devoid of content or internal determination; the interplay of Being and Nothing within Absolute Spirit results in Being as Becoming, the basic principle of the self-realization of Absolute Spirit in Nature and in human history.[40] But Being as Becoming results in *Dasein* (Being as present here and now), and *Dasein* is then itself further specified in terms of quality, quantity, and measure (*Mass*) as the unification of quality and quantity. Thus gathered into itself, Being becomes essence (*Wesen*), which Hegel describes as the truth of Being.[41] But essence likewise undergoes a threefold development, first considered as such in the abstract, then in terms of how it manifests itself existentially, and finally in the unity of reality and appearance as actuality (*Wirklichkeit*).[42] Finally, Being as actuality goes through three stages of self-unfolding: first, as immediate subjectivity, then as an objective principle at work within Nature at both the inanimate and the organismic levels of existence and activity, and finally as the Idea, the complete interpenetration of the subjective and objective dimensions of reality.[43]

Armed with these structural principles from reflection on the inner life of Absolute Spirit apart from creation, Hegel is then ready to plunge into his analysis first of the philosophy of nature and then of the philosophy of concrete spirit. With reference to the philosophy of nature, of course, Hegel has to deal with the transit from the world of forms (Logic) to the world of actuality in which they are to be embodied (Nature). Unlike Schelling, who attributed this "fall" from ideality into reality as a primordial free choice on the part of God and/or the primordial human being, Hegel presents it as a necessary step in the historical process of the self-realization of Absolute Spirit: "Nature is the idea in the state of otherness."[44] Being must posit itself as other than itself so as in the end to recover itself as Being both in and for itself. This assumption also gives Hegel an excuse for the sometimes awkward way in which his dialectical scheme is verified in the concrete workings of Nature, specifically in the move from a purely mechanistic to an organismic approach to physical reality. But, once having arrived at the level of the human being as the most perfect natural organism, he can shift into the Philosophy of Concrete Spirit.[45] Here too everything is arranged triadically. Under subjective spirit, he first takes up the doctrine of the soul as the substantial form or organizing principle of the body, then the development of human consciousness from common sense to rational self-awareness (basically a recapitulation of the contents of *Phenomenology of Mind*), and finally the notion of the free individual as a synthesis of mind and will, reason and feeling. The focus of the free individual, however, is not on itself in isolation but on life in community with other free individuals.[46]

At this point Hegel takes up consideration of objective spirit with its triadic division into individual rights (above all, the right of private property), morality or the duties of the individual vis-à-vis others in the community, and the synthesis of individual rights and moral obligation in the ethical life (*Sittlichkeit*).[47] Both individual rights and community obligations are "abstract" in Hegel's sense, since they do not adequately take into account the full context of the social reality of which they are parts. Hence, it is antecedently difficult to settle disputes over individual rights or even to decide for oneself between seemingly conflicting duties in terms of the common good. What is needed is the notion of the ethical life which unites the objective will of the group and the subjective freedom of conscience of the individual under the guidance of a universal rational will accepted by all parties.

But this universal rational will is likewise subject to a threefold articulation: the rational will as expressed in family life, civil society, and finally the state. Family life is heavily interpersonal; civil society is predominately impersonal in the way it lays down rules for individual members. Hence, the state must ideally combine feelings of intimacy as among family members with the relatively impersonal character of relations in civil society by presenting itself as a higher-order social reality or supra-individual personality. "In the state, men have borne home forcefully to them that they are free, personal subjects only within an encompassing whole, which is itself a self-conscious subject or social individual."[48] Only within the state do individuals fully exercise rational freedom vis-à-vis one another. The state within Hegel's scheme thus enjoys a mystique proper to itself as "the supreme actuality of the ethical idea and hence the objective manifestation of the divine idea [the *full* self-manifestation of Absolute Spirit] upon earth."[49]

Since Hegel in his position first as professor of philosophy and then as rector at the University of Berlin was subject to the authority of the Prussian government, some scholars have contended that he consciously shaped his theory of the state to please those same civil authorities. Others disagree, arguing that his concept of the ideal state was the logical outgrowth of his metaphysical system.[50] I would tend to agree with the latter group. The universal rational will is most clearly articulated in the decrees of a sovereign ruler, not in the sometimes messy will of the people as worked out in ongoing political debate and compromise. Likewise, since Hegel's predominant metaphor within his overall dialectical scheme was that of an organism with interdependent parts or members rather than that of a community with rival subgroups engaged in power struggles with one another, it is not surprising that Hegel preferred hereditary monarchy as the ideal form of government within the state.

The third and last subdivision of Hegel's doctrine of objective spirit is Absolute Spirit, which likewise has three stages of development in art, religion, and philosophy: "Art grasps the absolute spirit in concretely *sensuous intuitions*. Religion enjoys a direct feeling of union with the divine principle, and uses *symbolic representations* to express the nature of this principle. But the nature of the absolute spirit is adequately articulated only by philosophy, in the *rational concept*, which alone apprehends absolute spirit according to its own proper actuality."[51] "Philosophy" in this context is, of course, Hegel's own philosophy, which is as a result a self-sufficient whole or system of truths. Only in the whole as a system of interconnected partial truths is truth as such finally located.

Schelling in His Late Period

Beginning with his lectures at the University of Munich in 1827 and culminating in his professorship at the University of Berlin from 1841 until his death in 1854, Schelling began to distinguish between "negative" and "positive" philosophy.[52] Negative philosophy was pictured as a purely conceptual metaphysical scheme with logical consistency as its chief feature. Schelling regarded not only Hegel's philosophy but much of his own earlier attempts at explanation of the God-world relationship as negative philosophy, a triumph of speculative logic but without grounding in empirical reality.[53] Positive philosophy, accordingly, had to be grounded in empirical fact, that is, in a primordial free decision on the part of either God or the first human being.[54] This is hardly surprising, given Schelling's previous reflections on human and divine freedom in *Essay on Human Freedom* and in his efforts to explain the transition from past to present in the various drafts of the *Ages of the World* (*Weltalter*) in the years following *Essay*. But, in stipulating this difference between negative and positive philosophy, Schelling was implicitly calling into question the entire movement of German Idealism to which he himself had notably contributed.

That is, he still tried without success to explain in terms of his own dialectical scheme of the potencies (*Potenzen*) how the primordial free act of God in creation and revelation took place, and why the free response of human beings to that divine initiative necessarily followed. But simply by maintaining that the move from speculative thought to empirical reality cannot be made in virtue of a logical inference but only through appeal to an empirical fact outside the conceptual scheme and thus not controlled by it, Schelling restored the balance between realism and idealism within the history of Western philosophy that had been subverted, however unwittingly, by Fichte, Hegel, and Schelling himself. To put the same point more dramatically, whereas Hegel in his thought system subordinated religion, even revealed religion, to philosophy as the rational explanation of reality, Schelling at the end of his life was claiming that religion, which is heavily based on personal feeling and individual experience, is ultimately more important than philosophy for understanding what life in this world is all about.[55]

Schelling's philosophy of mythology and philosophy of revelation, as set forth in his lectures at the University of Berlin in 1841–1854, were still heavily idealistic in their orientation and articulation;

for that same reason those lectures were quite disappointing to Søren Kierkegaard and others who initially attended them in hopes of a fresh approach to philosophy.[56] But in principle Schelling had already taken the necessary first step in recovering the primacy of empirical fact as found in the details of human history over a priori first principles as the starting point for rational reflection on the meaning of life.

6

THE REVOLT AGAINST
SYSTEMS THINKING

As mentioned at the end of the last chapter, Søren Kierkegaard attended Schelling's lectures on positive philosophy at the University of Berlin in the mid-nineteenth century. Kierkegaard evidently did not find what he was looking for in terms of a new emphasis on the primacy of the individual human being over and against the grand metaphysical schemes of people like Hegel and Karl Marx. Hence, he created his own philosophy through thinking through what to do in terms of his own particular life situation and then generalizing upon that to offer a guide to other Christians in making their existential decisions. In that sense, Kierkegaard spearheaded a move from metaphysics into ethics as the proper focus of philosophical inquiry at the end of the nineteenth century. In this chapter, besides reviewing the writings of Kierkegaard on moments of self-doubt and anxiety within the Christian life, I analyze the work of two other religiously oriented philosophers, Emmanuel Levinas and Martin Buber. Both of them, largely on the basis of their adherence to Judaism and their regular reading of the Bible, came up with precious insights into human subjectivity as the necessary basis for one's relationships to God and to neighbor. Thus, all three philosophers in their own way stressed the need for moving beyond the self as object of thought within a metaphysical scheme to a new sense of the existential self who on the basis of a religious vision feels called to reach out to the Other, whether the Other be God, the neighbor, or, for Levinas, even the total stranger.

Søren Kierkegaard

Relatively few modern philosophers have used their personal lives for the starting point of their reflections as extensively as Søren Kierkegaard. Admittedly, he frequently used pseudonyms to disguise his authorship and in some cases to present opinions other than his own in the hope of provoking the reader into forming his or her own opinion on the issue in question.[1] But Kierkegaard's unusual personal life is still plainly reflected in all his major writings. Our point in this brief overview of his philosophy and theology, of course, is simply to make clear how he was consciously probing the depths of his own subjectivity so as to achieve a personal identity distinct from what either objective reason or the mores of contemporary society would see as acceptable. He had to go his own way, no matter what the cost to himself or others. In terms of the basic theme of this book, Kierkegaard was focusing on what it means to be a unique individual within a world governed largely by convention.

But this heightened sense of self-identity did not come to him all at once. In his mind there were three clearly differentiated stages of development or self-realization: the aesthetic, with its focus on the needs and desires of the solitary individual; the ethical, as the call of duty or the appeal of the universal (which is at once the antithesis and the sublation [in Hegelian terms, the *Aufhebung*] of the perspective of the solitary individual); and the religious, the synthesis of the particular and the universal in the extraordinary human being who goes beyond the ethical, trusting in one's status as a forgiven sinner in the eyes of God. In what follows, I briefly describe these three stages with appropriate references to some of Kierkegaard's works.

In the aesthetic stage, the individual is preoccupied with the world of sensuous experience—above all, the world of romantic love in which one as a master lover toys with the affections of innocent young women without sexually abusing them. Perhaps the clearest example of this is found in "The Seducer's Diary," a chapter within

Either-Or.[2] The seducer, an older man named Johannes, meets by chance a young girl named Cordelia and is deeply attracted to her beauty and innocence. Rather than court her directly, however, he arranges simply to be the companion and advisor of a much younger man who is consciously in pursuit of her hand in marriage. When the young man's efforts at courtship prove more and more futile, Johannes diverts Cordelia's attention to himself by indicating that he too is emotionally involved with her. Eventually he proposes marriage to her and she accepts. But then he must find a way to make her weary of his company and thus choose to break off the engagement. So, as Johannes later comments in his diary, he "lived much too intellectually to be a seducer in the ordinary sense. For him individuals were merely for stimulation; he discarded them as trees shake off their leaves—he was rejuvenated, the foliage withered."[3] Thus, in the end, his temporary engagement to Cordelia was part of a pact with himself as an aesthetic, one who seeks the subtler rather than the more obvious pleasures of romantic love.

Given that the term "either/or" points to a decision between alternative courses of action, it is not surprising that the second volume of *Either/Or* sets forth an alternative approach to fulfillment in life. The first chapter, "The Esthetic Validity of Marriage," is presented in the form of still another letter written to a close friend by a magistrate quite happily married for many years; his correspondent is someone like Johannes, a restless, novelty-seeking individual who for purely aesthetic reasons has never married. The magistrate seeks to explain to his friend that aesthetic fulfillment is to be found within marriage, not outside of it. Marriage and marital love are the "transfiguration" of first love or purely romantic love.[4] Thus, even though time can also be the enemy of true love since it sometimes produces boredom within marriage and a reduction of love to a mere sense of duty toward the other,[5] it can refine the quality of marital love and make clear to the marriage partners that duty is not the enemy of love but its friend.[6] Duty freely embraced sublates individual self-fulfillment into marital love.

In the second chapter, "The Balance between the Esthetic and the Ethical in the Development of the Personality," Kierkegaard has the letter writer of the first chapter continue his epistle to the solitary aesthetic by noting the importance of making choices. Only when one is in an either/or situation that demands a personal decision for the one or the other does one move from the aesthetic to the ethical stage of self-realization. The aesthetic individual is forever weighing possibilities for action and yet never committing himself/herself definitively to any one choice. The ethically oriented individual, on the contrary, realizes the need for a decision and actually makes a choice, thereby rising to a new stage of self-fulfillment in that he or she ultimately grounds his or her identity in that choice.[7] Since one can become quite depressed by failing to make a decision, the only practical solution is to choose, even if one chooses in despair of making the right choice. "When a person has truly chosen despair, he has truly chosen what despair chooses: himself in his eternal validity."[8] Only then is the individual truly free to be oneself. One thus moves through and beyond despair by embracing it freely and thereby taking full responsibility for oneself. One can make such a paradoxical concrete decision, however, only when one "repents," that is, when one recognizes the inevitable isolation from the rest of humanity, which is involved in such a personalized decision and then seeks reconciliation with God and other human beings through an act of repentance.[9]

At this point, the individual has already implicitly moved from the ethical to the religious stage of self-development. He has balanced particularity and universality in his own person; he is equivalently a Hegelian concrete universal. That is, he listens to the call of duty, feels the appeal of the universal norm. Yet he cannot take refuge in the security of the universal, what others acknowledge to be right and proper. He must choose on his own, in the light of his own concrete situation. In this way, he chooses himself more than any given course of action, and he chooses, feeling the need for repentance, because he has thereby distanced himself from the universal, the ethical norm (at least in principle, if not always in fact).

Toward the end of this second epistle, Kierkegaard takes note of the relation between an ordinary individual and an extraordinary individual. On the one hand, "The genuinely extraordinary person is the genuinely ordinary person. The more of the universally human an individual can actualize in his life, the more extraordinary a human being he is."[10] On the other hand, he may not be able to actualize the universal in his life. "He will realize that no particular is the universal."[11] He then must accept the pain and sorrow of such a defeat of his intentions and yet stay the course in making his own decision. "At this point, he says, I have placed myself outside the universal; I have deprived myself of all the guidance, the security, the reassurance that the universal gives; I stand alone, without fellow-feeling, for I am an exception."[12] This is the price to be paid for ascent to the religious stage of self-development; one must learn to live with anxiety and self-doubt.

Another work written shortly after the publication of *Either/Or* dramatically illustrates this last point. In *Fear and Trembling*, writing under a pseudonym (Johannes de Silentio) Kierkegaard makes use of the famous passage in Genesis 22:1–19 where Abraham is asked by God to sacrifice his heir Isaac even though God had previously promised to make Abraham the father of a great nation.[13] Kierkegaard's point is that there is a huge difference between a tragic hero like Agamemnon and a man of faith like Abraham.[14] Agamemnon reluctantly sacrifices the life of his daughter Iphigenia in obedience to what he sees as an ethical principle, the common good in the war with the Trojans, and is praised by everyone for his adherence to principle even at great personal cost. Abraham responds to a strictly personal call from God to do something absurd, namely, to give up his only chance to be the father of a great nation by sacrificing the son whom he loves more dearly than himself.[15] Yet he does it, trusting that Isaac will somehow still be saved from a premature death and become his heir. In this sense Abraham, the man of faith, suspends what is ethical and universally recognized as a higher good in response to an absolute, a personal call from God.[16] Yet he earns no praise from others as a result, but instead is regarded as a madman. Furthermore, even in his own mind he is not sure that he has properly understood the call of God and thus is making the right decision. Nor can he appeal to others for advice since it is a decision uniquely his own.[17] "The paradox of faith, then, is this: that the single individual is higher than the universal; that the single individual . . . determines his relation to the universal [ethical] by his relation to the absolute [God's call], not his relation to the absolute by his relation to the universal."[18] But it is a harrowing decision, fraught with uncertainty, that demands a level of self-investment significantly beyond that of the tragic hero. Only at the religious stage of self-development, therefore, is the individual a concrete universal, embodying both the particular and the universal in his own person.

Kierkegaard sums up this case study with further philosophical reflections in *Concluding Unscientific Postscript to Philosophical Fragments*.[19] Therein he asks himself whether objectivity or subjectivity is ultimately more important for assessing the truth of Christianity. He concludes that subjectivity is more important since "the issue is not about the truth of Christianity but about the individual's relation to Christianity."[20] Hence, Lessing's celebrated declaration that one cannot derive the eternal truth needed for salvation from study of contingent historical facts is refuted when one realizes that a "leap of faith" is required.[21] This leap of faith, however, is grounded in a personal decision rather than in an argument from logical premises: "Christianity is spirit; spirit is inwardness; inwardness is subjectivity; subjectivity is essentially passion, and at its maximum an infinite, personally interested passion for one's eternal happiness."[22]

In subsequent chapters of the *Concluding Unscientific Postscript*, Kierkegaard presses this last point home. He argues that what is important for ethical decision making is not reflecting on immortality in general but becoming aware of one's own immortality through self-appropriation of one's subjectivity or inwardness.[23] Similarly, truth is not the identity of subject and object in the act of knowing, but passionate faith in what is objectively uncertain.[24] God, after all, is a subject of existence, not an object of thought;[25] so God can be felt only in the inwardness of one's subjectivity, not in the world of external reality or in some speculative explanation of the truth of Christianity. "Subjectivity culminates in passion, Christianity is paradox; paradox and passion fit each other perfectly."[26] Kierkegaard, of course, is clearly overstating his case here. As Michael Polanyi points out in *Personal Knowledge* and other works, personal commitment is quite compatible with the search for objective knowledge.[27] One begins, trusting in one's intuitions based on personal experience, but one is not satisfied until one arrives at what is considered objectively real by others as well as oneself. Kierkegaard, however, was unable to grasp that point because of his passionate commitment to inwardness, individual subjectivity, as the only source of truth in this world.[28]

Emmanuel Levinas

Moving from Kierkegaard in the late nineteenth century to Levinas in the mid-twentieth century perhaps requires a preliminary word of explanation, especially since, as we will see below, Levinas makes frequent reference both in *Totality and Infinity* and his other major work *Otherwise Than Being: Or Beyond Essence* to the writings of Martin Heidegger, whose philosophy we do not consider until the next chapter of this book. What I have in mind here is a progression in thought, not a chronological sequence. As I see it, Levinas' emphasis upon responsibility for the Other even prior to a conscious decision to assist the Other challenges the impersonal character of classical metaphysics and thus logically follows upon Kierkegaard's efforts to free the individual self from blind submission to totalizing structures in his personal life. Likewise, the third thinker considered in the chapter, Martin Buber, offers in my judgment a way to balance Kierkegaard's focus on the individual self in its various stages of self-transcendence and Levinas' preoccupation with the "proximity" of the Other and one's consequent ethical responsibility for the Other. This is not to claim that Buber succeeded where Kierkegaard and Levinas failed, but only to propose that a middle ground between these two rival stances toward the self and the Other might be found in the admittedly elusive notion of the "Between" in Buber's reflections on the I-Thou relationship.

But first we must examine the approach of Emmanuel Levinas to the Other: "The other person as he comes before me in a face to face encounter is not an *alter ego*, another self with different properties and accidents but [otherwise] in all essential respects like me. . . . He is far from me and other than myself, a stranger, and I cannot be sure of what this strangeness may conceal."[29] In contrast to Hegel, therefore, Levinas does not use otherness as a logical tool to move from thesis to antithesis to synthesis within a philosophical system. Instead, he makes the otherness of the Other the starting point for a radical critique of all totalizing schemes in philosophy, above all, those that give priority to Being over beings.[30] For, how else does one break free from classical metaphysics with its emphasis on Being over beings except by acknowledging an interpersonal relationship, namely, my feeling-level sense of responsibility for the Other, as the starting point for philosophical reflection? Only when I feel the "proximity" of the Other with his or her demands on my time and resources even before I rationally think through the extent of my obligation to him or her am I free of preoccupation with myself and my own subjective interests. Only then am I truly open to the Good as transcendent reality: "To reduce the good to being, to its calculations and its history, is to nullify goodness. Goodness gives to subjectivity its irreducible signification."[31]

According to Levinas, therefore, self-transcendence is to be found in "substitution," total identification with the Other in his or her demands on the Self. "I exist through the other and for the other, but without this being alienation: I am inspired. This inspiration is the psyche."[32] Experiencing the otherness of the Other leads Levinas, accordingly, into the experience of infinity, not the infinity of God as an abstract object of thought, but the infinity of the subjectivity of the Other which I cannot comprehend or control. The Other always overflows whatever antecedent idea that I may have about him or her.[33]

In dealing with the human Other, for example, I can have a face-to-face encounter, but the face of the other human being does not fully disclose to me his or her subjectivity. Only in conversation does that person's unique subjectivity become clear to me, but never in such a way that I fully comprehend its depths. Conversation, says Levinas, can reveal something quite unexpected about the other person to me, and I belatedly realize that I am only beginning to understand that person.[34] In this sense, infinity can be found not only within the subjectivity of God but even within human subjectivity. I will never fully fathom the subjectivity of the Other, and I will never fully satisfy the demands of the Other upon me.[35] Thus understood, the notion of infinity repudiates totality, systematic understanding of the Other in terms of Reason, which in the end knows only itself and is always the same.[36]

Yet, if the face of the Other leads me to the idea of infinity, then I must at the same time assert my separation from the Other. "The idea of Infinity implies the separation of the same with regard to the other, but this separation cannot rest upon an opposition to the other which would be purely anti-thetical. Thesis and antithesis, in repelling one another, call for one another." [37] In conscious opposition to Hegel's dialectic of thesis, antithesis, and synthesis and the ideal of a systematic understanding of reality, Levinas maintains an irreducible duality between the self and the other. Thus, truth is not to be sought in identification of the individual self with Absolute Spirit, but in conversation between the self and the other. "Truth arises where a being separated from the other is not engulfed in him, but speaks to him. . . . Separation and interiority, truth and language constitute the categories of the idea of infinity or metaphysics."[38]

Language, however, speaks the truth only when through language the self or the other genuinely expresses itself. In conversation, to be sure, the self and the other "thematize" the world to which they both belong.[39] But this thematization of a common world is quite secondary to the mutual self-revelation of the self and the other to one another in spontaneous conversation. "The object of knowledge is always a fact, already happened and passed through. The interpellated one [the other in conversation with the self] is called upon to speak; his speech consists in 'coming to the assistance' of his word—in being present."[40] The experience of infinity or transcendence then is always to be found in a social relation, the relation between the self and the other. "It is here that the Transcendent, infinitely other, solicits us and appeals to us."[41]

The most important feature of Transcendence or Infinity for Levinas, however, is its ethical dimension. Transcendence implies responsibility for the Other and as a result a loss of personal freedom for the Self. "To welcome the Other is to put in question my freedom."[42] Admittedly, within the metaphysics of Spinoza and Hegel, freedom "is reduced to being the reflection of a universal order which maintains itself and justifies itself all by itself."[43] As Levinas sees it, however, truth and justice are to be found together in a face-to-face relationship, in conversation.[44] In *Otherwise Than Being*, however, Levinas qualifies that statement. Justice fully arises only when the asymmetrical relationship between the self and the other is broadened to include a third party:

To find that the one before whom and for whom I am responsible is responsible in his turn before and for another is not to find his order put on me relativized or cancelled. It is to discover the exigency for justice, for an order among responsibilities. And the entry of a third party, treating me as an other alongside of the other that I faced, first institutes a kind of common terrain among us. I am, thanks to him, someone to be concerned about, someone to answer for.[45]

The presence of a third party requires a move from the feeling-level sense of responsibility for the other to conscious reflection on responsibilities to the collective other besides this single other and even to responsibility for oneself. Yet in the end justice must be grounded in proximity, the felt sense of responsibility for the other: "Justice, society, the State and its institutions, exchanges and work are comprehensible out of proximity. This means that nothing is outside of the control of the responsibility of the one for the other.[46]

As already mentioned, Levinas has some critical remarks with respect to the philosophy of Martin Heidegger. Levinas studied with both Husserl and Heidegger at the University of Freiburg in his youth (1928–29). But over time he distanced himself from both of them—above all, from Heidegger in the latter's preoccupation with the question of Being (Why is there something rather than nothing?). As Levinas sees it, Heidegger thus ended up doing ontology rather than metaphysics, employing the impersonal notion of Being as an intermediary and unifying principle between the self and the other. "In Heidegger coexistence [*Mitsein*] is, to be sure, taken as a relationship with the Other irreducible to objective cognition; but in the final analysis it also rests on the relationship with *being in general*, on comprehension, on ontology."[47] Levinas, on the contrary, regards the Good as beyond Being. But, as already noted, the Good for Levinas arises out of the context of sociality, the ongoing conversation of the self and the Other. "Here the relation connects not terms that complete one another and consequently are reciprocally lacking to one another, but terms that suffice to themselves. This relation is Desire, the life of beings that have arrived at self-possession."[48] True intersubjectivity, in other words, demands the ontological separation of the self and the Other so as to generate a social relation between them rather than the absorption of both self and Other into a conceptual totality dominated by the notion of Being. Whether Levinas was being totally fair to Heidegger on this point, of course, is a question best left to the next chapter.

Martin Buber

In a Prologue to his translation of Martin Buber's *I and Thou*, Walter Kaufmann takes note of the way in which Buber may have oversimplified and romanticized complex human relations by his overly simplistic contrast of I-Thou and I-It relations. There are, for example, people who live equivalently in an I-I world; that is, they pay little or no attention to either people or things since they are almost exclusively preoccupied with themselves and the satisfaction of their own needs and desires.[49] Others are heavily involved in the world of I-It, not always for selfish reasons but often because of their devotion to their work. Thus they live unconsciously in a largely It-It world.[50] Still others have yet to gain a true sense of individuality because their subjective world is heavily oriented to We-We relations.[51] Finally, still others live in a world dominated by Us-Them, the mentality of the "good guys" vs. the "bad guys."[52] Furthermore, says Kaufmann, the word "Thou" is an anachronism, since it is seldom used any more in English except in liturgical prayers of petition to God.[53]

Yet Kaufmann with all these distinctions may have missed what I regard as Buber's key insight, namely, the radical difference between subjectivity and objectivity and the necessary dialectical relation between them. Neither can exist without the other; but two quite different experiential worlds emerge, depending upon one's decision to prioritize one over the other. Admittedly, there are degrees of personal involvement in both worlds. As Kaufmann himself concedes, the purest form of the I-Thou relationship is the relationship of the self with God since God cannot be seen or heard directly but only felt indirectly through some sensible medium, e.g., Sacred Scripture.[54] Hence, God can only be experienced in terms of the divine subjectivity, namely, as the One who above all others loves me and deserves my love in return. In this sense, one does not experience God even in the person of Jesus, except insofar as one penetrates beyond the life and teaching of Jesus as recorded in the Gospel narratives and makes contact with the subjectivity of Jesus as allegedly the most perfect finite reflection of the infinite subjectivity of God.[55]

Likewise, as Kaufmann notes, there are different ways to participate in a basically I-It relation: some clearly reprehensible in terms of a lack of respect and concern for those with whom one lives and works, others merely one-sided and quite unintentional. The key factor, however, in all these I-It relations is that one has consciously or more often unconsciously prioritized something purely objective over the subjectivity of the Other, whether the Other be God, another human being, or even a nonhuman created reality that somehow reflects the subjectivity of God for me at this moment but which for various reasons I chose to ignore. So Kaufmann is undoubtedly correct in claiming that Buber's intent in *I and Thou* and other writings was "to make the secular sacred" without becoming guilty of some form of pantheism.[56] But the secret of staying clear of pantheism (which in my judgment Buber also implicitly recognized) is to emphasize intersubjectivity, that is, the necessary ontological difference between the I and the Thou which in moments of "encounter" can be bridged with Buber's enigmatic notion of the "Between," as we shall see below.

Turning now to the text of *I and Thou*, I note, first of all, that Kaufmann translates the German *Du* as "You" rather than "Thou," in keeping with his comment on the strangeness of "Thou" in the English language, as noted above. To avoid switching back and forth between "Thou" and "You" in citing and then commenting on Kaufmann's translation, I likewise here use "You" rather than "Thou." In the first part of *I and Thou* Buber refers initially to "basic words": I, You, and It. He then continues: "Basic words are spoken with one's being. The basic word I-You can only be spoken with one's whole being. The basic word I-It can never be spoken with one's whole being."[57] This, as I see it, confirms what I said above about a different worldview, depending upon one's choice to think and speak in terms of I-You or I-It. As Buber says a little later in the text, "There is no I as such but only the I of the basic word I-You and the I of the basic word I-It."[58] Buber then proceeds to distinguish between "experience," which is oriented to perception of objects, whether animate or inanimate, and "relation," which only exists between subjects of experience in terms of an I-You relation. Thus I can "experience" a tree by taking note successively of its size, color, position in space with respect to other trees, and so on. But I can also stand in "relation" to a tree when it ceases to be an It for me and becomes a You, another subject of experience.[59] The tree acts on me as I act on it through this intersubjective relation: "What I encounter is neither the soul of a tree nor a dryad, but the tree itself"[60] as a concrete individual reality rather than an abstract object of thought.

Buber continues: "The You encounters me by grace—it cannot be found by seeking. But that I speak the basic word to it is a deed of my whole being, is my essential deed."[61] Hence, I am both passive and active in the encounter with the You: "I require a You to become; becoming I, I say You."[62] Distinguishing between the present (as opposed to the past and the future) and presence, Buber notes: "Only as the You becomes present does presence come into being."[63] This has some affinity with Heidegger's notion of the event of Be-ing as "prescencing," as we shall see in the next chapter. But, while Heidegger focuses on the encounter of Be-ing with *Dasein* (the human being in rare moments of insight), Buber focuses on the intersubjective character of the existential encounter, the I and the You in dynamic interrelation. In much the same vein, Buber distinguishes between "feelings" that I "have" as mine alone and "love," which is always both cause and effect of an event of encounter between an I and a You, hence, an interpersonal force acting on me and the other simultaneously.[64]

This last comment introduces the somewhat enigmatic notion of the Between for Buber. He first notes that "every You must become an It in our world. However exclusively present it may have been in the direct relationship—as soon as the relationship has run its course or is permeated by *means* [means-end thinking], the You becomes an object among objects, perhaps the noblest one and yet one of them, assigned its measure and boundary."[65] Thus, even in mentally passing from a You to a He or She in our speech, the Other becomes part of the I-It world and the Between characterizing an I-You encounter disappears. Primitive peoples and young children, to be sure, live easily and without interruption in an I-You world both because they lack sufficient self-awareness and because they feel the presence of a cosmic force at work binding them to all other entities within a common world.[66] But, as the I grows in self-awareness, it distinguishes itself from its environment and the I-It world begins to take shape.[67] Yet the I-You relation perdures in the longing for other subjects of experience with whom to relate (other You's).[68] So the adult human being ends up living in two worlds, the pragmatic world of I-It relations and the quasi-mystical world of I-You relations.[69]

In part 2 of *I and Thou*, Buber begins with the following lament: "However the history of the individual and that of the human race may diverge in other respects, they agree in this at least: both signify a progressive increase of the It-world."[70] As a result, an individual human being living in society finds himself or herself divided between an inner world of personal feelings and an outer world of public institutions (economic, political, social).[71] What the individual continues to yearn for, however, is a sense of community with others. Note, however, what Buber defines as community:

True community does not come into being because people have feelings for each other (though that is required, too), but rather on two accounts: all of them have to stand in a living, reciprocal relationship to a single living center, and they have to stand in a living, reciprocal relationship to one another. The second event has its source in the first, but is not immediately given with it.[72]

In other words, the individual community members have first to feel a relationship to a higher-order Thou (the God of the Hebrew Bible, as Buber makes clear in part 3 of *I and Thou*)[73] and then they can also relate effectively to one another as You. When that happens, Spirit awakens within human life. Spirit seems to be the same as the Between for Buber: "Spirit is not in the I but between I and You. . . . Man lives in the spirit when he is able to respond to his You."[74] Yet, given the complexity of contemporary human life in society, Spirit seems to come and go within human relations. The great danger is that human beings will no longer feel the presence of the Spirit in their lives as they find themselves either preoccupied with personal feelings in a self-centered way or engrossed in the life of public institutions in an equally self-centered manner. True actuality comes through participation in relationships.[75] But life in contemporary society all too often is devoid of significant relationships.

Finally, in part 3 of *I and Thou*, Buber takes up the notion of the divine Thou or God. As already noted, Buber believes that within the experience of every human You the divine You is also present. But unlike the human You, the divine You is never objectively present to the senses or even in thought. It becomes present when we address it as You in prayer and meditation.[76] Theology, accordingly, in speaking about God, actually is treating God as an object of thought, an It. Divine revelation takes place only in an I-You relation; thus it cannot be reduced to words without distortion.[77] The true test of the veracity of a divine revelation to someone lies in what it leads to by way of action in dealing with other human beings within daily life.[78] In this sense, divine revelation always carries with it a calling or sense of mission.[79]

Midway through part 3 of *I and Thou*, Buber denies that our human relationship to the divine You consists in a sense of dependence or "creature-feeling."[80] Rather, as he sees it, God needs us as we need God: "You need God in order to be, and God needs you—for that which is the meaning of your life."[81] Our lives give God a reason to create. What is important for Buber here is the necessary duality between God and ourselves, for that matter—between any I and You. The dynamics of the I-You relationship demand it: "In lived actuality there is no unity of being. Actuality is to be found only in effective activity; strength and depth of the former only in that of the latter."[82] Here we may respectfully differ from Buber. A metaphysical unity between I and You does exist but not at the price of the I being absorbed into the You or the You being absorbed into the unity of the I. It is rather, as noted above by Buber himself, the unity of the Spirit within community life or the unity of the Between. But paradoxically the unity of the Between is a unity achieved, not despite, but in virtue of the ontological distinction of the I and You. Only because the I and the You are irreducibly different from one another can a dynamic unity, a sense of common ground between the two, ever be achieved.

This last point should become clear when in a later chapter I take up the Christian doctrine of the Trinity as a model for reconciling unity and diversity within the created order but above all as a model for the workings of human community. The three divine persons are one God, not in spite of their irreconcilable differences as persons, but because of those same differences.[83] As noted earlier, Buber finds the reality of human community in the awakening of Spirit. But he represents Spirit as a higher-order You which links a finite I and You with one another. Yet, as Wolfhart Pannenberg points out in his *Systematic Theology*, "spirit" as applied to the Trinity has two references: the first is to the divine nature, that which makes God to be God; the other is to the "third" divine person who mediates between the Father and the Son in their ongoing relationship.[84] Much like Buber's understanding of Spirit, therefore, Spirit for Pannenberg is a dynamic reality. But it is in the first place not a subject of experience but the ground of being for the ongoing interrelationship of subjects of experience and only in the second place one of the divine persons within the community that it grounds.

What is ultimately at stake here in this distinction between rival meanings of the word "Spirit" are two different understandings of the One and the Many. The one is the classical understanding of the One and the Many grounded in the philosophy of Plato; the other

is a relatively new paradigm, grounded partly in modern evolutionary theory and partly in philosophical theology. The first assumes
that the One is a higher-order entity that exists over and above the
Many as their transcendent principle of order and intelligibility; the
other assumes that the One is rather an immanent activity at work
in the interplay of the Many with one another from moment to
moment. The first is linked to a philosophy of Being; the other, to a
philosophy of Becoming.

Further specification of these differences, however, is best left
to a subsequent chapter. Here it suffices to note how Kierkegaard,
Levinas, and Buber all sought to free themselves in different ways
from a systems orientation to reality whereby the individuality of
the Self or the individuality of the Other was subordinated to a contrived, purely man-made sense of unity represented by the thought
system as a "totality." Now it is time to turn to another modern
thinker, Martin Heidegger, who likewise by degrees saw the need
for a much more event-oriented approach to reality, a new appreciation of the uniqueness of the present moment. Heidegger, to be
sure, saw this new focus on ever-changing events rather than enduring things as "the end of metaphysics." But, as I shall make clear in
the next chapter, it can just as readily be interpreted as the beginning of a new metaphysics, grounded in time-bound principles of
becoming rather than in timeless principles of being.

STARTING WITH EVENTS RATHER THAN THINGS

Martin Heidegger is undoubtedly one of the premiere philosophers of the twentieth century, with wide-ranging influence on scholars in philosophy, theology, and the other humanities. His celebrated distinction between Being and beings at the beginning of his book *Being and Time* effectively called into question the entire previous history of the Western philosophical tradition from Plato and Aristotle onward.[1] But exactly what he meant by Being has to this day remained somewhat controversial. A later work, *Contributions to Philosophy (From Enowning)* [*Beiträege zur Philosophie: Vom Ereignis*], was written by Heidegger in 1936–1938 but only published after his death in 1976 and then translated into English in 1999.[2] Students of Heidegger's thought eagerly read the book, expecting to get the definitive answer to the question of Being in Heidegger's own words, but even then ambiguities remained. The book is divided up into 281 brief essays gathered under eight headings: Preview, Echo, Playing-Forth, Leap, Grounding, The Ones to Come, The Last God, and Be-ing. Where is one to look for the definitive answer to the question of Being?

There is, of course, much repetition of key themes out of *Being and Time* in the newer book. But what seems to stand out is an apparent turn (*Kehre*) in Heidegger's thinking from a basically phenomenological study of human temporal consciousness as the key to the meaning of Being in *Being and Time* to a new appreciation of be-ing (now called *Seyn*) as that which unexpectedly gives itself in an existential encounter with *Da-sein*.[3] *Da-sein* provides the "there (Da)," the site for the self-giving of be-ing in the event of "appropriation." But *Da-sein* must likewise "de-cide" in an "originary leap" (*Ursprung*) to participate in and make its own (appropriate) this meaning-giving event. *Da-sein* thus achieves a fleeting identity, as a singular and unrepeatable event of the self-giving of being.

But what does all this imply for the argument of the present book, namely, that a new philosophical worldview or metaphysics is needed to facilitate discussion between people in the humanities and natural and social sciences on issues of common concern? As I see it, with his distinction between Being and beings, Heidegger was forcing a reevaluation of the classical paradigm for the relationship between the One and the Many. Being for him is not synonymous with God as the Supreme Being. Being is an activity immanent in this world to make things be. Being, in other words, is a verb, not a noun. So understood, Being is still transcendent of the Many. But it is transcendent as an activity, a self-giving or "presencing" to beings rather than a transcendent entity, a Creator God who brings into existence entities other than himself.

To illustrate my point here, I call attention to the philosophy of Heidegger's contemporary, Alfred North Whitehead, who seems to have made a similar distinction between Being as an activity and the individual beings of this world. In his major work *Process and Reality*, Whitehead stipulates that there is an ongoing dynamic relation between what he calls "creativity," the basic principle of process whereby at every moment "the many become one and are increased by one,"[4] and "actual occasions," momentary self-constituting subjects of experience that are in his judgment "the final real things of which this world is made up."[5] Creativity, then, as an activity rather than an entity, thus makes use of—or, in Heidegger's words, "appropriates"—individual actual occasions in order to pass from potentiality to actuality in and through them at every moment. That is, it has no identity in itself beyond being an activity that exists in its concrete momentary instantiations. Individual actual occasions, for their part, must likewise "appropriate" the power of creativity in order to take account of their specific location within the world in which they find themselves and then to make a self-constituting decision with respect to the present and the future of the cosmic process to which they belong before they themselves expire and make way for new actual occasions in the next moment of the cosmic process. In this way, actual occasions in general but, above all, actual occasions on the level of human consciousness seem to bear some analogy to what Heidegger has in mind with *Da-sein*, the site of the appropriation of be-ing as cosmic self-giving.

Both men, in other words, seem to be responding to what they perceive as a crisis in Western civilization, the one from the perspective of a natural scientist with interest in the humanities, the other from the perspective of a philosopher trained in the humanities but with keen awareness of the inherent limitations of scientific method for answering life's deeper problems. Both are critical of the tendency in classical metaphysics to give priority to "things" in terms of their universal representations or essences over "events" in their irreducible concrete particularity. *Da-sein*, for example, is not just a particular instance of humanity as a universal concept. *Da-sein* is not even an instance of universal human subjectivity, but is more properly an event, something that happens, which can in some measure be repeated in the next moment of existence for a given human being but never exactly duplicated within the life either of that same person or of other persons. This is presumably why Heidegger laid such stress on the relative rarity of the event of appropriation in human life.

Whitehead came to a similar conclusion about the priority of events over things in our human understanding of ourselves and the world around us. He stipulated a dynamic relation between creativity and individual actual occasions as the ultimate units of reality. Their mutual "appropriation" of one another at every moment of the cosmic process is what allows for the ongoing move from potentiality to actuality both within the world process as a whole and within human consciousness. This ongoing movement from potentiality to actuality within human consciousness, of course, is rarely noticed by human beings in their preoccupation with the "things" or the beings of this world. Here the value of Heidegger's *Being and Time* comes to the fore, in that therein he explicitly calls attention to the radical temporality of human existence, namely, *Da-sein* as a "being unto death" that forces one to think more seriously about the meaning and value of one's life.[6]

There is, accordingly, an unexpected congruence in the thinking of these two otherwise quite different philosophers about what is fundamentally wrong with contemporary Western culture. Both argue that we Westerners are immersed in a world of finite material things that we try to control for our own individual purposes but which in the end control us because we have lost perspective on how to deal with them in meaningful ways. Furthermore, Heidegger and Whitehead have in their own way focused on what has been a key factor in this book, namely, what is meant by individuality or concrete particularity in a thought world dominated by universal concepts (as in the ancient and medieval worlds) or by strictly determined laws (as in the modern period). Both question how we come to know an individual entity in its concrete particularity, in terms of what makes it different from other entities of the same class or species rather than in terms of what it has in common with those same entities.[7] Likewise, both ask themselves how a human being (for Heidegger) or for that matter any created reality (for Whitehead) itself becomes unique, something truly different from other members of its own species or class.

Whitehead's answer to the second question is that only momentary self-constituting subjects of experience, given that they give order and shape to their lives by their own decision from moment to moment, can qualify as truly individual entities. Heidegger, on the contrary, was wary of human subjectivity as a "trap" for a false sense of objectivity in human knowledge.[8] But with his careful analysis of the event of appropriation whereby be-ing and *Da-sein* mutually condition one another, he was clearly at work on a much deeper understanding of subjectivity in terms of authentic human existence. Furthermore, since both Heidegger and Whitehead were constantly probing for what makes individuals different from one another, they both had to deal with the further issue of philosophical atomism, how presumably unique events can have value and significance for the future.

In the following pages, accordingly, I set forth some of the key ideas in Heidegger's *Contributions to Philosophy* and compare them with various features of Whitehead's metaphysical scheme in *Process and Reality*. Given the sheer number and complexity of the 281 essays in Heidegger's book, however, I have chosen to be guided by a recent commentary on Heidegger's text entitled *The Emergency of Being: On Heidegger's Contributions to Philosophy*.[9] Therein the author, Richard Polt, provides a relatively straightforward exposition of the thought content of the book and in addition offers a translation of key terms in the German text that make more sense to me than the translation of the same terms in the standard English version of the text. Reference to Heidegger's text in the original German, however, is also regularly provided in the endnotes.

In chapter 1 of his book, entitled "Toward Appropriation," Polt makes clear the logical connection between *Being and Time* and Heidegger's later reflections on be-ing and *Da-sein* in *Contributions to Philosophy*. As Heidegger realized already in *Being and Time*, we accept without thinking the givenness of the world around us and most of the things within it. It takes an "emergency," a break in our everyday consciousness, to become aware of what is always already there awaiting our response. Only then do we personally appropriate what we are otherwise passively experiencing.[10] Early in his career at Freiburg University in Germany with Edmund Husserl, Heidegger found himself taking issue with his senior colleague's focus on universal meaning (essences) as the way to transcend the countless particularities within human experience.[11] For Heidegger, on the contrary, true meaning was to be found only in the concrete events of a particular person's life, even though such a stance seemed at first to imply that truth is relative, something available to me only from my own limited perspective.[12] As Heidegger saw it, a new approach to the study of human nature was needed that would focus on events happening to the individual in his or her unique existential context.

The result, of course, was the composition of *Being and Time*, which began by raising the issue of the meaning of being and the possible distinction between being as such and individual beings but then focused on *Dasein* in its temporality or historicity as the privileged way to raise the question of being.[13] In the next section of the book, Heidegger probed the experience of temporality within human beings, the way in which past, present, and future implicitly condition one another at every moment of conscious experience.[14] We find ourselves, for example, at every moment "thrown" into a situation partly created by our own past decisions and partly determined by the decisions of others. Likewise, at every moment we anticipate our future in the form of possible courses of action as we decide how to respond to the situation within which we find ourselves. Given the radical finitude of our lives, a major question looms. Will we by our decision in the present moment strive for personal "authenticity," conscious appropriation of our particular place in the world here and now as *Dasein,* or will we succumb to "inauthenticity" by simply going along with conventional patterns of thinking and behavior?[15]

Throughout *Being and Time*, therefore, Heidegger keeps returning to the question of what it means to be, whether there is a legitimate distinction between being as such and individual beings. Being is truly experienced only when the individual human being chooses to be authentic as *Dasein.* So being depends upon *Dasein.* "In turn, without being, there is no being-there [*Dasein*], for being-there is precisely the entity who has an understanding of being."[16] *Dasein*, in understanding its own way of being, understands the being of everything else as well; it thus "appropriates" its world as belonging both to itself and others. But this can only happen within the context of *Dasein's* basic temporality, the ongoing interplay of past, present, and future within consciousness.[17] In *Contributions to Philosophy*, however, the focus shifts from *Dasein* (now spelled as *Da-sein* or "there-being") to be-ing (*Seyn*), the self-giving of being, the way in which the meaning of being comes to be for *Da-sein* here and now.

In *Contributions*, for example, time is linked with space to become space-time or "the site of the moment."[18] *Da-sein*, accordingly, is not something already present within human consciousness but has to be grounded through an originary leap (*Ursprung*) into a clearing or open space in which being can be given. *Da-sein* thus belongs to be-ing because it exists only in responding to the claim that be-ing makes on it.[19] Perhaps better said, be-ing and *Da-sein* appropriate each other in a singular historical event (*Ereignis*), which establishes them as necessarily interdependent.[20] As Polt explains, *das Seyn west als das Ereignis*.[21] *Das Seyn*, or the self-giving of being, is not itself an entity but an event, something that happens, an activity that has no logical ground or vital source beyond itself.

Turning now to Alfred North Whitehead's understanding of creativity in *Process and Reality*, we note first of all how he describes it as "the universal of universals characterizing ultimate matter of fact. It is that ultimate principle by which the many, which are the universe disjunctively, become the one actual occasion, which is the universe conjunctively."[22] Hence, creativity, the many, and the one are always linked; together, they constitute the Category of the Ultimate, the principle from which everything else flows in Whitehead's metaphysical scheme. Even God within Whitehead's scheme is a "creature" of creativity since the inner life of God, the ongoing interplay between the primordial and consequent natures of God, is characterized by the operation of creativity, the many becoming one and being increased by one.[23] Finally, and perhaps most importantly for comparison with be-ing (*Seyn*) in Heidegger's thought, creativity is not an entity but an activity that exists, has actuality, only in its concrete instantiations, God, and created actual occasions.[24] In this sense, it is both like and unlike Aristotle's "prime matter." It is never without forms, yet not reducible to them (thus akin to prime matter for Aristotle). But, unlike Aristotelian prime matter, it is active rather than passive. It individuates forms not simply by receiving them into itself (as with prime matter) but by empowering them to become themselves.[25]

As might be expected, not all Whiteheadians agree on the function of creativity within the cosmic process.[26] For some, the term "creativity" is simply an empirical generalization. Something is needed to enable each actual occasion to be *causa sui*, that is, to exist in virtue of its own self-constituting decision. As such, creativity is a necessary principle of novelty within the cosmic process. But it has no actuality apart from its individual instantiations, actual occasions that come into being and then expire. Others contend that creativity is not only the principle of novelty within the cosmic process but also the principle of creative advance or transition. It explains why there is always a succession of actual occasions, why when one actual occasion expires, another immediately takes its place. Creativity, accordingly, is to be found not only within actual occasions but also between them. In this instance, creativity is identified with the entire past world "as it conspires to produce a new [actual] occasion."[27] Thus creativity is the activity of transcendence within the cosmic process, "permeating the whole of reality, transcending what is and yet carried by it, leading to ever new becoming."[28]

But what has all this to do with Heidegger's notion of be-ing or *Seyn*, the giving of being to *Da-sein*? As I see it, Whitehead's creativity, understood as both a principle of novelty and as a principle of transition within the cosmic process, illustrates how be-ing (*Seyn*) is not simply a giving of being in general to *Da-sein* but a giving of a definite way of being or a pattern of being (*Sein*) to Da-sein for just that special moment.[29] If this analogy between be-ing and Whiteheadian creativity is valid, be-ing both shapes and is shaped by *Da-sein* in the event of their mutual appropriation. That is, be-ing encounters *Da-sein* in a definite space-time, a context where the event of appropriation here and now will take place.

As Polt comments in *The Emergency of Being*, "Only in a place can beings make a difference to us. Only at a time can we receive and interpret a legacy for the sake of a possibility, cultivating and eliciting historical import."[30] But, in thus providing a specific context to *Da-sein* for *Da-sein's* activity of self-appropriation, be-ing or *Seyn* (like Whiteheadian creativity) is itself shaped by *Da-sein's* response to that context. Be-ing is not the same as before this particular event of mutual appropriation. This is not to claim that be-ing is an entity undergoing accidental changes over time, but only that even as an activity which is in itself formless or indeterminate it is qualified by the ways in which it is instantiated.[31] Akin to Whiteheadian creativity, then, be-ing or *Seyn* is a principle of transition as well as a principle of novelty in the event of appropriation. Heidegger's emphasis, to be sure, is on be-ing as a principle of novelty. But it has to be simultaneously a principle of transition for the human being(s) affected by that event. Otherwise, the event of appropriation would have no significance beyond its brief moment of existence.

In the second chapter of *The Emergency of Being*, entitled "The Event of Thinking the Event," Polt shows how Heidegger tries to bypass commonsense thinking with its focus on things as abstract objects of thought so as to see them in a new light, to think of them in a way which is itself an event of appropriation. Polt labels this more original way of thinking "bethinking" or "inceptive thinking."[32] As such, it seems to bear a resemblance to what Whitehead calls the "concrescence" of an actual occasion. That is, a concrescing actual occasion is initially passive in its reception of objective patterns and subjective feelings from its predecessor actual occasions both in the society to which it immediately belongs and in the world at large. Then the developing actual occasion tries to unify for itself this multiplicity of objective data and subjective feelings. Finally, when it has achieved a novel togetherness or sense of "satisfaction," it ratifies its own process of concrescense through a self-constituting "decision."[33] The parallel between the concrescence of an actual occasion and bethinking or inceptive thinking in Heidegger is that in neither case does one know in advance what the result of this process of unification of feelings and data will be. Risk is thus involved in the process of concrescence for an actual occasion, and risk is involved in "bethinking" as opposed to the nonrisk associated with commonsense representational thinking.

The actual occasion, to be sure, at the beginning of its concrescence receives from God an "initial aim" or felt sense of directionality for its self-constitution, but it is free to depart from that initial divine aim with its own slowly developing subjective aim which is itself fully formed only in the moment of self-constituting "decision."[34] In similar fashion, Polt uses various examples to make clear what he means by bethinking or inceptive thinking: for example, writing poetry in which something quite familiar is transformed into something new and original; the Japanese tea ceremony, which is indeed heavily rule-bound but in which the rules serve as "occasions for carrying out each action in an inceptive, unique way."[35] The key point here is that the emergence of something new is not known in advance but only realized in its accomplished actuality at the end of the process: for Whitehead, the process of concrescence of an actual occasion; for Heidegger, the event of the mutual self-appropriation of be-ing and *Da-sein*.

Yet, one may object, for Heidegger the event of appropriation or the event of inception is very rare. It cannot be something that happens everywhere and all the time within the cosmic process as innumerable actual occasions undergo their individual processes of concrescence. But Whitehead himself distinguishes between different kinds of actual occasions, most of which involve little or no novelty or difference from their predecessors, and only the highest kind or "grade" of actual occasions functions at the level of human self-consciousness.[36] Furthermore, even at this level Whitehead allows for degrees of self-awareness.[37] Hence, even from a Whiteheadian perspective one can agree with Heidegger that the event of appropriation between be-ing and *Da-sein* is rare within human history.

The analogy between the thought of Whitehead and the thought of Heidegger is grounded, not in the frequency of the event, but in its basic structure. That is, the event of mutual appropriation of be-ing and *Da-sein* seems to follow a structure that, as Whitehead sees it, is everywhere present in the cosmic process and in human consciousness. But it is seldom noticed because, as Heidegger claims, human beings have become forgetful of the difference between be-ing and beings. Be-ing has become identified with presence as a fixed state rather than with presencing as an activity.[38] Human beings are preoccupied with objective forms of intelligibility rather than with their vital subjective source or ground in be-ing. Be-ing, after all, is what gives beings their very "beingness," their intelligibility or specific pattern of existence (as opposed to nothingness).[39]

In chapter 3 of *The Emergency of Being*, Polt lists "straits" (*Grundzüge*) of the event of appropriation, that is, characteristic features of events that do not necessarily coalesce to form an overall logical pattern or system. The first of these "straits" is the withdrawal of be-ing in its very act of unconcealment within the event of appropriation.[40] How can it be thus both present and absent at the same time? Here I find help in Whitehead's notion of an actual occasion as both subject and superject, that is, an inner power of radical self-constitution and its necessary objective self-manifestation.[41] As I see it, Whitehead is thereby claiming that an actual occasion is both potentiality and actuality, but in the end more a potentiality than an actuality. That is, actual occasions invariably require a successor (or successors) because the potentiality latent within the overall context is never exhausted by what an individual actual occasion de facto becomes. There is, to be sure, no notion of a permanent "soul" or "spiritual substance" at work here in Whitehead's thought. Every actual occasion is closely linked to its predecessors and its successors in the same "society" or series of actual occasions; but it is always in the first place a unique though strictly limited instance of the conversion of potentiality into actuality within the cosmic process.

Heidegger's notion of "abyss" as the "Nothing" (*das Nichts*) operative within the self-revelation and self-concealment of be-ing in the event of appropriation seems likewise to reflect this contingent movement from potentiality to actuality and back again to potentiality: "Be-ing *calls* for grounding in a way that is urgent, rather than logically necessary. If the grounding were logically necessary, then be-ing would have some sort of a priori guarantee. Instead, it happens contingently, in a decisive emergency, an originary leap."[42] Yet, understood as a contingent leap into an abyss, the event of appropriation is more than just another actuality but a newly realized potentiality that may or may not endure. Like an actual occasion in Whitehead's scheme, the leap into the event of appropriation between be-ing and *Da-sein* can be unsettling because of its unpredictability. What will follow upon this originary leap into provisional actuality remains unclear. At the same time, pure chaos does not take over; there is "mastery" (*Herrschaft*) likewise present in the event of appropriation since the leap originates spontaneously from within the encounter of be-ing and *Da-sein*, not in virtue of some purely external force or violence.[43]

Another "strait" of appropriation is *Da-sein* as "ownness" or self-appropriation. Not only the self-giving of be-ing but also the self-giving of *Da-sein* is needed for the event of mutual appropriation.[44] As such, *Da-sein* is not simply equivalent to the generic notion of humanity, as reading Heidegger in *Being and Time* might have led one to believe. *Da-sein* is humanity only in its special moments, in its authenticity, when the individual abandons the familiar ground of everyday life in order to risk the "originary leap" into the encounter with be-ing.[45] One attains true selfhood in listening to the call of be-ing and "insisting" on letting it happen, staying in the place of encounter with be-ing.[46]

A third "strait" or enduring characteristic of the event of appropriation, accordingly, is space-time, the time and the place where the event of appropriation between be-ing and *Da-sein* necessarily takes place. It has little or nothing to do with space-time as a mathematical construct but with the co-inherence of past, present, and future as a constitutive feature of the event of appropriation: "Appropriation takes time—not just because it lasts a while, but because it requires remembrance and awaiting as our belonging to a past and future. Appropriation also takes place—it stakes out the site that is our own, a 'there' where beings can be given to us as beings."[47] An affinity with Whitehead's understanding of the self-constitution of an actual occasion can be seen in the fact that for Whitehead too space-time is not in the first place an external reality but rather the "standpoint" of each actual occasion in its self-constitution relative to other actual occasions, past, present, and future.

By its "decision" ending the process of concrescence, the individual actual occasion creates its own space-time relative to these other actual occasions with their standpoints or space-time parameters. Only in the inevitable interrelation and overlap of such particular space-time parameters for the individual actual occasions is the "extensive continuum" or the physical counterpart for the mathematical construct of space-time brought into being. "This extensive continuum is one relational complex in which all potential objectifications [of actual occasions] find their niche. It underlies the whole world, past, present, and future."[48] Such an approach to space-time seems to be akin to Heidegger's thought in *Contributions to Philosophy* when he suggests that, while the event of mutual appropriation between be-ing and *Da-sein* is unique, it is still necessarily conditioned by what has already happened and what is still to come in human history. As Polt comments, "The past and the future need a place into which they can be gathered, and conversely, the place needs to serve as the site for the gathering of past and future."[49]

Two final "straits" of the event of appropriation are first simultaneity and sheltering and then the activity of the "gods" in the event of appropriation. With reference to the former, Polt notes how for Heidegger be-ing as the giving of the significance of beings to *Da-sein* is necessarily simultaneous with *Da-sein*'s appropriation of that gift of meaning and value. Beings, in other words, enter the clearing of *Da-sein* when they are seen as "sheltering" the truth of their own being. "When sheltering takes place, the clearing is grounded in the beings that lie open within it (including things, tools and artworks). . . . Unconcealment properly happens only if we encounter beings in their connections to the entire field of significance that is shared by a community, while remaining aware of the contingency and limits of this field. Since the field is historical, it is always finite and open to new possibilities."[50] The truth of be-ing then is not to be found in beings in isolation from one another but only insofar as they constitute a web of meaning and value not just for the individual but for the group to which the individual belongs.

As Polt indicates, there is for Heidegger a tension between "earth" and "world" in the event of appropriation. "The world is a people's understanding of the being of beings. The *earth* is the unmastered and uninterpreted basis of experience, the non-sense that sustains yet resists our understanding."[51] Hence, the tension between world and earth is crucial to sheltering the truth of beings. *Da-sein* must see how beings both belong to a given world and yet how they are more than this belonging. For this to happen, however,, *Da-sein* must first be silent so as to allow the mystery of be-ing represented by the earth to set limitations for the truth of be-ing as represented by the world. Here is where the last "strait" of the event of appropriation—namely, the activity of the "gods" and, above all, of the "final god"—plays its role in the entire process. As Polt makes clear, the "gods" for Heidegger are not higher-order beings but "existential possibilities that inform a people's interpretation of itself and the world around it."[52] Precisely as possibilities and not actualities, the "gods" give meaning and value to our human activities, whether these activities are explicitly religious or not. The "final god" is then the ultimate existential possibility—in the language of the Bible, the *kairos* moment—that must be taken advantage of, grasped as it "passes by," if both the individual human being and the people are to experience the fullness of the event of appropriation, the decisive encounter of be-ing and *Da-sein*.[53]

There is no exact parallel to this line of thought in Whitehead's

Process and Reality. In part 5 of that book, entitled "Final Interpretation," however, Whitehead offers some reflections on the inevitable limitations of a philosophy of becoming such as he has presented in earlier parts of the book. "The ultimate evil in the temporal world is deeper than any specific evil. It lies in the fact that the past fades, that time is a 'perpetual perishing.' Objectification involves elimination. The present fact has not the past fact with it in any full immediacy."[54] In the language of Heidegger, worlds of meaning and value come and go for Whitehead, together with the beings that gave those worlds meaning and value. *Da-sein* is itself destined for nonbeing or extinction. No event of appropriation, no meaningful encounter with be-ing, can save it from ultimate meaninglessness.

In the face of such ultimate meaninglessness for the cosmic process as a whole and for human life in particular, Whitehead in his final chapter of *Process and Reality* proposes that the divine consequent nature—that is, the reality of God as affected by events taking place in the world—manages to reconcile with one another and to integrate into a meaningful whole all the individual creaturely events taking place within the world process at any given moment:

The revolts of destructive evil, purely self-regarding, are dismissed into their triviality of merely individual facts; and yet the good they did achieve in individual joy, in individual sorrow, in the introduction of needed contrast, is yet saved by its relation to the completed whole. The image—and it is but an image—the image under which this operative growth of God's nature is best conceived, is that of a tender care that nothing be lost.[55]

Many Whiteheadians, to be sure, dismiss this image of God "saving" the world as it passes into the immediacy of God's own life, as a deus ex machina on Whitehead's part, designed to soften the logical consequences of a philosophy based on becoming rather than being. But, with due qualification, it seems to bear some affinity to Heidegger's concept of the "final god." That is, it offers hope for a better future, all appearances to the contrary notwithstanding. The differences between Whitehead and Heidegger on this point, however, are equally valid. Whereas Heidegger projects into a distant future the emergence of the "final god" in human history, Whitehead claims that the divine consequent nature of God is at work at every moment of the cosmic process "behind the scenes," so to speak. Only because of the divine consequent nature does the cosmic process continue as a relatively integrated reality rather than dissolve into virtual chaos and effectively come to an end.

In the last chapter of his book, entitled "Afterthoughts," Polt expresses his reservations about the suitability of the notion of appropriation, the fateful encounter of be-ing and *Da-sein*, for contemporary human life. While conceding the validity of Heidegger's critique of the complacency or lack of urgency about the deeper meaning of human life within contemporary Western civilization, Polt feels that Heidegger has somehow overstated his case. Especially with respect to the "second inception," the future encounter of be-ing and *Da-sein* that will presumably reshape the worldview of all reflective people in the West, Heidegger's thought is "saturated with emergency, drunk on apocalypse."[56] Accordingly, Polt himself proposes as one of his "afterthoughts" that "events of appropriation happen countless times in our lives, though not at every time."[57] The point of my own comparison of Heidegger and Whitehead on the event of appropriation has been to argue that in fact it does happen all the time, not only to human beings in their personal history, but also to every actual occasion in its individual process of concrescence. That is, the actual occasion moves from a purely passive reception of data and feelings from the world in which it originates (in Heideggerian terms, from its experience of "thrownness" within this world) through a series of subjective unifications of these objective feelings and data so as to establish its own unique standpoint in the world in virtue of a self-constituting "decision." It may be only marginally different from its predecessors in the same society of actual occasions, but it is still something new, something that never existed before.

Yet Polt would certainly be correct in counterarguing that the encounter between be-ing and *Da-sein* is not subjectively experienced and recognized as such by human beings on a regular basis. Only in unexpected moments do we suddenly become aware of the radical contingency of the meaning and value that we customarily attach to our thoughts and actions and thus are psychologically readied for a new encounter with be-ing, its gift of a new way of looking at ourselves and the world in which we live. Precisely in these revelatory moments we experience ourselves as the unique individuals whom we have always been but seldom acknowledged in our preoccupation with the persons and things of this world. In this respect, both Heidegger and Whitehead in different ways contribute significantly to one of the basic questions of this book: first, what does it mean to be an individual entity in a world structured by principles of order and intelligibility largely not of one's making, and second, how does one recognize and preserve this uniqueness for oneself and others even as one strives with those others to refashion the existing world of meaning and value which in one way or another we all must inhabit? It is the age-old problem of the One and the Many in a new context.

THE ONE, THE THREE, AND
THE MANY

In the Introduction to this book, I made the claim that a new paradigm for the relationship between the One and the Many was one of the more urgent philosophical issues of our time. Given the explosion of diverse thought and behavior patterns available to contemporary human beings as a result of global electronic communication and other forms of modern technology, one has to work much harder to achieve a strong sense of personal and communal self-identity. The temptation is either to withdraw from those notably different from oneself or to seek to impose one's sense of self-identity, one's own beliefs and values, on others by whatever means one has at one's disposal. Persuasion to one's point of view through dialogue with others is often seen as too time-consuming and apparently fruitless. Hence, at least for those in "power-positions" within contemporary society, the urge is to use force or at least the threat of force to get one's way with others. Yet the sense of mutual trust and harmony among individuals and groups that is sorely needed for the nurturing of a new world culture or civilization is then almost totally lacking, and the fear of escalating violence among rival groups becomes almost overpowering.

Among contemporary philosophers and theologians who have grasped the seriousness of this problem for our day is the late Colin Gunton, who published his Bampton Lectures at the University of Oxford, England, in 1992 under the title *The One, the Three and the*

Many: God, Creation and the Culture of Modernity. In what follows I first summarize his views on a new paradigm for the One and the Many, paying particular attention to the way in which for this purpose he employs the classical understanding of the Christian doctrine of the Trinity at the hands of the Cappadocian Fathers in the Greek-speaking church of the ancient world. Then I indicate how my own Trinitarian reinterpretation of Whitehead's metaphysics nicely complements Gunton's scheme for the relation between the One and the Many and perhaps even improves on it by putting it in a more properly philosophical (rather than strictly theological) context. One should not, in other words, have to be a Christian who believes in the doctrine of the Trinity in order to see the significance and value of this new paradigm for the One and the Many. The classical Greek understanding of the doctrine of the Trinity should only serve as an apt illustration of a transcultural philosophical hypothesis.

Gunton divides his book into two parts. In the first part he analyzes what he considers to be the major problems of modernity and postmodernity (in his mind, late modernity), and in the second he sets forth his solution to those problems, namely, finding a new way for human beings to relate to one another and to God without sacrificing their proper sense of self-identity along the way. The problems of modernity are summed up in the word "disengagement," a strong tendency to deal with others not as persons or ends in themselves worthy of one's respect and affection but more or less as instruments or means for the achievement of one's own goals and values.[1] This pervasive feeling of disengagement, of course, did not arise by chance but has a long history, beginning with two ancient Greek philosophers, Heraclitus and Parmenides.

Heraclitus, focusing on the experience of change or becoming, emphasized the priority of the empirical Many over the rationally conceived One; Parmenides, focusing on permanence and continuity within human experience, emphasized instead the priority of the timeless One over the time-bound Many.[2] Plato attempted to mediate between these two extremes but basically favored the One over the Many with his doctrine of the universal forms. Likewise, early Christian theologians tended to emphasize the priority of the One over the Many but with the understanding that the transcendent One was not the form of the good as with Plato but the God of the Hebrew and Christian Bible.[3] Beginning with Descartes in the early modern era, however, the role of the One as transcendent over the Many shifted again. This time the One was no longer God the Creator but the individual human being in her or his personal subjectivity. Yet, since such a theoretical standpoint is impossible to sustain in ordinary life, human beings either consciously or unconsciously surrender their personal autonomy in favor of a "false universal," some finite goal or value as a substitute for God.[4] Thus, says Gunton, "the paradox of the modern condition is that a quest for the freedom of the many has eventuated in new forms of slavery to the one."[5]

In the remaining chapters of part 1, Gunton analyzes still other issues related to the problem of the One and the Many in modern life. For example, philosophers and theologians influenced by Plato have notably underestimated the importance of the body for understanding human individuality and particularity. In their eyes, "The true person is the soul, so that the material body comes to be understood as that which *divides* one human being from another rather than *relates* them to one another."[6] Truth is to be found in what the mind grasps, namely, the universal form, rather than in what the senses perceive, the particular material reality. But, as Gunton points out and as we have seen earlier in this book, universal forms establish what individuals have in common, not what makes them different from one another. In similar fashion, the value of the present moment with its opportunity for meaningful encounters between individuals has been undercut by still other abstractions—for example, time as "the moving image of eternity"[7] or time as the "fourth dimension" in the space-time continuum (see below, chap. 11).

Gunton's conclusion at the end of part 1 of his book, therefore, is that contemporary human beings are overwhelmed by the reality of the Many, the sheer diversity of lifestyles and perspectives in modern life, and so find themselves unable to make a decision as to what is true and good except in terms of individual preference. As a result, they are characterized by what he calls a "rootless will," that is, "a will conceived in abstraction from any foundation in other aspects of the person or in its broader environment."[8] The historical source for this arbitrary approach to human decision making is to be found in Ockham's distinction between the absolute and the ordinate will of God and even earlier in Augustine's theory of double divine predestination.[9] But its immediate antecedent is Kant's notion of the categorical imperative, which presupposes a rational will but one that has "no necessary reference except to itself."[10]

Gunton's solution to these problems of modernity and postmodernity is to make a careful study of the doctrine of the Trinity set forth by the Greek Fathers of the church and to find therein new Trinitarian "transcendentals."[11] Instead of Unity, Truth, Goodness, and Beauty as in the classical tradition, Gunton proposes *perichoresis*, particularity or substantiality, and relationality (or sociality at the human level of activity). The key to all three, however, is *perichoresis*: "In its origins, the concept was a way of showing the ontological interdependence and reciprocity of the three persons of the Trinity . . . so that for God to be did not involve an absolute simplicity, but a unity deriving from a dynamic plurality of persons."[12] The transcendental Unity of God in the classical tradition was absolutely simple and undifferentiated, because to have parts or members was considered an imperfection, characteristic of finite being.[13] But from a Trinitarian perspective the Unity of God must be differentiated, a unity-in-diversity or community of three co-equal but radically distinct divine persons. Furthermore, since the world of creation should reflect its Creator, it too "is perichoretic in that everything in it contributes to the being of everything else, enabling everything to be what it distinctively is."[14] The world is a cosmic community of entities that find their self-identity not in themselves but in their ongoing relations to one another.

This leads into discussion of the second Trinitarian transcendental, namely, particularity or substantiality. Whereas in modernity and postmodernity the individual entity is one among many things of the same kind, a homogeneous unit, particularity or substantiality insists that each individual entity in its concreteness is unique. Just as "the *substantiality* of God resides not in his abstract being, but in the concrete particulars that we call the divine persons, and in the relations by which they mutually constitute one another,"[15] so individual material things are constituted in their particularity not by what they are in themselves but by what they are in relation to one another: "Something is real—what it is and not another thing—by virtue of the way it is held in being not only by God but also by other things in the particular configuration of space and time in which its being is constituted."[16] Drawing the parallel with the doctrine of the Trinity even closer, Gunton argues that, just as the Holy Spirit within the inner life of the Trinity not only unites the Father and the Son but makes them "to be particular *persons* in community and as communion,"[17] so the work of the Holy Spirit in the world of creation is to relate to one another individual entities or groups of entities (institutions) which seem to be opposed or separate: "That which is or has spirit is able to be open to that which is other than itself, to move into relation with the other."[18]

The third and last Trinitarian transcendental is relationality with respect to all created entities and sociality with respect to other human beings. "Personal beings are social beings, so that of both God and man it must be said that they have their being in their personal relatedness: their free relation in otherness. This is not so of the rest of creation, which does not have the marks of love and freedom which are among the marks of the personal. Of the universe as a whole we should conclude that it is marked by relationality rather than sociality."[19] Relationality, accordingly, is a transcendental because it applies to all finite entities, both inanimate and animate, to indicate their necessary ontological interdependence. Sociality is not a transcendental in the strict sense since it applies only to entities who are likewise persons capable of relating to one another in freedom and love. Human sociality, in other words, should mirror the sociality of the divine persons, their free self-gift to one another and their ongoing reception of that self-gift from one another within the communion of the divine life.[20]

Accordingly, the ideal of human interpersonal relations is not individual self-fulfillment in distinction from the other but ongoing mutual transformation through self-gift to the other and reception of that same self-gift from the other. Some sacrifice of self-interest will inevitably be involved in this exchange but such sacrificial acts are transformative, not demeaning.[21] Moreover, through the dynamic of gift and reception among human beings, the rest of creation can be incorporated into the rhythm of the divine life: "The sacrifice of praise which is the due human response to both creation and redemption takes the form of that culture which enables both personal and non-personal worlds to realize their true being."[22]

At this point we are ready to consider my own Trinitarian reinterpretation of the concept of God within Whitehead's metaphysics. What I wish to stress at the beginning, however, is that the doctrine of the Trinity within my scheme serves as an illustration rather than an argument or proof for the validity of my philosophical hypothesis. My proposal is that reality is intrinsically social, constituted by innumerable momentary self-constituting subjects of experience that through their dynamic interrelation from moment to moment spontaneously co-generate higher-order unities which Whitehead calls "societies" and which I call "structured fields of activity" as their ongoing principle of order and continuity. This is then my solution to the problem of the One and the Many. The One is emergent out of the interplay of the Many with one another from moment to moment rather than timelessly transcendent of them as their enduring principle of order and intelligibility. At the same time, as I explain below, the One is not thereby an incidental byproduct of the interaction of the Many with one another. Rather, as the necessary context or condition for the ongoing interaction of the Many, the One as a Whiteheadian society (field of activity) preserves the structure or pattern that holds them together as this particular socially organized group of entities rather than some other group.

All of this, of course, applies nicely to the Christian doctrine of the Trinity if one thinks of the Trinity as an ongoing communion or community of three co-equal divine persons. But the argument or proof for the proposal is not to be found in an appeal to divine revelation (as in Gunton's theory) but in recourse to a new philosophical scheme, the metaphysics of universal intersubjectivity already suggested in previous chapters of this book. Thus, my focus (as opposed to Gunton's) is on human reason rather than divine revelation for its principle of verification. At the same time, however, for Christians who likewise believe in the reality of the Trinity as a communion of three co-equal divine persons, the proposal offers welcome confirmation of their religious beliefs. Creation, after all, is supposed to be fashioned in the image of God its Creator.

Alfred North Whitehead claimed in *Process and Reality* that "the final real things of which this world is made up"[23] are actual occasions or the momentary self-constituting actual occasions referred to above. My counterclaim is that he was only half-right with this hypothesis. The "societies" or socially organized units into which actual occasions consolidate should likewise be counted among "the final real things of which this world is made up." For, as Whitehead himself years later conceded, "An actual occasion has no history. It never changes. It only becomes and perishes."[24] Thus, unless it is viewed as the latest member of a "society" which alone endures and has "an essential character,"[25] an actual occasion is equivalently a "trivial puff of existence in far-off empty space"[26] without further meaning and value.

Furthermore, if one thinks of Whiteheadian societies as likewise constituting the building blocks or "final real things of which this world is made up," then from still another perspective one can say that reality is intrinsically social. That is, reality is not made up simply of individual entities whose membership in various "societies" or socially organized units is something derivative or purely contingent. On the contrary, reality is made up precisely of such socially organized unities or totalities in virtue of the dynamic interrelation of their constituent parts or members. The totalities, admittedly, cannot exist apart from the activity of those interrelated parts or members, but their parts or members only make sense as parts or members of a more comprehensive social reality. There are, accordingly, innumerable levels of social organization within the human world and the world of Nature. Atoms, for example, have dynamically interrelated parts or members (electrons, protons, and neutrons), but are themselves constitutive parts or members of molecules which in various combinations make up the living and nonliving things of this world. Human beings are born and die within hierarchically ordered communities (local, regional, national, international). Everywhere one looks in this world, reality is socially organized, composed of individuals and groups that themselves upon further inspection are dynamic unities of interrelated parts or members.

Does such a scheme lead to totalitarian ways of thinking in which the good of the individual entity is always subordinated to the good of the totality to which it belongs? My contention is that this would indeed be the case if "the final real things of which this world is made up" were subatomic particles. Subatomic particles have little or no value in themselves except insofar as they can be combined to constitute the persons and things of this world. But if "the final real things of which this world is made up," as Whitehead claims, are self-constituting subjects of experience, this danger seems to be eliminated. A self-constituting subject of experience by definition has sufficient ontological integrity to be partially independent of the social context out of which it is arising and to which it contributes its own pattern of existence and activity. A Whiteheadian society, after all, depends for its continued existence on the interplay of its constituent actual occasions as much as they depend on it as the necessary context or environment for their origination and the survival of their distinctive pattern of existence and activity.

Let us assume, for example, that not momentary subjects of experience but subatomic particles are "the final real things of which this world is made up." The world in effect is then a cosmic machine with seemingly interchangeable parts since the parts themselves, the subatomic particles, have meaning and value only with reference to the atoms and molecules into which they aggregate. Moreover, if the world is thus viewed as a cosmic machine, there is reason to wonder about the origin of life on this planet. Evolution or the emergence of new life forms within Nature, as we shall see in a later chapter, seemingly demands more than simply a rearrangement of previously existing parts. Natural selection as a principle of evolution, in other words, seems to involve an interplay between the organism and its environment that is very difficult to explain on purely mechanical grounds.

But, if for that reason we allow for self-organization at the level of physics and chemistry, where does it come from and how does it function so as to guarantee order and stability within the world of Nature? Here Whitehead's approach makes sense. If the world is made up of actual occasions or momentary self-constituting subjects of experience that both condition and are conditioned by the environment in which they arise, then order arises spontaneously out of successive generations of actual occasions that have basically the same pattern of interrelation and which pass on that basic pattern to subsequent actual occasions in the same society or field of activity. At the same time, as David Griffin has pointed out, this does not imply pan-psychism, the belief that even inanimate things possess consciousness or self-awareness.[27] All that Whitehead proposes is that the ultimate components of inanimate things (i.e., subatomic particles) must be minimally aware of and responsive to one another so as consistently to aggregate into the higher-order unity first of an atom and then of a molecule.[28]

Hence, to claim that there are subjects of experience everywhere within Nature, even at the subatomic level of existence and activity, is not as outrageous as it might seem at first reading. All that is thereby being stipulated is that an actual occasion at that primitive level of existence and activity within Nature is somehow aware of its predecessor within the electromagnetic field and responds to it as the situation demands. In this way, it repeats and passes on to its successor basically the same pattern of existence and activity which it inherited from its predecessor in that subatomic "society" or ongoing series of actual occasions. The further challenge, of course, is to explain how what works at this subatomic level of Nature can account for the existence of the highly complex world in which we live. How, in other words, can we claim that all the persons and things of commonsense experience are the natural outgrowth and development of such an elementary process on the subatomic level of existence and activity within Nature?

For the purpose of argument, let us assume that every Whiteheadian society is in fact what I call a structured field of activity or lawlike environment for its constituent actual occasions from moment to moment. Normally, each new set of constituent actual occasions simply repeats the structural pattern already present within the field by reason of the interrelated activity of its predecessors. But in principle, any given set of actual occasions can take on a new pattern of interrelation in virtue of their common "prehension" or feeling-level grasp of new factors in their external environment. When this happens, the structure of the field is altered, however subtly. At this point, the next set of actual occasions must "decide" either to accept this new pattern of interrelation derived from their immediate predecessors or revert to the older pattern derived from still earlier sets of actual occasions. If this next set of actual occasions decides to stay with the new pattern as the structure of their own interrelationship, then a new Whiteheadian society with a new pattern of interrelation for its constituent actual occasions has emerged, different from the old society and the previous pattern of interrelation. The Whiteheadian society as a structured field of activity and its constituent actual occasions thereby depend on and mutually condition one another's existence.

At this point it should be clear why I prefer to describe White-headian societies as structured fields of activity for their constituent actual occasions rather than as collections of individual actual occasions with a "common element of form" or analogous self-constitution, as Whitehead himself proposes in *Process and Reality*.[29] For, in that case, there really is no One, no objective higher-level unity proper to the society as such. Whatever alleged unity the society possesses is only an abstract and partial reflection of the concrete unity of each constituent actual occasion in and through its process of individual self-constitution.[30] Admittedly, there are according to Whitehead likewise "structured" societies of actual occasions corresponding to organisms of various kinds. These "structured societies" have an objective principle of unity and organization, due to the activity of a "regnant nexus" of actual occasions (in most cases a "soul") in its relations with all the subsocieties of inanimate actual occasions constituting the "body" of the organism.[31] But this arrangement seems to be an instance of the older Platonic paradigm for the One and the Many, whereby the One as a higher-order entity gives order and intelligibility to the Many as its multiple subordinate entities.

What I am proposing, however, is that the One is in the first place a unifying activity rather than a higher-order entity and that what it produces by way of a unitary objective reality is a field of activity or ongoing environment for successive generations of these constituent actual occasions. Thus understood as a lawlike field of activity for constituent actual occasions, the One is emergent out of the ongoing interplay of the Many (the constituent actual occasions) with one another and thus is as much dependent upon them as they are dependent upon it as the One.

This is not to deny, of course, that a "soul" or "regnant nexus" of actual occasions at work within a Whiteheadian structured society will inevitably play a larger role in structuring that society (field of activity) than any of the other subsocieties of actual occasions. But the activity of the "regnant nexus" has to be coordinated with the activities of all the subsocieties of inanimate actual occasions at any given moment in order to produce the here-and-now unity of the overall structured society or organism. I am, for example, at every moment the unity of all the events (actual occasions) taking place in my body. Everything going on inside me contributes to who I am at every moment; I am not just a "mind" in a body.

Whitehead is certainly not opposed to a gradual growth of complexity within Nature; he explicitly says that the emergence of complex structured societies "exemplifies the general purpose pervading nature."[32] But in my judgment he fails to explain how this emergence of higher-order ontological unities realistically takes place. If "agency belongs exclusively to actual occasions,"[33] and if the "common element of form" for the society is only analogously present in each constituent actual occasion at any given moment,[34] how do these analogously related actual occasions together ever produce something new and quite different from themselves as individual subjects of experience? What is really needed to explain the emergence of higher-order complexity within Nature, as I see it, is my own revised understanding of a Whiteheadian society as a structured field of activity for its constituent actual occasions.

The field already has a form proper to itself as a society as a result of the interplay of antecedent sets of actual occasions. But that form can gradually undergo change as a result of minute changes in the relationship of new constituent actual occasions to one another with the passage of time. There is, then, a reciprocal relationship between the field with its relatively stable structure and ever new sets of actual occasions that in responding to one another and to their common environment will over time assume new patterns of interrelation. The actual occasions co-generate the new common element of form for their interaction here and now, but the society as the environment or enduring field of activity for the ongoing succession of actual occasions transmits that changed pattern of interrelation to the next set of constituent actual occasions in their processes of concrescence.

Only with this combination of bottom-up causality exercised by the constituent actual occasions in co-generating their "common element of form" for the society to which they belong and the top-down causality exercised by the society as an already existing but still flexible structured field of activity for those actual occasions can one explain how Nature is not dead but alive, capable of spontaneous self-organization even at inanimate levels of existence and activity. As we shall see in the next chapter of this book, emergence of new forms of self-organization within Nature only makes sense when one has recourse to both bottom-up and top-down causality within the entity undergoing transformation. Reliance on either one in exclusion of the other produces insuperable problems. Likewise, such an adroit combination of bottom-up and top-down causality illuminates how a Creator God can be active in a world governed by relatively fixed patterns of operation. Especially when top-down causality likewise implies communication of information or informational causality, then the much sought after "causal joint" between divine primary causality and creaturely secondary causality may well be at hand. As we shall see in chapter 11, God provides what Whitehead calls "divine initial aims" or feeling-level promptings to creaturely actual occasions at every moment, but the actual occasions decide whether or not to accept these divine "lures" in their individual processes of self-constitution.

For the moment, however, this chapter should have made clear how Colin Gunton's resolution of the perennial problem of the One and the Many in terms of *perichoresis*, the unity-in-diversity of the divine persons within the Christian doctrine of the Trinity, can be transposed to a more purely philosophical level of reflection. If one reinterprets Whiteheadian societies as structured fields of activity for their constituent actual occasions, then one has at hand a strictly philosophical paradigm for validating Gunton's new understanding of the One and the Many. In this way, belief in the reality of the Christian God as a community of three co-equal but radically different divine persons is not a prerequisite for acceptance of a new approach to reality in terms of a metaphysics of universal intersubjectivity. As I see it, only the presupposition of ongoing intersubjectivity between two or more individual self-constituting subjects of experience over an extended period of time allows for both particularity and universality, ongoing change and enduring order. Only thus can one explain first the emergence and then the consolidation of genuinely new forms of existence and activity at all levels of Nature in a lawlike manner.

9

OPEN-ENDED SYSTEMS

In earlier chapters of this book, I indicated how the systems approach to reality employed by Kant and the German Idealists, notably Hegel with his notion of Absolute Spirit as the beginning and end of cosmic history, was strongly resisted by Kierkegaard in the nineteenth century and then by Levinas, Buber, and Heidegger in the mid-twentieth century with their focus on individual subjectivity and attention to historical context. But, given the nature of the ongoing dialectic between the One and the Many, a strong emphasis on the necessary particularity of the Many will inevitably produce a counteremphasis on the need for an overarching unity represented by still another understanding of the One. So it is not surprising that, above all in scientific circles in the twentieth century, thinking in terms of systems for the organization and analysis of empirical data has made a strong comeback.

The difference, of course, between systems thinking as represented by Hegel's *Encyclopedia* and the hypothesis of self-organizing systems set forth by Stuart Kauffman and others to explain the phenomenon of emergence in evolutionary theory is that the older systems were basically closed and the newer systems are unpredictable in terms of their precise outcome and to that extent open-ended. That is, the timeless reality of Absolute Spirit was both the starting point and the final stage in Hegel's philosophical system; in this way, the system would be self-validating. For Kauffman and other contemporary systems thinkers, on the contrary, self-organizing systems, while clearly lawlike in their procedure, do not presuppose their final outcome. So one has to take into account the past history of the system as well as its here-and-now lawlike regularities, if one is to anticipate what will happen next.

Ervin Laszlo's Systems Approach to Reality

Before launching into further study of the hypothesis of self-organizing systems, however, I first call attention to the work of an earlier systems thinker, Ervin Laszlo, who in the mid-twentieth century was already at work in constructing a systems-oriented worldview, a project which with modifications he is still promoting today. In his *Introduction to Systems Philosophy* published in 1972, for example, Laszlo maintains that the basic components of the physical universe are social realities or systems.[1] Systems can be divided into natural and artificial (humanly constructed) systems. In either case, a system is a "nonrandom accumulation of matter-energy in a region of physical space-time which is nonrandomly organized into coacting interrelated subsystems or components."[2] This definition, of course, would also apply to my understanding of Whiteheadian societies as structured fields of activity for their constituent actual occasions, with one key exception. As noted above, for Laszlo the components of systems are subsystems. This would fit Whitehead's notion of a "structured society" and my own understanding of a more complex structured field of activity inclusive of other more limited fields of activity. But here I agree with Whitehead that the ultimate components of societies/structured fields of activity are actual occasions, momentary self-constituting subjects of experience. These ultimate components are individual entities, albeit individual entities that are normally not found in isolation from one another but only in dynamic interrelation with each other. They are not social realities (systems) made up of still other social realities (subsystems), as Laszlo seems to have in mind.

Admittedly, actual occasions are themselves the result of a process of unification of physical and mental "prehensions," that is, feeling-level responses to physical data and structures of intelligibility ("eternal objects") coming from the external environment.[3] So they could possibly be considered mini-systems in Laszlo's sense except for one all-important reason. Actual occasions are in the first place subjects of experience, not objective organizational realities. As such, systems do not fit into a metaphysics of universal intersubjectivity as "the final real things of which the world is made up."[4] They are instead the result or byproduct of subjects of experience in dynamic interrelation. To claim that the components of systems are always other systems is, accordingly, to postpone the question of the ultimate constituents of reality. Within a metaphysics of universal intersubjectivity, the final real things of which the world is made up must be individual subjects of experience, not systems.

Yet in other respects Laszlo's systems approach to reality is quite compatible with my own field-oriented understanding of Whiteheadian societies. For example, with the notion of system Laszlo has a metaphysical category that applies equally well to the inorganic, organic, and supraorganic (institutional) levels of reality.[5] This is also true of my concept of field. That is, "system" and "field" are both analogical rather than univocal concepts. They both refer to a dynamic unity of interrelated parts or members. But the further specification of both the unity and the parts or members varies widely, depending upon the type of system or field being considered. An intentional field co-generated by human beings in ongoing conversation is quite different, for example, from the electromagnetic or gravitational field in physics. Yet in all three cases I maintain that an objectively structured reality is generated through the ongoing interaction of its component parts or members. Thus, everything from atoms to physical organisms to human communities and physical environments can be described as a field or a system.

Still another point of comparison between Lazlo's notion of system and my own understanding of a Whiteheadian society as a structured field of activity for its constituent actual occasions is the way in which both systems and fields are inclusive rather than exclusive of one another. Unlike the notion of substance in classical metaphysics, therefore, in which substances mutually exclude one another, a more complex or more expansive field of activity or system can integrate within itself a simpler or more geographically limited field of activity or system without loss of ontological integrity on either side. The lower-level field of activity or system thereby provides the infrastructure for the existence and operation of the higher-level field or system, and the higher-level field of activity or system in turn provides the superstructure for the further existence and activity of the lower-order field of activity or system. Atoms, for example, as miniature fields of activity or systems both condition and are themselves conditioned by their existence and activity within a molecule as a higher-order and more expansive field of activity or system. Thus, for both Laszlo and me, reality is hierarchically ordered with a wide range of interrelated systems or fields of activity from the smallest to the largest, and from those that are relatively simple in terms of structure and organization to those that are much more complex.

For Whitehead, on the contrary, there is no all-inclusive understanding of "society" that applies equally well at all the levels of organization within Nature. Inanimate "societies," for example, are little more than aggregates of actual occasions, all of which have a similar self-constitution or "common element of form."[6] Organic "structured societies"—that is, societies made up of subsocieties of actual occasions—have an internal principle of unity and organization in virtue of a "regnant nexus" of actual occasions within the structured society.[7] But molecules are also described by Whitehead as "structured societies."[8] How is one to understand a "regnant nexus" within a molecule as a presumably inanimate entity?[9] In similar fashion, supraorganic realities like human communities and physical environments seem to have defining characteristics that make them different from one another. Yet here too the notion of a "regnant nexus" of actual occasions for the community or environment seems out of place. Within Whitehead's scheme, therefore, what works well for organisms with a "soul" or internal principle of unity and organization does not work so well for entities on the inorganic or supraorganic levels of existence and activity within Nature.

Another feature of Laszlo's systems approach to reality that I find compatible with my own notion of Whiteheadian societies as structured fields of activity for their constituent actual occasions has to do with the notion of agency. According to Whitehead, only actual occasions exercise agency.[10] Thus inanimate societies, those without an internal principle of organization and control, are little more than purely passive aggregates of similarly constituted actual occasions, as noted above. Organisms or "living societies" exercise agency in and through their "regnant nexus" of actual occasions, but supraorganic realities like communities or environments are also lacking in agency from the top down. Laszlo argues that systems have to possess direct agency in order to function as a unified reality. I basically agree with Laszlo on this point, but with a qualification that keeps me still quite close to Whitehead's understanding of agency.

I argue that the agency of a Whiteheadian society or structured field of activity is different from the agency of its constituent actual occasions. The agency proper to an individual actual occasion is twofold. It exercises final causality in its self-constitution or "concrescence" as a subject of experience. It exercises efficient causality as a "superject" when it transmits its energy-content or feeling-level "satisfaction" to successor actual occasions.[11] The agency proper to the society, however, is an instance of formal or what might be called "informational" causality. From moment to moment it is, to be sure, derivative from the dynamic interrelation of its constituent actual occasions. But this "common element of form" gives a specific intelligibility or structure to the society or field of activity as a whole for each moment. Furthermore, it provides the objective pattern for the self-constitution of the next set of constituent actual occasions and thereby guarantees the enduring ontological identity of the society as a whole over time. In human beings, this formal or structuring cause operative within consciousness is easily recognizable as habit or character, a persistent way of thinking and acting from moment to moment.

Finally, in a book published a few years ago, Laszlo used field imagery in setting forth a revised systems approach to reality. Therein he explains how physical, biological, and what he calls transpersonal phenomena are best understood in terms of fields in which parts or members are connected to one another and to the system as a whole quasi-instantaneously.[12] He concludes that while fields are not themselves directly observable, they produce clearly observable effects and hence must be considered as physical realities, not simply as mental constructs.[13] As I have explained in greater detail elsewhere,[14] Laszlo's systems approach to reality in this book is closely connected to my own field-oriented reinterpretation of Whiteheadian societies. In both his theory and mine, Nature is hierarchically ordered, made up of "'a nested hierarchy of nonlocally connected coherent systems. Lower-level systems exist as semi-autonomous realities within higher-level systems, thereby setting limits to the functions of the higher-level systems, just as the higher-level systems provide additional 'in-formation' to the operation of the lower-level systems."[15] Laszlo's notion of "information" provided by higher-level systems to lower-level systems corresponds nicely to my understanding of the formal causality proper to the society as a structured field of activity for its constituent actual occasions. Furthermore, it explains what I earlier described as top-down and bottom-up causation within a Whiteheadian structured society. That is, it explains how the common element of form for a society is the immediate source for the "information" guiding the dynamic interrelation of actual occasions moment by moment. Moreover, this notion of the common element of form as a structuring cause in the emergence and the ongoing organization of Whiteheadian societies will also play a key role in our assessment of the systems theory of Stuart Kauffman.

Stuart Kauffman's Notion of
Self-Organizing Systems

In the Preface to his book *At Home in the Universe*, Stuart Kauffman challenges the claim that natural selection is the exclusive mechanism for biological evolution: "Another source—self-organization—is the root source of order. The order of the biological world, I have come to believe, is not merely tinkered, but arises naturally and spontaneously because of these principles of self-organization—laws of complexity that we are just beginning to uncover and understand."[16] Natural selection, in other words, comes into play only after a certain level of self-organization has been already achieved. At that point natural selection decides which such novel experiments in self-organization will survive and prosper and which for various reasons (both internal and environmental) will inevitably fail. Thus, only a combination of self-organization and natural selection ultimately explains first the emergence of life from nonlife and then the amazing diversity of biological species that have historically come into existence in the last 4 billion years on this planet.

Kauffman readily concedes that there is as yet no commonly accepted conceptual framework among biologists for conjoining the principle of natural selection with principles of self-organization within Nature.[17] But in *At Home in the Universe*, and in a later, more technically written book, *Investigations*,[18] he sets forth a generalized formula for the way in which self-organization and higher orders of complexity spontaneously appear not only in the lifeworld but also in economic and political systems. This is a very ambitious project undertaken by Kauffman and his associates in the Santa Fe Institute in New Mexico. In these pages I content myself first with analyzing the general principles for his approach to spontaneous self-organization within Nature and then indicating how my own understanding of Whiteheadian societies as structured fields of activity for their constituent actual occasions might provide a clue to that generalized "conceptual framework" that he still at present finds lacking in his own and others' work.

In an early chapter of *At Home in the Universe*, for example, Kauffman claims: "Life is a natural property of complex chemical systems, that when the number of different kinds of molecules in a chemical soup passes a certain threshold, a self-sustaining network of reactions—an autocatalytic metabolism—will suddenly appear."[19] Let us now compare Kauffman's proposal with Whitehead's understanding of a "society":

A nexus enjoys "social order" [is a society] where (i) there is a common element of form illustrated in the definiteness of each of its included actual entities, and (ii) this common element of form arises in each member of the nexus by reason of the conditions imposed upon it by its prehensions of some other members of the nexus, and (iii) these prehensions impose that condition of reproduction by reason of their inclusion of positive feelings of that common form.[20]

For Whitehead, accordingly, each actual entity/actual occasion is a unique subject of experience with its own pattern of existence and activity. Yet all the actual entities within a society still have an analogous self-constitution by reason of their common prehension of the pattern proper to the self-constitution of their immediate predecessors in the same society. This common element of form carried over from one set of constituent actual occasions to another constitutes their group identity as a society.

Structurally, Kauffman's notion of self-organizing chemical systems and Whitehead's notion of a "society" as a set of actual occasions linked by a common element of form are quite similar. Self-organizing chemical systems for Kauffman and societies for Whitehead are both socially organized realities emergent out of the dynamic interplay of their component parts or members. In *Investigations* Kauffman frequently uses the term "autonomous agents" to describe self-organizing systems as entities emergent out of the interplay of their component parts or members.[21] Corresponding to "autonomous agents" for Kauffman would presumably be "structured societies" or societies composed of subsocieties of actual occasions for Whitehead. But here one must be careful. The agency proper to a Whiteheadian "structured society" is not quite the same as what Kauffman has in mind for self-organizing systems. That is, whereas Kauffman believes that life spontaneously emerges from the dynamic interaction of nonliving components (chemical systems), Whitehead claims that structured societies which are "living" have a "regnant nexus" of entirely living actual occasions which is supported by but still functionally superior to the other subsocieties of actual occasions that are inanimate, nonliving.[22]

What Whitehead thereby leaves unresolved is the question of the origin and the perpetuation of this nexus of "entirely living" actual occasions. How did it emerge out of a background composed of inanimate actual occasions? Likewise, once emergent, how was it sustained and carried forward to the next set of actual occasions within that structured society? Whitehead claims, for example, that "the growth of a complex structured society exemplifies the general purpose pervading nature"[23] and then attributes this growth in complexity or emergence of new order to an increased intensity of experience among the constituent actual occasions. But how does this increased intensity of experience arise in the first place, and how is it then communicated to future actual occasions? The problem is that Whitehead attributes agency exclusively to individual actual occasions and does not seem to recognize the validity of a collective agency for the society as a whole so that it can function as a reality in its own right. As a result, Whitehead's system by his own admission is a type of metaphysical atomism: "the ultimate metaphysical truth is atomism."[24] Actual occasions "are the final real things of which this world is made up."[25] But, if so, it is difficult to see how Whiteheadian societies as aggregates of similarly constituted but independently existing inanimate actual occasions can bring about a life form radically different from themselves as individuals.

Thus, if one wishes to claim with Kauffman that life is naturally emergent from the dynamic interplay of nonliving components (chemical systems), then some rethinking of the dynamism at work within a Whiteheadian structured society is required. I suggest for this purpose three further specifications or modifications of Whitehead's scheme: (a) that there is an agency proper to the various subsocieties within a structured society over and above the agencies of their component actual occasions, (b) that this agency functions as the structuring principle or common element of form for the sub-society as such and not simply for its component actual occasions in their individual self-constitution, and (c) that the structured society as a whole and all its subsocieties be conceived as a set of interconnected and hierarchically ordered fields of activity.

Given these modifications, life can emerge from the dynamic interplay of inanimate actual occasions, as Kauffman maintains is the case within chemical systems. That is, a single set of inanimate actual occasions within a given subsociety of the overall structured society could by their dynamic interrelation in response to changes in the external environment spontaneously generate a significantly new common element of form for their collective reality as a subsociety within that same larger structured society. Furthermore, if this new common element of form with its potential for higher-order existence and activity is not immediately rejected but rather sustained and supported by the next set of actual occasions (and their successors) within that same subsociety, then the subsociety could evolve over time into what Kauffman earlier in this chapter called a "self-sustaining network of reactions" or the "autocatalytic metabolism" characteristic of life as opposed to nonlife. Functioning as an "autocatalytic metabolism," this subsociety could then bring it about that the structured society as a whole eventually makes the transition from nonlife to life.

Key here is the way in which change normally takes place among subsocieties of a larger structured society. For, if and when a novel form of existence and activity is introduced within a single subsociety through the collective activity of its constituent actual occasions, then all the actual occasions within the other subsocieties have to adjust to what has happened in their midst, either by incorporating the change of pattern into their own individual self-constitution or by rejecting it. If they in some way incorporate this structural novelty into their own pattern of operation, then the structured society as a whole will be altered and thus could over time make the transition from nonlife to life. If, however, the actual occasions within the other subsocieties do not accept this change of pattern proposed by some of their predecessors, then the future actual occasions of the subsociety within which the change of pattern originated will either revert to their previous pattern of inanimate co-existence or break up altogether as a subsociety within the larger structured society. The actual occasions within the other subsocieties will have equivalently suppressed this novel advance within their midst so as better to preserve the order and directionality received from the rest of their predecessors in the structured society.

This account differs from Whitehead's own explanation of the growth of complexity within the cosmic process because it focuses better on the role that societies play in sustaining and transmitting a new pattern of existence and activity once it originates within a given set of actual occasions. The societies, in other words, constitute the necessary principle of continuity within a metaphysical scheme in which individual actual occasions arise and perish with such rapidity. Furthermore, this revised understanding of Whiteheadian societies seems to correspond nicely with what Kauffman in *At Home in the Universe* says about the relatively haphazard and unpredictable way that life emerges from nonlife. He notes, for example, that "life evolves toward a regime that is poised between order and chaos."[26] It is never certain whether life will prevail over nonlife and, if it does prevail, what precise form or structure it will take. "In such a poised world, we must give up the pretense of long-term prediction. . . . Only God can foretell the future."[27] Likewise, in this field-oriented approach to Whiteheadian societies a delicate balance between novelty and order is achieved. The constituent actual occasions by their dynamic interrelation at any given moment account for the unexpected emergence of novelty. But the society as the context or field of activity within which the actual occasions arise and to which they contribute their momentary pattern of interrelation changes in its overall structure much more slowly.

Whitehead, to be sure, likewise makes this point in *Process and Reality*: "Error is the price which we pay for progress."[28] If the need for order prevails over the desire for novelty within the creative process, then stagnation at a given level of existence and activity ultimately prevails. But the opposite alternative is not simply the case. Unbridled desire for novelty undermines the order requisite for stable existence. In brief, then, a balance between order and novelty within a Whiteheadian structured society is the only way for it to survive and prosper: "A complex inorganic system of interaction is built up for the protection of the 'entirely living' nexus [of actual occasions], and the originative actions of the living elements are protective of the whole system. On the other hand, the reactions of the whole system provide the intimate environment required by the 'entirely living' nexus."[29] Yet, beyond this generalized statement, Whitehead does not further specify how this crucial correlation between bottom-up and top-down causality actually works within structured societies.

Granted this need for further precision in working out the details of his metaphysical scheme, there are many other interesting points of comparison between Whitehead's approach to reality and Kauffman's notion of self-organizing chemical systems. Given that "structured societies" are Whitehead's generic term not only for inanimate compounds, but also for organisms (plants, animals, human beings), even for supraorganic realities like human communities and physical environments, Whitehead as well as Kauffman seems to be saying that the same basic laws of self-organization are operative everywhere in the cosmic process. Kauffman, for example, compares the explosion of new species at the beginning of the Cambrian Era on earth to the rapid spread of new technologies in modern times and then remarks: "I am not an expert on technological evolution; indeed, I am also not an expert on the Cambrian explosion. But the parallels are striking, and it seems worthwhile to consider seriously the possibility that the patterns of branching radiation in biological and technological evolution are governed by similar general laws."[30] Likewise from a Whiteheadian perspective, the issue is at least worth exploring. After all, the laws governing the aggregation of actual occasions into societies (structured fields of activity) are everywhere the same. What happens on the organic and, above all, the supraorganic or institutional level is only a more complex version of what happens at the inorganic level of atoms and molecules. In every instance, novelty arises within a society with the slow growth in complexity of constituent actual occasions, provided that the change in the "common element of form" from a single subsociety within a structured society to the structured society as a whole can be sustained and deepened over time.

Another feature of Kauffman's hypothesis in *At Home in the Universe* which seems to resonate nicely with a Whiteheadian approach to reality is to be found in Kauffman's reference to the "logic of patches."[31] His basic argument here is that complex self-organizing systems achieve maximal efficiency in dealing with conflict situations if their individual parts or members stay focused on their own tasks and effectively ignore what is happening to others in the group: "if the conflict-laden task is broken into the properly chosen patches, the coevolving system lies at a phase transition between order and chaos and rapidly finds very good solutions."[32] Note how this compares with Whitehead's description of a society in which the common element of form "arises in each member of the nexus by reason of the conditions imposed upon it by its prehension of *some other* members of the nexus."[33] If all the actual occasions prehend the common element of form from their predecessors in exactly the same way, then nothing changes from moment to moment. But, on the contrary, if all the actual occasions in the society prehend the common element of form from their predecessors in totally different ways, then the society itself as the principle of order and continuity between successive sets of actual occasions collapses. Hence, just as Kauffman says about the logic of patches in self-organizing systems,[34] a Whiteheadian society only works well if it too is carefully poised between order and chaos in its internal constitution.

Kauffman also uses the term "receiver-based communication."[35] All the agents in a chemical system are in ongoing communication with one another but decide to respond positively only to some of their contemporaries in the achievement of some projected "team goal."[36] This too seems to correlate well with Whitehead's metaphysical scheme, specifically, his distinction between positive and negative prehensions in the self-constitution of an actual occasion:

An actual entity has a perfectly definite bond with each item in the universe. This determinate bond is its prehension of that item. A negative prehension is the definite exclusion of that item from positive contribution to the subject's own real internal constitution. . . . A positive prehension is the definite inclusion of that item into positive contribution to the subject's own real internal constitution.[37]

Thus an "agent" within a chemical system for Kauffman and a concrescing actual occasion for Whitehead share the same principle of self-organization; each is in broad communication with its surrounding world but chooses positively to incorporate into its self-constitution only some of what it knows (prehends). In both cases what might be called enlightened self-interest on the part of the chemical agent or actual occasion paradoxically works quite well to achieve goals and values bigger than itself and its own immediate self-interest.

One should not, of course, overestimate these similarities between Kauffman and Whitehead on the overall pattern of self-organization and the emergence of novelty within Nature. Yet both are clearly opposed to a purely mechanistic approach to the phenomenon of change or development within an evolutionary worldview. Throughout *At Home in the Universe*, Kauffman makes clear his belief that natural selection alone does not explain the emergence of life from nonlife or, even more generally, the unexpected emergence of novelty within natural processes: "And so we return to a tantalizing possibility: that self-organization is a prerequisite for evolvability, that it generates the kind of structures that can benefit from natural selection. . . . These two sources of order are natural partners."[38] For his part, Whitehead in an early philosophical work, *Science and the Modern World,* made clear his opposition to a purely mechanistic understanding of Nature.[39] Then in *Process and Reality* he specified that "the final real things of which the world is made up" are not material atoms in purely mechanical interaction but actual occasions, momentary self-constituting subjects of experience in dynamic interrelation.[40] Finally, near the end of his life Whitehead published *Modes of Thought*, in which he called attention to the different methodologies involved in treating Nature first as lifeless and then as alive.[41] Even though one achieves considerable success in the mathematical formulation of the laws of Nature, the task of understanding what is really going on within the world around us and within us is at best only half-done.

Accordingly, Whitehead's metaphysical cosmology, modified along the lines suggested above, might well be a candidate for the much-needed new conceptual framework to which Kauffman alludes in *At Home in the Universe*: "Nowhere in science have we an adequate way to state and study the interleaving of self-organization, selection, chance, and design. We have no adequate framework for the place of law in a historical science and the place of history in a lawful science."[42] In the next two chapters of this book, I summarize the reflections of two other natural scientists on the need for a new philosophical conceptuality in the religion and science debate. Paul Davies focuses on the dynamics of the part/whole relationship in theoretical physics and evolutionary biology, and Russell Stannard asks whether the notion of a "block universe" in theoretical physics might illuminate the relationship between time and eternity in theology. In both cases, the authors are consciously or unconsciously dealing with the overall problematic of this book, namely, how to understand the enduring relationship between the One and the Many in ever-new contexts or situations. Not surprisingly, I maintain that the modified understanding of Whitehead's category of "society" developed in these pages could be quite useful in addressing these issues.

PARTS AND WHOLES IN
CONTEMPORARY NATURAL
SCIENCE

In *The Cosmic Blueprint*, recently republished by Templeton Foundation Press, the Australian physicist Paul Davies notes: "Today, the truly fundamental material entities are no longer considered to be particles, but *fields*. Particles are regarded as disturbances in the fields, and so have been reduced to a derivative status."[1] Later, in discussing the differences between inanimate compounds and living organisms, he remarks:

The activity of fields could help explain biological forms because fields, unlike particles, are extended entities. They are thus better suited to accounting for long-range or global features. However, there still remains the central problem of how the genetic information containing the global plan which supposedly resides in particle form in the DNA, communicates itself to the fields and manages to impose upon them the requisite pattern. In physics, field patterns are imposed by boundary conditions, i.e., global, holistic control.[2]

These remarks by Davies in my judgment open up the possibility of a new philosophical understanding of the complex relationship between particles and fields, or more generally between parts and wholes, in the natural sciences. That is, in the world of Nature higher-order forms of existence and activity seem to have historically emerged out of the interplay of component parts at a lower-level stage of existence and activity (e.g., the emergence of molecules out of preexisting atoms, cells out of dynamically interrelated molecules, etc.), even though this violates the classical metaphysical belief that no effect is ever greater than its antecedent cause. Some scientists, of course, still implicitly endorse this metaphysical premise so as to justify a strictly analytical or mechanistic approach to their discipline. But others, like Stuart Kauffman, seem to be looking for a more synthetic or organismic approach, one in which genuinely new levels of existence and activity can legitimately be said to emerge over time within lower-level natural processes.[3]

Hence, even though the age-old philosophical problem of the relation between the One and the Many is not uppermost in the minds of these scientists, it is still tacitly there in the background. As Davies comments, "There is a growing dissatisfaction with sweeping reductionism, a feeling that the whole really is greater than the sum of its parts. Analysis and reduction will always have a central role to play in science, but many people cannot accept that it is an exclusive role."[4] Not only in the analysis of organisms but also in the study of open systems or "dissipative structures" at the inanimate level of existence and activity within Nature, new levels of self-organization and complexity seem to spontaneously emerge. Ilya Prigogine and Isabelle Stengers made this claim some years ago in their book *Order Out of Chaos*.[5] Now Kauffman and his colleagues at the Santa Fe Institute are proposing the same ideal on the basis of their work with computer-generated models.

Hence, in dealing with these issues Davies and others find themselves rejecting vitalism and mechanism as explanations for the emergence of life out of nonlife. What is needed is a combination of top-down and bottom-up causation that neither vitalism nor mechanism by itself can provide: "The real challenge is to demonstrate how *localized* interactions can exercise *global* control. . . . It is the relationship between the *locally* stored information [in the DNA molecules] and the *global, holistic* manipulation necessary to produce the relevant patterns which lies at the heart of the 'miracle' of morphogenesis."[6] "Morphogenesis," of course, refers to the theory that the antecedent structure of a field influences the way in which entities within the field interact.[7] Thus with the use of the term Davies is thinking once again in the context of fields and their components. But, as already noted, field theory presents conceptual problems: "If the fields tell the DNA molecules where they are located in the pattern, and the DNA molecules tell the fields what pattern to adopt, nothing is explained because the argument is circular."[8] The proper relation between the parts and the whole remains unclear.

Here in my judgment is where the field-oriented understanding of Whiteheadian societies developed in this book might be quite useful as a new theoretical paradigm for understanding the complex relationship between fields and their components in the natural sciences. As already mentioned in chapter 9, there are different kinds of causality at work in a Whiteheadian society. The actual occasions exercise final causality in and through their individual processes of concrescence, which always end in a self-constituting decision, a state of "satisfaction" for each actual occasion. They exercise efficient causality in transmitting that energy content or feeling-level "satisfaction" to their successors in that same society.[9] But the common element of form for the society as a whole likewise exercises causality, namely, formal or informational causality with respect to the next set of constituent actual occasions. That is, because it already has a determinate structure as a result of the structural pattern inherited from antecedent sets of actual occasions, the common element of form is a major conditioning factor in the self-constitution of all subsequent sets of actual occasions. Thereby it "informs" their pattern of dynamic interrelation and, as I see it, gives them an ontological unity proper to their status as a society rather than simply a collection of similarly constituted actual occasions.[10]

Furthermore, unlike an Aristotelian substantial form, the common element of form for a Whiteheadian society is not forever fixed in its intelligibility or ontological status. As an ongoing reflection of the dynamic interplay between successive sets of actual occasions, the common element of form over time undergoes gradual transformation. Once again, the individual actual occasions are the efficient causes of this transformation of structural pattern since in their self-constitution from moment to moment, they reflect various changes in the environment and thereby produce a new common element of form for their co-existence as a society. But since each actual occasion presumably reflects those environmental changes in a manner slightly different from its contemporaries in the same society, it is crucially important that this new common element of form or "complex eternal object" for the society as a whole both reflect and yet be different from its particular instantiation in individual actual occasions.

In this sense, the common element of form is a "concrete universal" rather than an "abstract universal."[11] That is, it is not an abstraction from the concrete reality of its constituent actual occasions but the synthesis or full embodiment of the complex eternal object imperfectly realized in each of its constituent actual occasions at any given moment. Whitehead himself seems to allude to this point when in his definition of a society he notes that "this common element of form arises in each member of the nexus by reason of the conditions imposed upon it by its prehension of *some other* members of the nexus."[12] All the constituent actual occasions reflect in their self-constitution this complex eternal object but in different ways and in differing degrees. For that very reason, the common element of form cannot be exclusively located in the self-constitution of individual actual occasions but has to enjoy a separate existence as the overall structure of their conjoint field of activity.

But how can this field-oriented approach to Whiteheadian societies assist Davies in solving the problem of the interrelationship of the One and the Many as exemplified in the dialectical relation between the information-laden DNA molecules and the global pattern or plan of the organism? Davies, for example, asks: "If every molecule of DNA possesses the same global plan for the whole organism, how is it that different cells implement different parts of that plan? Is there, perhaps, a 'metaplan' to tell each cell which part of the plan to implement?"[13] Within my own field-oriented understanding of Whiteheadian societies, the solution seems simple enough. The "metaplan" is to be found in the common element of form for the Whiteheadian society as a whole. Since actual occasions are self-constituting and thus by definition similar to but not identical with their contemporaries, they all implement the common element of form in slightly different ways. Yet these differences remain consistent with one another because of the overall structuring activity of the common element of form or "metaplan." This unique blending of formal causality exercised by the common element of form and the combination of final and efficient causality exercised by the constituent actual occasion solves the "mystery" of morphogenesis, namely, how an organism or a nonliving "dissipative structure" at the inorganic level within Nature can successfully evolve into a higher level of self-organization and complexity without considerable risk of chaos or at least regression to a lower-level pattern of organization than it previously possessed.

Elsewhere in *The Cosmic Blueprint* Davies takes note of the work of Rupert Sheldrake in *A New Science of Life* with respect to the structure and function of morphogenetic fields but rejects the latter's hypothesis as "a revival of old-fashioned teleology."[14] According to Sheldrake, "morphogenetic fields correspond to the *potential* state of a developing system and are already present before it takes up its final form."[15] The metaplan for the organism is thus fixed from the beginning, and the possibility of change or development through chance factors such as environmental changes or random gene mutations is in principle excluded. In addition, there is the question of the origination of the form as contained in the field rather than in its molecular components. Is the field somehow active in its own self-constitution, or is it subject to external influences (e.g., from God as the Cosmic Architect)?[16]

Here, too, I believe that the field-oriented approach to Whiteheadian societies proposed above can be of assistance in vindicating the theory of morphogenetic fields without lapsing into "old-fashioned teleology." For the common element of form in a Whiteheadian society is the ongoing product of the interplay of its constituent actual occasions. As such, it can and indeed should undergo gradual transformation as new sets of actual occasions arise and "prehend" their ever-changing environment in new ways, thus giving rise to a new common element of form as a result of their dynamic interrelation. But even as a product of the activity of its constituent actual occasions, the common element of form exercises formal or informational causality vital for the continuing existence of the society. It guarantees the basic continuity of form or relative self-identity of the society in a constantly changing world. In Davies' terminology, it provides a "metaplan" for the organism but not one that is fixed in every detail. Hence, one can make the claim that the common element of form in a Whiteheadian society is a developmental teleology in which the final outcome is not guaranteed in advance but rather progressively worked out over time. In this sense, the Whiteheadian common element of form is purposive or teleonomic rather than purposeful or strictly teleological in its operation. That is, there is a telos or goal at work in the functioning society but it always remains somewhat indeterminate until the end of its process of development.

Implicit here in this discussion of "morphogenetic fields" is the desire on the part of many contemporary evolutionary thinkers to find a middle ground between physical reductionism and vitalism in the explanation of the phenomenon of emergence within evolutionary biology. Physical reductionism argues that the emergence of more complex organisms is simply due to the chance reordering of already existing components (atoms and molecules) together with the mechanism of natural selection to weed out less successful combinations of such elementary parts. Vitalism argues that a separate life-principle or the equivalent of an Aristotelian entelechy is needed for the components successfully to come together into a more complex physical organism and survive various environmental risks. While physical reductionism is evidently a form of monism in that the organism as a whole is simply the sum of its component parts, vitalism is just as clearly a form of dualism in that the necessary life principle or entelechy is an immaterial or spiritual principle distinct in kind from the material component parts.[17]

What has been set forth as a compromise position between these two alternatives is called "emergentist monism." As Philip Clayton explains, this term presupposes that (1) Nature is uniform; there is only one kind of physical "stuff" in the world. But (2) this "stuff" is hierarchically organized into progressively higher levels of existence and activity emergent out of lower levels of existence and activity. Likewise, (3) this happens in virtue of roughly similar patterns of self-organization with downward causation in some form or other normally present. Finally, (4) consciousness or mind (if not a soul in the classical sense, at least mental properties) is thus emergent out of matter (that is, the brain with its neural networks).[18] This is not dual-aspect monism or something akin to the philosophy of Spinoza in which the one divine substance is both mind and body under different "modes" (see above, chap. 4). Rather, there is real causal interaction between higher and lower systems within Nature and within a given system between higher and lower components (e.g., molecules as combinations of atoms).[19]

In line with my own field-oriented approach to Whiteheadian societies, I would propose instead what might be called "emergentist non-dualism." That is, every physical reality is composed of two dynamically interrelated dimensions or parts: momentary self-constituting immaterial subjects of experience and the material fields of activity out of which they originate and to which upon cessation of their process of concrescence they contribute their individual pattern of self-constitution. Together they constitute a single nondual psychophysical reality. Neither "spirit" nor "matter" can exist without the other. At lower levels of existence and activity within Nature, the constraints of "matter" on the activity of "spirit" are considerable, but at higher levels of existence and activity (e.g., human beings and the institutions they co-create) the flexibility and spontaneity of "spirit" come more and more to the fore.

Whitehead himself proposed that an actual occasion is a "subject/superject."[20] As a subject of experience, an actual occasion is a strictly immaterial reality that must be materialized or become physically objectified as a superject in order to be "prehended" by subsequent actual occasion.[21] The superject of an actual occasion is an energy-laden combination of physical and conceptual "feelings" organized in terms of an immanent self-constituting "decision." Both energy content and organizational pattern are then incorporated into the structured field of activity out of which the actual occasion originated. In this way, the individual subject of experience perishes but its particular energy content and pattern of self-constitution survive in modified form. Whitehead himself notes in *Process and Reality*, "In the philosophy of organism it is not 'substance' which is permanent, but 'form.'"[22] I simply add the qualification that the ongoing transmission of energy and organizational pattern from one actual occasion (or set of actual occasions) to another is guaranteed by an enduring field of activity common to both.

In his book *Mind and Emergence* Clayton makes clear at several points his opposition to "panpsychism," the belief that "it's mind all the way down" within Nature; empirical evidence for the reality of panpsychism is highly debatable.[23] Moreover, panpsychism seems to imply spiritual monism, namely, the belief that only immaterial subjects of experience exist. What I am urging, however, is not spiritual monism but nondualism, the contention that spirit and matter are necessarily interrelated. Subjects of experience as such are immaterial realities and for this reason cannot be directly observed or studied. But subjects of experience express themselves as material realities; that is, they are superjects with a specific energy content and pattern of self-constitution. Both energy content and pattern, moreover, contribute to the energy level and structure of the field of activity to which the subjects of experience belong. The fields as such are invisible to the eye; but, as Ervin Lazlo comments in *The Connectivity Hypothesis*,[24] the observable empirical effects of such fields (e.g., the electromagnetic field) are unmistakable.

One could label this proposal "panexperientialism."[25] But more precisely, my theory should be called pan-agency; agency in some form or other exists at all levels of existence and activity within Nature. An actual occasion, after all, is the agent of its own process of self-constitution and likewise active in transmitting its energy content or "satisfaction" to successor actual occasions in the same society. It thus exemplifies what Whitehead calls the principle of creativity: "the many [past entities] become one [currently develop-ing actual entity] and are increased by one."[26] Hence, if, as White-head claims, actual occasions are "the final real things of which this world is made up," agency in some minimal form is present every-where in Nature, even at the level of a subatomic particle (e.g., a proton or electron understood as an ongoing society of actual occa-sions). Agency, accordingly, is not first emergent at higher levels of existence and activity within Nature in order to explain the reality of "spirit" or self-conscious agency.[27] Rather, "spirit" in this sense is simply a higher form of agency present everywhere in Nature.

Admittedly, "agency" is not a univocal term. As already noted in this chapter, the agency proper to a society or structured field of activity is different from the agency proper to its constituent actual occasions. It is an agency derivative from the collective activity of its constituent actual occasions in their individual processes of self-constitution and transmission of form or pattern to their successors. As such, it is an instance of formal or informational causality, not of final or efficient causality as in the case of the constituent actual occasions. That is, the society or structured field of activity provides the ongoing pattern or "metaplan" for the dynamic interrelation of successive sets of constituent actual occasions.

Clayton claims that personhood is the best example of what he means by spirit or self-conscious agency: it is "that level that emerges when an integrated state is established between a person and her body, her environment, other persons, and her overall mental state, including her interpretation of her social, cultural, historical, and religious context."[28] But, if so, is personhood rooted in the exercise of efficient causality or in the exercise of formal or informational causality? That is, is not personhood the ongoing result of a variety of agencies both internal and, as Clayton points out, external to the human being as an individual entity? Is it not, in other words, within the consciousness of each human being the abiding "metaplan" or higher-order structured field of activity which informs the way in which that person achieves self-identity in a complex, multidimensional world? Seen in this light, Clayton's rejection of the notion of morphogenetic fields in *Mind and Emergence* may have been premature.[29] For, not simply in terms of personal identity for human beings but everywhere in Nature, structured fields of activity seem to be the necessary principle of continuity for the preservation of form or pattern for all the interrelated energy events taking place within those fields. This continuity of pattern or structure is, of course, likewise subject to gradual change or development in the light of new events taking place in the field.

Before concluding this chapter, I will make reference to some other anomalies or "mysteries" within the natural sciences to which Davies refers in *The Cosmic Blueprint*. Perhaps a field-oriented approach to Whiteheadian societies might likewise be worth considering here. In a chapter entitled "The Quantum Factor," Davies notes that quantum states differ from physical states in classical mechanics because they do not yield relative certainties about the entities therein contained but only probabilities. The quantum state is described by a wave function whereby the relative probabilities either of the momentum or of the position of a subatomic particle can be mathematically determined.[30] Yet the wave function itself evolves deterministically: "Knowing the state of the system at one time (in terms of the wave function), the state at a later time can be computed, and used to predict the relative probabilities of the values that various observables will possess on measurement. In this weaker form of determinism, the various probabilities evolve deterministically, but the observable quantities themselves do not."[31]

As I see it, this "weirdness" of quantum physics by comparison to classical mechanics may possibly be explained philosophically by comparing the role of the wave function in quantum physics to the operation of the common element of form in a Whiteheadian society. The latter is, as noted above, a "complex eternal object" or a quasi-Platonic form. Yet it does not exist by itself in a world of forms as in Plato's philosophy but is only actual in its physical instantiations, the constituent actual occasions of the society. Thus, while in itself a well-defined information-bearing reality, the common element of form cannot be physically measured or otherwise observed except in terms of its contingent actualization in ongoing sets of actual occasions. It is accordingly determinate and indeterminate at the same time. It is determinate insofar as it here and now transmits the overall pattern of intelligibility for a given Whiteheadian society as a result of the dynamic interplay of an antecedent set of constituent actual occasions; and it is indeterminate insofar as it awaits further instantiation and specification in the next set of constituent actual occasions for the same society. Thus, to paraphrase Davies' remarks cited above, the various probabilities for the ongoing structure of the common element of form "evolve deterministically"; one can predict from moment to moment the likely structure of a given Whiteheadian society. But "the observable quantities"—namely, the events taking place in the field (the actual occasions)—are never the same from moment to moment. They represent the principle of novelty within the society.

Still another form of "weirdness" within quantum mechanics is the way in which the act of measurement is said to "collapse" the wave function:

Although the microworld is inherently nebulous, and only probabilities rather than certainties can be predicted from the wave function, nevertheless when an actual measurement of some dynamical variable is made a concrete result is obtained. The act of measurement thus transforms probability into certainty by *projecting out* or *selecting* a specific result from among a range of possibilities. Now this projection brings about an abrupt alteration in the form of the wave function, often referred to as its "collapse," which drastically affects its subsequent evolution.[32]

From within the field-oriented scheme for Whiteheadian societies, however, the clear distinction between observer and thing observed, the act of measurement and thing measured, seems to disappear. That is, whereas the act of measurement of a subatomic particle in quantum physics is conventionally assumed to be the work of a human being making use of some scientific apparatus, within a Whiteheadian worldview the act of measurement can be understood as the "prehension" of data pertinent to its own self-constitution by an actual occasion in its process of concrescence. This means, however, that there are not only human observers but nonhuman "observers" at every level of existence and activity within Nature. Moreover, every actual occasion is first "observer" in its own process of concrescence and then "something observed" by other actual occasions in the next moment of the cosmic process. Within a Whiteheadian context, therefore, the "collapse" of the wave function in virtue of a scientific measurement is not an anomaly but a necessary part of a much broader conversion of potentiality to actuality within the cosmic process that surpasses the capacity of human beings accurately to calculate and measure.

I am, of course, aware that I am dealing here with the notion of decoherence and other highly technical issues in quantum physics for which I have no special competence.[33] My only objective in this chapter has been to make clear that there are philosophical issues involved in contemporary natural science whose resolution might go far to clear up the "mystery" in the alleged functioning of morphogenetic fields and the "weirdness" of quantum mechanics. What seems to be needed, in other words, is a new process-oriented worldview with verifiable applicability both in the sciences and in the humanities. My own wager for many years now has been that this new worldview will inevitably reflect many of the metaphysical insights of Alfred North Whitehead. But the burden of this chapter and much of this book has been to make clear that Whitehead's metaphysical scheme itself needs some revision if it is to be equal to that task. Whitehead's basic insight that the final real things of which this world is made up are not inert bits of matter but momentary self-constituting subjects of experience is truly revolutionary in its scope and implications. But his understanding of "society" as a higher-order reality emergent out of the interplay of these same actual occasions is curiously very traditional, based on a seemingly Platonic understanding of the relationship between the One and the Many.

That is, Plato conceived the One as the principle of order and intelligibility for the Many; the transcendent One thereby exercises top-down causality on the otherwise disordered empirical Many. Whitehead himself and most Whiteheadians, as I see it, have implicitly adopted this Platonic paradigm for the relationship between the One and the Many in their explanation of societies as more than simple aggregates of actual occasions. They stipulate, in other words, a "regnant" subsociety of actual occasions to give further order and unity to a structured society otherwise made up of loosely organized subsocieties of actual occasions. Or, as in the case of Lewis Ford and possibly David Griffin,[34] they postulate the existence of more comprehensive "higher-order" actual occasions which are inclusive of lower-order actual occasions. Yet Ford and Griffin thereby likewise endorse a Platonic understanding of the relationship between the One and the Many, namely, the ontological priority of the single long-term actual occasion over its many short-term subordinates.

In my own approach to Whiteheadian societies, however, another paradigm for the relationship between the One and the Many is at work. Here the One is described as emergent out of the dynamic interplay of the Many with one another. As a result, the One is not transcendent of the Many as in the Platonic paradigm, but emergent out of the Many in their ongoing dynamic interrelation. Yet at the same time in the further existence of the society the One exercises formal or informational causality upon the Many as their immanent principle of order and intelligibility. In this way one can philosophically account for the phenomena of emergence or genuine novelty within the world of Nature. That is, there is both top-down and bottom-up causality at work in natural processes, but primacy is always given to bottom-up causality so as to account for the emergence of genuine novelty. Doubtless, acceptance of this new philosophical insight into the age-old problem of the relationship between the One and the Many does not solve all the questions involved in the understanding of "emergence" at various levels of existence and activity within Nature, if only because there are so many different ways that it takes place.[35] Hence, dealing with these more empirical questions is best left to scientists at work in their respective fields.[36]

TIME AND ETERNITY IN RELIGION AND SCIENCE

In an article entitled "God in and beyond Space and Time," the British physicist-turned-theologian Russell Stannard discussed the differences between objective time as measured in theoretical physics and subjective time or time as experienced by human beings in normal consciousness. Since objective time or four-dimensional space-time for the physicist does not change but exists all at once (past, present, and future plotted on a graph together with the spatial coordinates), Stannard then argued that this is presumably how God views time from eternity which is beyond time. We human beings, on the contrary, are limited to experiencing the moments of time successively and thus cannot know the future as already existing in the same way that God does. Stannard conceded that not all scientists and philosophers agree with the notion of space-time as a "block universe," but he argued that it is consistent with the mathematics of relativity theory.[1]

In this chapter I argue that Stannard is basically correct in his theological assumptions about God's understanding of time but that his explanation would be more persuasive within the context of the neo-Whiteheadian metaphysics that I have developed in this book. The key point in that metaphysics is that Whiteheadian "societies" are to be understood as structured fields of activity for their constituent actual occasions. Given such a field-oriented understanding of Whiteheadian societies, one can stipulate with Stannard that God is both in time and beyond time and that God knows past, present, and future simultaneously somewhat akin to the "block universe" as employed in theoretical physics.

By way of explanation, I first cite here a key passage out of Stannard's essay and then indicate how it can be reinterpreted in neo-Whiteheadian terms:

We are so accustomed to thinking in terms of us all sharing the one space and the one time, that it requires a severe mental wrench to conceive of something radically different: namely, that we each inhabit our own space and our own time, and these will differ from each other if we are in relative motion. The reason most people go through life unaware of this is that for the speeds we normally encounter in everyday life, the differences between our various estimates of distance and time are so small as to make no practical difference. Nevertheless, the effects are there all the time.[2]

Where I would differ from Stannard is in proposing that we not only exist within our own space and time but unconsciously create our own space and time in successive moments of existence. That is, if an individual's consciousness is understood as an ongoing intentional field of activity for successive moments of experience (actual occasions), then this field should have its own space-time structure. The actual occasion of the moment, in other words, is at the center of its own spatial world and finds itself integrating past events and future possibilities in its self-constituting "decision" here and now. That structure will, of course, inevitably change as new moments of experience add their own pattern of spatial and temporal self-awareness to the overall structure of the field. But the intentional field remains stable enough so that the individual experiences an enduring sense of self-identity as he or she moves about and experiences the flow of events in and around himself or herself. In this way the ongoing structure of the field is the concrete basis for our memory of the past and our anticipation of the future. Yet in the end it is only our own world, not the world, which we thus inhabit.

Why isn't this apparent to us? Why do we human beings normally think of ourselves as existing in space and time rather than as creating our own space and time? Stannard claims that we do not notice the difference between our subjective estimates of time and space because they are minimally different from one another, given our modest differences in movement relative to one another. Without denying this clear implication of relativity theory, I would further argue that it is because our individual worlds or fields of activity sufficiently overlap so that we end up co-creating a common field of activity with approximately the same space-time parameters for all of us. This commonly structured field of activity is, to be sure, dependent upon the dynamic interrelation of all the actual occasions at work both within us and in other individuals (other societies of actual occasions) at any given moment. Yet such intense activity is always below the level of conscious experience. Instead our commonsense experience leads us to believe that space and time are objective realities existing independently of us rather than in total dependence on us and our contemporaries.

Here, of course, I am making a metaphysical claim about the nature of space-time as a strictly intersubjective reality, namely, something co-created by subjects of experience in dynamic interrelation. Carefully observing standard procedure in theoretical physics,[3] Stannard limits himself to a statement about how to measure space and time, given sufficiently large differences in motion between observer and thing observed. He makes no explicit claim about the reality of space and time as such. But he does seem to make an implicit metaphysical claim with his further statement that in relativity theory we are dealing with interrelated events in space-time rather than with the things of common sense experience.[4] For, he is thereby implicitly shifting from a metaphysics of being in which things first exist in their own right and then interact with one another to a metaphysics of becoming in which events come and go and only the patterns of their dynamic interrelation remain.

This is much akin to Whitehead's claim that there are no separately existing *things* that need time to move spatially from one place to another; there are only dynamically related *events* of approximately the same duration rapidly succeeding one another and sometimes involving change of place.[5] If then the pattern of succession of actual occasions within ourselves and our neighbors is more or less the same, our commonsense experience tells us that we are living in a world of space and time independent of ourselves. Yet it is also part of our commonsense experience that we often feel the passage of time as faster or slower than originally expected, and that we necessarily occupy different places with respect to one another and thus inevitably have a somewhat different view of what is happening all around us than our contemporaries. Hence, upon further reflection it becomes clear that we do indeed live within our own subjective space-time worlds even as we share and co-constitute a conjoint field of activity that we simply call the world.

Turning now to consideration of the God-world relationship and of the way in which God presumably experiences events taking place within the space-time continuum, I propose in line with chapter 8 that God is not unipersonal but tripersonal, three eternally coexisting divine subjects of experience. Each of these divine persons is in Whiteheadian terms a personally ordered society of actual occasions presiding over a completely unlimited field of activity. Yet these three fields of activity necessarily merge to constitute a single all-inclusive shared field of activity so as to guarantee the reality of the three divine persons as one God rather than simply three gods in relatively close association. The structure of that common divine field of activity is, moreover, determined by the ongoing relations of the three divine persons to one another as set forth in classical Trinitarian theology. The Father is the source of the divine life; the Son is the self-expression or Word of the Father; the Spirit is the Mediator between the Father and the Son in their ongoing relations to one another.[6]

Is there likewise a space-time structure for the divine persons within this divine field of activity? I would argue yes, given my earlier presupposition that Whiteheadian actual occasions or self-constituting subjects of experience necessarily co-constitute a common space-time structure for one another through their ongoing dynamic interrelation. Yet within this divinely constituted space-time structure God is, as Alan Padgett maintains, "relatively timeless."[7] That is, with respect to our human standards of measurement, namely, our finite frame of reference based on observation of the laws of Nature, we cannot judge how long a single moment for the divine persons lasts and how it would compare with a single moment in the lives of each of us. The divine duration or sense of time is an intersubjective experience reserved to the divine persons alone.

Likewise, I stipulate that the world of creation originally came into being and still continues to exist within this divine field of activity.[8] Since the divine field of activity is infinite or strictly unlimited, creation cannot exist apart from God but only in God. Yet since creation as a whole is to be understood as a complex set of overlapping and hierarchically ordered fields of activity for created actual occasions, it can exist within the divine field of activity and yet retain its own ontological identity apart from the three divine persons. As already noted at different points in this book, fields, unlike Aristotelian substances, can interpenetrate and be layered within one another without loss of ontological identity. Lower-level fields at the atomic and molecular levels of existence and activity, for example, evidently provide the infrastructure for the operation of higher-level fields of activity at the organic and environmental/communitarian levels of existence and activity within Nature. The higher-level fields of activity in turn set necessary parameters for the further existence and activity of the lower-level fields of activity upon incorporation into a higher-level field of activity.

The divine persons existing within the all-encompassing divine field of activity thus experience what is going on within the world of creation and are able to respond to events taking place within creation even more accurately and completely than the mind or soul within a human being is able to monitor what is happening in one's own body and respond to it with one's own decisions. What is key here, of course, is that the space/time structure proper to the world as a whole and its various subdivisions is thus in God rather than that God is somehow constrained by the space-time parameters of this world in dealing with creation.

Hence, while I agree with Padgett that God is both the ground of time and the Lord of time so that in effect we exist in God's time rather than that God exists in our time,[9] I interpret the experience of time or duration both within God and in the world of creation somewhat differently than he does. I agree that God and creatures experience past, present, and future; but, contrary to Padgett, I propose that within every such moment of experience both for the divine persons and also for all creaturely actual occasions there is what may be called a "B-series" understanding of past, present, and future.[10] That is, past, present, and future simultaneously coexist as ordered to one another sequentially in terms of "before" and "after" rather than exist separately from one another as "earlier" and "later." Unlike past, present, and future in an "A-series" in which only the present actually exists at any given moment, past, present, and future in the B-series are all present to and impact upon one another in each successive moment of eternity for the divine persons and in each successive moment of time for all creatures.

I am indirectly appealing here to Robert Neville's understanding of eternity as the "togetherness" of past, present, and future in his book *Eternity and Time's Flow*.[11] That is, the three dimensions of time are always co-involved in the making of a decision at the present moment. What I decide here and how is limited by past decisions along the same line made by myself and others and is normally made with an eye to the future, once again both for myself and others. Hence, "Not only is something new always becoming— the present is steadily moving on to new dates—but the past is always growing and the structure of future possibilities is constantly shifting in responses to the decisions made in each moment of present actuality."[12] Yet eternity, in contrast to time's flow, is not still another temporal dimension but "rather the condition for and inclusive of all the changes involved in temporal togetherness."[13] Eternity holds together in a dynamic unity the entire past, the present moment, and the anticipated future for a finite subject of experience at a given moment, and this experience of togetherness is a privileged insight into the reality of eternity as opposed to time's flow.

Whitehead describes the process of concrescence for actual occasions in similar fashion. That is, an actual occasion becomes itself by making a self-constituting "decision" in the present moment. This decision, however, is heavily conditioned by the past, both the past of the society to which it immediately belongs and the past of the broader world out of which it is emerging. Likewise, it makes this decision in anticipation of the future, once again the future of both the society to which it immediately belongs and of the bigger world to which it is making a contribution.[14] For Whitehead, then, each of the three time dimensions is actively interrelated with the other two in the concrescence of an actual occasion, its movement from potentiality to actuality at any given moment. Creaturely actual occasions, of course, can only appropriate part of their past and part of their future into the present moment. God, on the contrary, incorporates the entire past of the cosmic process into what Whitehead calls the divine consequent nature[15] but not the future of the cosmic process except as a set of possibilities. As Whitehead sees it, the future of the cosmic process has not happened yet even for God and thus cannot be "prehended," incorporated into the divine mind as an existing actuality.[16]

Here is where I consciously differ from Whitehead in terms of my own understanding of the God-world relationship. On the assumption that eternity, the duration proper to the divine persons, is not coterminous with but rather inclusive of the space-time continuum, the duration proper to this world, it is entirely possible that our entire cosmic epoch is already present to the divine persons as an existing actuality, and not simply as a combination of past actuality and future potentiality. In this way, the divine persons would overview the historical sequence of events within creation in such a way as to see each event as it happens in the context of its significance or value for the created process as a completed whole within the broader parameters of the divine communitarian life. Equivalently, they would "see" what is happening in creation in terms of a B-series rather than an A-series. That is, they would see events in the created order as before and after other events but not as earlier and later—that is, as past, present, and future in the strict sense.[17]

Here I am in some measure borrowing from the analysis of time and eternity offered by Wolfhart Pannenberg in his *Systematic Theology*, volumes 1 and 3.[18] Pannenberg claims that the divine persons need full knowledge of the past, present, and future of the cosmic process; for if they were limited simply to conjecture about the future, their ordering activity for the present moment would be severely hampered.[19] Where I possibly differ from Pannenberg is in the claim that, while the divine persons thus know every event as it happens in this cosmic epoch, they do not directly will it or otherwise make it happen one way rather than another.[20] Rather, more in line with the thinking of Whitehead on this point, I propose that the principal activity of the divine persons with respect to their creatures is in terms of final rather than efficient causality. That is, they continually order into a more comprehensive whole what creatures decide in virtue of the creatures' own finite self-constituting "decisions" from moment to moment. Hence, instead of unilaterally causing what the creature will decide from moment to moment, they simply empower the creature to make its own decision by imparting to it a share in their own creativity, their own divine decision-making power.[21]

Thus, there is no doctrine of divine predestination in this approach to the God-world relationship. The divine persons, to be sure, communicate at every moment what Whitehead calls divine "initial aims" to their creatures to inspire a good rather than a bad decision.[22] But the actual decision is always the responsibility of the creature. The chief responsibility of the divine persons at every moment of the divine life is to keep ordering and reordering into an ever-expanding intelligible whole the decisions of their creatures within the temporal order. This is certainly akin to what White-head had in mind with his concept of the divine consequent nature. But, whereas Whitehead envisions God as totally involved with the cosmic process from moment to moment and thus as not knowing future events as factual until they actually occur, I propose, as noted above, that the divine persons are present to each moment of the cosmic process as it happens even though they are likewise present to the cosmic process as a completed actuality. In this way, they can offer "initial aims" to their creatures without violating the spontaneity or, in the case of human beings the freedom, of the created subject of experience to make its own self-constituting "decision." Yet, being likewise present to the cosmic process as a completed whole, the divine persons can at every moment give each such decision its place in that completed whole.

In brief, then, in this matter of God's knowledge of the future it should be possible, as Stannard suggests, to use a conceptual model based on contemporary understanding of relativity theory better to illuminate and further explain problematic issues in theology, namely, time and eternity, human freedom, and divine providence. But this is only possible if one also makes a move from classical metaphysics with its emphasis on the timeless, strictly unchanging character of God in dealing with an ever-changing world of creation to a process-oriented metaphysics in which God is in some measure affected and changed by what happens in the material world. I say "in some measure" deliberately because, as I made clear above, Whitehead's model for the God-world relationship in which God and the world are totally interdependent seems to be a move too far in the opposite direction. As a result, cherished beliefs about the transcendence of God to the world of creation within the three great monotheistic religions (Judaism, Christianity, and Islam) are thrown into jeopardy. For many educated people, this is too high a price to pay for theoretical consistency within one's worldview. As a result they find themselves in a quandary, fretting about the lack of an adequate metaphysical foundation to deal with complex issues arising out of the interface of religion and contemporary science and yet thus far unable to come up with a suitable alternative to classical metaphysics.

But where does one begin in developing an alternative to classical metaphysics? My argument throughout this book has been that only a new process-oriented understanding of the relationship between the One and the Many will be key to such an enterprise. For example, the relationship between time and eternity discussed in the current chapter reduces, in my judgment, to one's antecedent philosophical conviction about the relationship between the One and the Many. If one believes that the One is fully transcendent of the Many as their unchanging principle of order and intelligibility, then one will be inclined to think that eternity is a timeless reality which gives order and direction to the otherwise purely contingent events taking place in the temporal order. This is the position of classical metaphysics.[23] If one thinks that the One is completely immanent within the Many, then eternity becomes synonymous with unending time or time without beginning or end. This is the position of many process-oriented metaphysical schemes (including that of Whitehead as already noted). But, if one thinks that the One is both transcendent of and yet immanent within the Many, then one tends to think of eternity as indeed involving duration or a sequence of events but without a strict one-to-one correlation with events taking place within the temporal order. The process of becoming proper to the One thus includes within itself the process of becoming which governs the relations of the Many to one another. But it does so from a position of transcendence, at a higher level of existence and activity.

As we saw in chapter 9 with the discussion of the phenomenon of "emergence" within the natural order, the higher-order level of activity (the One) is both immanent within and at the same time transcendent of the lower-level fields of activity (the Many) within its boundaries. Likewise, if, as claimed in this chapter, eternity is the "togetherness" of past, present, and future, then eternity is both immanent within the three time dimensions of the created order and yet likewise transcendent of them. It is their higher-order unity guaranteeing their necessary functional interdependence. But it is not dependent on these time dimensions for its own reality and intelligibility as a different kind of duration. That is, it is not simply the summation of past, present, and future for the cosmic process but a different, transcendent reality that gives these temporal dimensions their interrelated meaning and value. As Pannenberg claims in his *Systematic Theology*,[24] it is eternity that gives meaning and value to time rather than vice versa. Without an antecedent sense of the whole, an anticipation of what should logically come next, time with its ongoing sequence of purely contingent events would make no sense at all.

12

CONCLUSIONS

As already mentioned in the Introduction to this book, one of the persistent themes in the history of Western philosophy has been the problem of the One and the Many. Naturally, it takes somewhat different forms in different eras and at the hands of different thinkers. But the results of my survey of the history of Western philosophy should have made clear that there are two basic paradigms for understanding how the One and the Many can and should be related to one another. The first paradigm might be called the classical understanding of the relationship between the One and the Many since it originated with the philosophy of Plato and Aristotle in antiquity and was then adopted with key modifications by Christian philosophers and theologians in the Middle Ages and well into the modern period. It is idealistic rather than empirical in its approach to reality since it presupposes the ontological priority of universal concepts to particular facts. The One, accordingly, is a universal form or principle of intelligibility that gives meaning and value to the otherwise disorganized data of sense experience. Since the data of sense experience are in constant flux, the forms are necessarily perceived as permanent and unchanging. They represent what is true under all circumstances as opposed to what just happens to be the case here and now.

The second paradigm is of more recent origin. As we have seen above, in the modern period the focus of attention first among natural scientists and then among more empirically oriented philosophers shifted to careful analysis of empirical data and away from heavy reliance on a priori concepts. Unconsciously the classical priority of the One over the Many was thereby being called into question. Not the rationally conceived One but the empirical Many became the final court of appeal in questions of truth and certitude. Yet the presumed hegemony of the empirical Many over the rationally conceived One cannot long endure; the human mind becomes confused with the presence of so much undifferentiated diversity. Hence, it is not surprising that in recent decades of the past century systems-oriented thinking has once again come to the fore: not the closed conceptual systems of the German Idealists, but the open-ended systems of natural scientists trying to cope with the experience of novelty and change within an evolutionary cosmic process.

What seems to have emerged from this new form of systems-oriented thinking is an alternate paradigm for the One and the Many, whereby the One is not understood as a higher-order entity as in the classical paradigm, but as a synthesizing activity that links the empirical Many with one another in progressively more complex and far-reaching syntheses. Yet one must still ask where this synthesizing activity within the cosmic process comes from. What is its source? Here I introduced my own hypothesis, namely, that this synthesizing activity, what Alfred North Whitehead calls the principle of creativity, is the nature of the triune God, that which enables the three divine persons of the Christian doctrine of the Trinity to co-exist as one God within an all-comprehensive divine field of activity; furthermore, that in virtue of a free choice on their part the divine persons have communicated this principle of creativity to all their creatures so as by degrees with the cooperation of their creatures to build up the world of physical reality within the "space" proper to their own divine field of activity. This is a hypothesis grounded not only in Trinitarian theology but in a careful rethinking of what Whitehead had in mind with his key concept of "society" as a grouping of contemporary actual occasions linked together by a common element of form.

To make clear the differences between the two paradigms for the One and the Many and, as far as possible, to argue for the preferability of the second paradigm over the first for opening up lines of communication between scientists and theologians in the contemporary religion and science dialogue, I set forth in the preceding chapters of this book an overview of the way in which key figures in the history of Western philosophy addressed the problem of the One and the Many for their own time: for example, in ancient and medieval times how philosophers and theologians routinely accepted the priority of universal concepts over sense experience of concrete individuals; at the beginning of the modern era, how other thinkers came to understand and appreciate the workings of the human mind in unifying the data of sense experience; and finally at the present time, how scientists and theologians are trying to explain novelty and spontaneity within a causally determined evolutionary process.

But one can readily lose the forest for the trees in such a rapid overview of major thinkers with their different perspectives on reality. Hence, in this final chapter, I want as briefly as possible to state the conclusions that I drew from this historical survey first for recognizing the differences between the two paradigms for the One and the Many and then for deciding between them in any given situation. As I mentioned earlier, one cannot evade making at least an implicit decision on this matter. Whether one is doing scientific research, reflecting philosophically or theologically on the God-world relationship, or simply coping with reality in the practical affairs of life, one is always working with a tacit understanding of the relationship between the One and the Many.

To begin, in chapter 1 I focused primarily on the work of medieval theologians in thinking through the intellectual heritage of Plato and Aristotle on the issue of universals. As noted therein, some, like John Scotus Erigena, were ultra-realists, claiming extramental existence for the universal concept. Others, like Abelard and Gilbert Poiree, maintained that a universal concept existed one way in the human mind and another way in the physical world, but this approach to the problem ran the danger of conceptualism or even pure nominalism. With his typical sense of balance, Aquinas found the middle ground with his threefold distinction between universals *ante rem*, *in re*, and *post rem*. But John Duns Scotus moved beyond Aquinas in recognizing that universals still fall short in describing concrete individual existents. His solution to the problem—namely, yet another universal form called *haecceitas* or "thisness"—seems quaint in retrospect. But Scotus did see the limitations of the Platonic-Aristotelian worldview much better than Aquinas and thereby prepared the way for Ockham and a new, more empirical approach to reality in the early modern period.

After taking note of how Francis Bacon, Galileo Galilei, and Isaac Newton implicitly changed the rules for research and reflection in the philosophy of nature (as natural science was known at that time), I indicated in chapter 2 the particular impact that Descartes on the continent and Locke in England had on the early modern approach to physical reality. Descartes was more rationalist in his thinking, laying heavy stress on deduction from innate ideas or intuitively known first principles. Locke was more empirically minded with his "historical, plain" method of investigation into the workings of the human mind. But in the end they were both conceptualists in that they saw themselves as dealing with ideas as imperfect representations of extra-mental realities rather than universal forms that really exist, albeit in different ways, both in the mind and in physical reality. In this sense, Descartes and Locke both gave philosophical backing to the notion of a split or unavoidable dualism between mind and matter that lingers in the popular imagination even to this day.

Likewise, in terms of the problem of the One and the Many, both philosophers had an enduring impact on their successors. While both continued to believe in God as the transcendent Creator of this world, each in his own way maintained that the starting point for philosophical reflection, equivalently the unchanging

One as the ordering principle for the ever-changing Many within one's philosophical system, should be not God, but the human being in one's subjective consciousness. In this way, they addressed the problem of the individual concrete existent much better than their predecessors in the Middle Ages, who were preoccupied with grand schemes for the God-world relationship. But both of them remained in the classical tradition by focusing their attention on the generalized relations of the self to the outside world rather than on the self's personal feelings where differences in perspective inevitably play a much greater role.

Given the dualism between mind and matter set up by Descartes and Locke in their respective philosophical schemes, it was virtually inevitable that attempts to overcome this dualism would play a prominent role in the thinking of their successors. On the continent, Spinoza decided that mind and matter are interrelated attributes of the one divine being or world-substance and that all the finite things of this world as contingent modes of the divine substance are inevitably a mixture of mind and matter in different proportions. Even more aggressively, Leibniz claimed that matter is simply the humanly perceptible byproduct of monads or strictly immaterial mini-subjects of experience in dynamic interrelation. For both Spinoza and Leibniz, therefore, matter is best understood as the physical counterpart or necessary self-expression of mind or spirit.

In England Berkeley went even further with his contention that in the end only minds exist with God as Infinite Mind supplying the ideas of a material world to human beings in their practical dealings with one another. There are, as a result, objective laws of Nature but they correspond to the unchanging relations between ideas in human minds rather than between an extra-mental physical reality and its representation within the human mind. As an empirically oriented thinker more in line with the "historical, plain" method of Locke, Hume dismissed Berkeley's idealistic approach to material reality and focused once again on the data of sense experience as his starting point for philosophical reflection. But in the end he too may have been out of touch with reality with his insistence that there is no logical proof of the reality of objective laws of Nature or even of the existence of one's own mind to understand and interpret those laws for making decisions in the practical order. Yet both Berkeley and Hume indirectly contributed major new insights to what it means to be a subject of experience in a material world. Berkeley made clear how matter in some form or other is the necessary medium of communication between minds. Hume challenged the classical notion of the self as an unchanging spiritual reality. If the world around it is never the same from moment to moment, how can there be a self impervious to change?

Hence, in chapter 4 I analyzed Kant's attempt to counter the skepticism of Hume about the possibility of human knowledge either of the self or of the world around it. In what he called a second "Copernican Revolution," he stipulated that the self is real enough but that it is manifest to consciousness only as a transcendental activity, never as a direct object of thought. Likewise, he borrowed from Hume the novel idea that human imagination is ultimately responsible for our habitually linking distinct sense impressions in terms of cause and effect. In Kant's hands, this became the basis for his doctrine of the "schematism" of the a priori concepts of understanding to the data of sense experience. With the image of a dog in mind, I can implicitly organize the data of sense experience and confidently say to myself, "This is a dog." Thus Kant made clear the constructive role of the human mind in coming to understand the laws of Nature and thereby provided theoretical justification for what the natural scientists of his day were already doing, namely, "constraining nature to give answers to questions of reason's own determining."

But this singular achievement was also his undoing in that he could not adequately explain the experience of permanence in time (substance), cause and effect, and simultaneity or reciprocity simply in terms of the synthesizing activity of the human mind. Not simply a succession of sense perceptions, but only a necessary connection between an earlier and a later perception is needed for the category of causality to apply to the data of experience. But where does this necessary connection come from, from the synthesizing activity of the mind or from the "phenomenal object," for example, a ship moving downstream in a river? Within the limits of his conceptual scheme Kant could not give a fully satisfactory answer to that question. He thus could not logically bridge the gap between phenomena and noumena, the world of mentally organized sense experience and Nature as an independent reality with its own patterns of organization and activity.

Yet Kant still deserves praise for calling attention to the primacy of subjectivity over objectivity in human cognition. It is not what the human subject of experience receives from the outer world that is all-important but what it does with the data after it has been received into consciousness. Furthermore, he thereby shed new light on what it means to be a concrete individual existent. Only subjects of experience are true individuals in this world. For subjects of experience alone have the power to create themselves anew moment by moment out of the fusion of sense data and a priori categories. Kant himself, of course, was still a thinker in the classical tradition since he presumed that his schematism of the pure categories of understanding would function basically the same way in the mind of every human being. But he nevertheless pointed the way to a new understanding of the problem of the One and the Many. The One is primarily a subject of experience; the Many are the objective data which it needs for its ongoing self-constitution. The German Idealists effectively grasped this insight and proceeded to explore it systematically.

In chapter 5, accordingly, I reviewed the metaphysical systems of the three major German Idealists, Fichte, Schelling, and Hegel. The link between the three was the way in which each of them dealt with the issue of the empirical Other within their schemes. For Fichte, the non-ego was the point of resistance (*Anstoss*) initially to the activity of the finite ego but ultimately to the striving of the Absolute Ego for self-realization through the establishment of a universal moral order. For Hegel, somewhat akin to Fichte, the empirical Other existed only as an antithetical moment in the dialectical unfolding of Absolute Spirit. That is, at every stage of the dialectic an antithesis is needed as counterbalance to the original thesis so that a synthesis, the negation of the negation presented by the antithesis, might be generated and the dialectical process can begin all over again. So both for Fichte and Hegel, the empirical Other plays only an instrumental role in the development of their theoretical scheme.

Schelling's understanding of the empirical Other is more complex since his own thought went through different stages of development. In his early years he stipulated that Spirit and its empirical Other, Nature, were different dimensions of one and the same ontological reality, the Absolute Identity of subjectivity and objectivity. In his middle period, Schelling was strongly influenced by the writings of the German mystic Jacob Böhme and proposed that the physical world originated from a divine ground of being which is nonrational, a principle of vitality rather than a supreme mind. Hence, for both God and all God's creatures there is an ongoing internal tension between a nonrational and a rational principle within their being. Within God the rational principle always prevails, but within creatures the nonrational principle can get the upper hand and bring evil/sin into the world. So for "middle" Schelling the nonrational principle is the equivalent of the empirical Other, that which must be overcome by the rational principle if order in the world is to prevail. Finally, the "late" Schelling in his positive philosophy correctly identified the empirical Other as that which is not part of the conceptual system but for the same reason is its necessary starting point. Schelling, in other words, belatedly recognized that no speculative system can be self-validating without running the risk of a vicious circle, that is, ultimately presupposing what the system is designed to prove.

Chapters 6 and 7 carry forward Schelling's insight into the inherent limitations of speculative philosophy and theology. Comprehensive overviews of the God-world relationship almost always reduce the concrete individual existent to a bit player in a cosmic drama. Hence, Kierkegaard in the nineteenth century and Levinas, Buber, and Heidegger in the twentieth century each in his own way called into question the value of traditional metaphysics as practical guide for life in this world. Authentic human life is only lived in response to a personal calling, an intersubjective relation between the Self and the Other, whether the Other be understood as God, the neighbor, both God and the neighbor, or finally (in Heidegger's philosophy) Being itself as an elusive cosmic "prescencing."

Of the four thinkers, Kierkegaard was unquestionably the most autobiographical in his philosophical reflections. The move from the aesthetic to the ethical and finally to the religious stage of self-realization was almost certainly grounded in his own ill-fated relationship with Regine Olsen and perhaps other young women of his day. But, above all in the *Concluding Unscientific Postscript* where he spoke more generally about embracing Christianity in a passionate "leap of faith" rather than as a result of a careful investigation of historical data, Kierkegaard was able to convert his personal experience into an effective philosophical argument for the truth of Christianity against convinced rationalists like Gotthold Lessing. In any case, he is a key figure in what emerged later in the twentieth century as a deep suspicion of metaphysics as a "totalizing" approach to reality that disguises its covert desire for intellectual dominance and control in an appeal to objectivity. In different ways, Levinas, Buber, and Heidegger all share this conviction in their writings.

Levinas, for example, contrasted the notions of totality and infinity in one's approach to reality. Those who think in terms of totality implicitly absorb both the self and the other into an impersonal conceptual scheme that deprives both of them of their integrity as mutually independent subjects of experience. One finds infinity, on the contrary, in the "face" of the other as the natural symbol of inwardness and subjectivity, something that rational reflection by itself can never comprehend. Moreover, ethics can never be grounded in purely rational reflection since the latter is always subtly biased in favor of the interests of the self. One must recognize the ontological priority of the other to the self, my responsibility to the other even at cost to my own personal freedom. Buber is even more emphatic on this point with his celebrated distinction between the thought-worlds of I-Thou and I-It. There is no I as such for Buber, but only the I of the I-Thou relation in which one experiences an interdependence with the other, or the I of the I-It relation in which one consciously or unconsciously subordinates the other to one's own self-interest and -desires. In the first case, the I lives in a genuinely subject-subject or intersubjective world; in the second case, one lives in a subject-object world in which the needs/desires of the self are paramount and consideration for the needs/desires of the other recedes in importance.

As Walter Kaufmann points out, Buber is clearly oversimplifying highly complex human relations in ordinary life. But in my judgment, even more importantly, Buber did not reflect deeply enough on what he meant by the "Between," the moment of genuine encounter between an I and a Thou. If the Thou always becomes an It when the moment of encounter is ended, then pessimism about long-term human relations is virtually inevitable. Likewise, in claiming that the Spirit which he sees at work in human life is the personalized embodiment of the Between, Buber implicitly falls back into the older Platonic understanding of the One and the Many, namely, the subordination of the empirical Many to the ontological primacy of the immaterial One. Instead, as I make clear in chapter 6, Buber would have been greatly assisted in his spirited defense of intersubjectivity or I-Thou relations if he had claimed that the Spirit as the Between for an I and a Thou is not an entity but a unifying activity that sustains the ongoing exchange between the I and the Thou. Even within Christian Trinitarian theology (as I indicate in chapter 8), God as Spirit is in the first place a transcendent activity that links the three divine persons (including the Holy Spirit) to one another.

In chapter 7 where I took up the philosophy of Martin Heidegger, I consciously embarked upon what might be called a *Gedanken-Experiment* (thought experiment). That is, simply as an exercise in imaginative thinking, I juxtaposed Heidegger's notion of Be-ing as event (*Ereignis*) which is "appropriated" by there-being (*Da-sein*) in its existence here and now with what Whitehead calls "creativity," that which exists, passes from potentiality to actuality, only in its concrete instantiations, namely, actual occasions or momentary self-constituting subjects of experience. To establish some historical connection between the two philosophers on this point might well be impossible. But to compare their seemingly independent insights into this process-oriented reality of the self and the world around it could be very useful, above all, for illuminating the elusive relationship between the One and the Many. As I see it, both of them identified the One in the first place not with an unchanging being or a transcendent Creator-God but with a cosmic activity that does not so much control the finite entities constituting the Many but rather empowers them to become more authentically themselves by means of an internalized subjective "decision." Heidegger evidently thought that he was thereby proclaiming the end of metaphysics, but in point of fact along with Whitehead he may have been simply pointing in the direction of a new metaphysics which, on the one hand, gives much more emphasis to the subjectivity of the concrete individual and, on the other hand, grounds human understanding of the overall cosmic process in generic principles of becoming rather than in unchanging structures of being.

In chapter 8 I chose to focus on the thought of a theologian rather than still another philosopher, namely, Colin Gunton. Like myself, Gunton saw the importance of rethinking the traditional understanding of the One and the Many in order to deal effectively with the strong sense of diversity among peoples and cultures at the present time. Likewise, he too found inspiration for that task in the way that the early Greek Fathers of the church understood the Christian doctrine of the Trinity. But, whereas Gunton more or less presumed antecedent belief in the doctrine of the Trinity in setting forth his Trinitarian "transcendentals," namely, *perichoresis*, particularity or substantiality, and relationality (or sociality at the human level of activity), I preferred to see this communitarian approach to the doctrine of the Trinity as an illustration of a basically philosophical issue, how the Many become One without losing their individuality or particularity as the Many. For this purpose, I revised the Whiteheadian doctrine of "society" because it readily lent itself to the understanding of socially organized realities everywhere in the world of Nature.

I assumed, in other words, that Whiteheadian "societies" are ongoing structured fields of activity for successive sets of constituent actual occasions. They are not simply aggregates of actual occasions which are organized sometimes democratically with no internal principle of unity and order among themselves, and sometimes monarchically with a "regnant nexus" of actual occasions to give order and unity to various inanimate actual occasions within the "society." On the contrary, whether it is organized democratically or monarchically, a "society," as I see it, should possess an internal coherence or ontological unity which is emergent out of the dynamic interplay of its constituent actual occasions from moment to moment. With this revised understanding of Whiteheadian "societies," one has a plausible explanation for both top-down and bottom-up causality within the different levels of existence and activity in Nature. The constituent actual occasions exercise bottom-up causality in determining here and now their "common element of form" or emergent pattern of interrelation, and the society thus structured exercises top-down causality in perpetuating that pattern for future sets of constituent actual occasions.

The same combination of bottom-up efficient causality and top-down formal causality, moreover, provides a plausible explanation of the Christian doctrine of the Trinity. That is, the three divine persons by their dynamic interrelation co-generate a structured field of activity for their joint existence and operation. Because they equally share in one and the same field of activity, they are one God. The field with its pregiven structure acts as their ontological principle of unity. Yet they each contribute to the structure of that field in a unique way, from a privileged perspective. So there is real diversity among the divine persons or bottom-up causality as well as top-down causality in virtue of the ongoing structure of their commonly shared field of activity. In the end, however, this is only a corollary of a basically philosophical argument derived from my reinterpretation of Whitehead's notion of "society."

In chapter 9 I continued this same line of thought in reviewing the growth of systems theory in the mid-twentieth century. With Ervin Laszlo I agreed that systems (like "societies" in my reinterpretation of Whitehead) are specifically social realities that exist in their own right even though they are necessarily dependent upon the dynamic interplay of their constituent parts or members. With Whitehead, however, I argued that the ultimate parts or members of these systems must be actual occasions or momentary self-constituting subjects of experience, not subsystems as with Laszlo. Finally, agreeing with Laszlo once again, I claimed that both systems and Whiteheadian societies must exercise agency if they are to function as unified realities within Nature. Yet the agency which they exercise should be described as a collective agency, derivative from all the interrelated individual agencies of their constituent parts or members (actual occasions). Provided that the system/society is seen as a structured field of activity for those constituent parts or members, then, as noted above, bottom-up efficient causality and top-down formal causality are both simultaneously operative to produce the unified agency of the system/society as a whole.

Then I reviewed the work of another systems thinker, Stuart Kauffman, who proposes that life is spontaneously emergent out of the dynamic interplay of molecular components under certain conditions. I speculated that such a complex chemical system bears a distinct resemblance to Whitehead's description of a society as a set of actual occasions governed by a "common element of form." In both cases, what seems to be happening is the emergence of a new form of the One out of the dynamic interplay of the Many with one another over a period of time. Yet, once arisen in this way, the common element of form (the One) exercises a type of formal or informational causality over the ever-changing activity of the Many in their dealings with one another. Top-down and bottom-up causality both thus seem to be at work within Kauffman's complex chemical systems and in the operation of Whiteheadian societies as I understand them.

Kauffman further proposes that the structure of a complex chemical system whereby its inanimate molecular components spontaneously self-organize so as to produce life from nonlife can be found in many other areas of existence and activity within human life (e.g., economic and political systems). This fits very nicely, of course, with the basic Whiteheadian dictum that "the final real things of which this world is made up" are actual occasions. All that I add is that the societies into which these actual occasions aggregate in virtue of a "common element of form" are equally foundational to the structure of everything that exists in this world. The entire universe is thus radically intersubjective in its constitution. What applies at one level of self-organization within the cosmic process should, mutatis mutandis, likewise be applicable to all the other levels as well. Moreover, as Daniel Depew and Bruce Weber point out in their historical review of Darwinism as a research tradition,[1] this does not mean that natural selection is thereby set aside as the preferred mechanism of evolution. Instead, it can and should be integrated with a generalized law of self-organization within Nature so as to produce an even more convincing explanation of the overall phenomenon of evolution. As Stuart Kauffman comments, "Only those systems that are able to organize themselves spontaneously may be able to evolve further."[2]

Chapters 10 and 11 represented rewritten versions of articles already published in academic journals dedicated to the religion and science dialogue. In both cases, I was trying to make clear how my revision of Whitehead's category of society in the direction of a metaphysics of universal intersubjectivity can possibly solve problems both in contemporary natural science and in current theology, all of which bear one way or another on the proper understanding of the relationship between the One and the Many. In chapter 10, for example, I first noted the comments of Paul Davies in his book *The Cosmic Blueprint* about the mysterious way in which DNA molecules trade information and thereby set up global patterns of interaction within a broader field of activity. From my perspective this is still another version of the problem of the One and the Many that could possibly be solved by appeal to my own approach to Whiteheadian societies as structured fields of activity for their constituent actual occasions. After all, bottom-up causality and top-down causality seem to be simultaneously at work in these "societies."

Davies also makes reference to what he calls the "weirdness" of quantum mechanics in comparison with the workings of Newtonian mechanics. The wave function of a quantum state is mathematically predictable even though the position and momentum of particles governed by the wave function remain indeterminate until a given measurement is made and the wave function "collapses." This paradox, as I see it, is illuminated by the dynamic relation between Whiteheadian actual occasions and the structured field of activity out of which they originate and to which they contribute. The wave function corresponds to the determinate "common element of form" in a Whiteheadian society (structured field of activity for a set of concrescing actual occasions). Yet, since those actual occasions are self-constituting out of various factors besides the common element of form inherited from the previous set of actual occasions in the society, they remain indeterminate until they become "superjects" available for "prehension" (objectification) by other actual occasions. The "collapse" of the wave function when a human being makes a scientific measurement, accordingly, may be just one more instance of the move from potentiality to actuality within the cosmic process as a whole.

In chapter 11, I started with the reflections of a physicist-turned-theologian, Russell Stannard, on the relations between religion and science. Noting that the model of a block-universe in relativity theory equivalently turns time into a fourth spatial dimension, Stannard speculated that perhaps God sees events taking place within the temporal order from a similar timeless perspective. God, in other words, sees events within the cosmic order as before and after one another rather than as past, present, and future. Partly agreeing with Stannard on this point, I first argued that Whiteheadian societies as structured fields of activity for their constituent actual occasions generate their own space-time parameters. That is, past, present, and future exist only within the structured field of activity proper to each society. Then, presupposing that the three divine persons of the Christian doctrine of the Trinity share a common field of activity with space-time parameters proper to themselves alone, one can claim that the space-time continuum of the created order is contained within eternity, the broader space-time continuum of the divine field of activity.[3] Hence, just as in a block universe for the theoretical physicist, the three divine persons are able to see events in the temporal order as before and after one another but not necessarily as past, present, or future in terms of their own divine duration. There is, in other words, no one-to-one correspondence between events in time and eternity.

Yet this does not end up as a result in the doctrine of divine predestination. One can distinguish between what God knows and what God makes happen. God uses what Whitehead calls divine "initial aims" to prompt creatures to do what is right but gives them the "freedom" to make their own decisions at every moment. Thus God's principal activity in dealing with the world is to order events as they happen into the more comprehensive reality of the "divine consequent nature" and then on this basis communicate still another set of divine initial aims to creatures for the next set of self-constituting "decisions." Not being bound by the sense of past, present, and future in the temporal order, the divine persons are thus in a unique position to keep the cosmic process moving in a given direction without sacrificing the freedom of their creatures at any given moment to make their own decisions.

Furthermore, this approach to the relation between time and eternity is still another reworking of the problem of the One and the Many. The One is represented by eternity; the Many, by events in time. Eternity as the One should not be timeless, that is, totally different from or transcendent of the Many (events in the temporal order) as in classical theology. Nor should eternity be unending time (as Whitehead himself seems to presuppose in *Process and Reality*). Rather eternity and time, the One and the Many, should be seen as distinct but not separate, thus a nondual reality, with the field of activity proper to the temporal order enclosed within the field of activity proper to eternity. There is ongoing interplay between what happens in time and what happens in eternity, but there is no one-to-one correspondence between a moment in time and a moment in eternity.

To sum up, then, this book has been an extensive review of the problem of the One and the Many from both a historical and a contemporary perspective. Given the enormous length of the Western philosophical tradition and the complexity of the positions therein represented, of course, it has been necessary to be quite selective in choosing which authors to include in the survey. Likewise, given the various fields of activity in which the problem of the One and the Many is at least implicitly a major factor, it has been necessary to pick out one area for special attention, namely, the contemporary religion and science dialogue, above all, the knotty problem of emergence, the appearance of genuine novelty within the cosmic process.[4] But, limited as this survey necessarily has been, it should still be clear that there are at least two different paradigms for the relationship between the One and the Many with major implications for how one looks at reality and tries to deal with it. This is not to claim, of course, that reflective individuals must definitively choose one paradigm over the other. Clearly there are situations where one paradigm will be much more applicable to the analysis of what is happening than the other. But the burden of this book has been to make clear that it makes a real difference which of the two one chooses in the analysis and explanation of whatever reality one is trying to comprehend. Whether that reality is the relation of God to the world, the underlying structure of the overall cosmic process, or of any of the individual events taking place within that process, one will inevitably employ one or the other paradigm. At the very least, therefore, one should be aware of the strengths and limitations of whatever paradigm one chooses for that task.

NOTES

Introduction

1. Alfred North Whitehead, *Process and Reality: An Essay in Cosmology*, corrected ed., ed. David Ray Griffin and Donald W. Sherburne (New York: Free Press, 1978), 18.

2. Ibid., 35. In his earlier philosophical works such as *An Inquiry concerning the Principles of Natural Knowledge* and *The Concept of Nature*, Whitehead was more preoccupied with the spatial-temporal context of events rather than with the events themselves as individual actual occasions, momentary self-constituting subjects of experience (see here Paul Grimley Kuntz, *Alfred North Whitehead* [Boston: Twayne, 1984], 33–42).

3. See here W. Norris Clarke, *The One and the Many: A Contemporary Thomistic Metaphysics* (Notre Dame, IN: University of Notre Dame Press, 2001), 245–60. To his credit, Clarke seeks in this book to reconcile Thomistic metaphysics with the widely accepted notion of biological evolution. But, since he is committed to the classical principle that no effect is greater than its antecedent cause (247), he feels obliged to give cautious endorsement to the contemporary "intelligent design" movement, which most practicing natural scientists, even those who profess belief in a Creator God, reject as lacking empirical confirmation. Likewise, Clarke's appeal to the primary causality of God as an invisible factor in the working of the secondary causes of the natural world is certainly commendable. But the argument remains inconclusive because it too cannot be empirically verified and thus appears to be reductively a deus ex machina explanation.

4. See Josiah Royce, *The Problem of Christianity* (Chicago: University of Chicago Press, 1968), esp. part 2, 229–405.

Chapter 1. The Individual in a World of Universals

1. Karl Jaspers, *The Origin and Goal of History*, trans. Michael Bullock (New Haven, CT: Yale University Press, 1965), 1–21.

2. Plato, *The Republic,* trans. Francis MacDonald Cornford (New York: Oxford University Press, 1962): Bk. VI, 509D–511B; Bk. VII, 514A–521B.

3. Aristotle, *Metaphysics*, 1038b–1040a8. See also Richard I. Aaron, *The Nature of Universals*, 2nd ed. (Oxford: Clarendon Press, 1967), 7–10, where he notes how Aristotle's distinction between "thisness" and "suchness" is critical to his metaphysics.

4. W. T. Jones, *The Classical Mind: A History of Western Philosophy*, 2nd ed. (New York: Harcourt, Brace and World, 1952), 224.

5. Alfred North Whitehead, *Process and Reality: Essay in Cosmology*, corrected ed., ed. David Ray Griffin and Donald W. Sherburne (New York: Free Press, 1978), 18.

6. Ibid., 28.

7. W. T. Jones, *The Medieval Mind: A History of Western Philosophy*, 2nd ed. (New York: Harcourt, Brace and World, 1969), 141. See also Aaron, *The Nature of Universals*, 1–17.

8. Frederick Copleston, S.J., *A History of Philosophy*, vol. 2, parts 1 and 2 (Garden City, NY: Doubleday Image Books, 1962), 2/1:159.

9. Ibid., 2/1:162.

10. See here Aaron, *Theory of Universals*, 20: "The distinction between conceptualist and nominalist must lie finally in this, that the former asserts the existence of a concept along with the name, whereas the latter denies the need for the concept and holds that the universal is merely the name."

11. Copleston, *History of Philosophy*, 2/1:164–66.

12. Ibid., 2/1:172.

13. Ibid., 2/1:174.

14. Ibid.

15. Ibid., 2/1:175–76. See also Thomas Aquinas, *Scriptum super Libros Sententiarum Magistri Petri Lombardi Episcopi Parisiensis*, vol. 2, ed. R. P. Mandonnet, OP (Paris, P. Lethielleux, 1929), Dist. 3, q.3, a.2, ad 1.

16. Copleston, *History of Philosophy*, 2/1:175–76.

17. Ibid., 2/2:111. See also Thomas Aquinas, *Summa Theologiae*, I, q.85, a.2.

18. Copleston, *History of Philosophy,* 2/ 2:11–12. See also Aquinas, *Summa Theologiae*, I, q.86, a.1.

19. Aquinas, *Summa Theologiae*, I, q.86, a.1, ad 3.

20. Ibid., q.87, a.1.

21. See here Mary Beth Ingham and Mechthild Dreyer, *The Philosophical Vision of John Duns Scotus: An Introduction* (Washington, DC: Catholic University of America Press, 2004), 1–9.

22. Ibid., 25–31. See also William A. Frank and Allan B. Wolter, *Duns Scotus, Metaphysician* (West Lafayette, IN: Purdue University Press, 1995), 184–87, 196–97.

23. Copleston, *History of Philosophy*, 2/2:213–17.

24. Ibid., 2/2:216.

25. Ingham and Dreyer, *Philosophical Vision of John Duns Scotus*, 101–16. Scotus claimed that *haecceitas* or the principle of individuation "contracts" the common nature (*natura communis*, a term derived from the philosophy of Avicenna) to the concrete reality of the individual existent. But that still leaves in question how *haecceitas* achieves this contraction differently in different individuals of the same species.

26. See Aquinas, *Summa Theologiae*, I, q.82, a.4, ad l.

27. Copleston, *History of Philosophy*, 2/2:261–64. See also Frank and Wolter, *Duns Scotus*, 186–95, 200–203.

28. Copleston, *History of Philosophy*, 2/2:268–73.

29. Ibid., 2/2:273.

30. Ibid., 2/2:302–3.

31. Ingham and Dreyer, *Philosophical Vision of John Duns Scotus*, 33–38.

32. See Aquinas, *Summa Theologiae*, I, q. 3, a.4. See also Copleston, *History of Philosophy*, 2/2:51–54.

33. Copleston, *History of Philosophy*, 2/2:233.

34. Ibid., 2/2:224–31; also 2/2:77–78, where Copleston discusses the difficulty of giving any positive content to analogical concepts applied to God, e.g., intelligence: "We either attain a positive concept of the divine intelligence as such [which Aquinas denies in virtue of the *via negativa*] or we attain a concept of the 'essence' of intelligence, apart from finitude or infinity, which would seem to be univocal in respect of God and creatures [Scotus' position]."

35. Ibid., 2/2: 229: "for there is no greater analogy than that of the creature to God *in ratione essendi*, and yet *esse*, existence, belongs primarily and principally to God in such a way that it yet belongs really and univocally to the creature; and similarly with goodness and wisdom and the like." See also *Duns Scotus: Philosophical Writings*, ed. Allan Wolter, OFM (London: Nelson, 1962), 14–33 ("Man's Natural Knowledge of God").

36. Jones, *Medieval Mind*, 316.

37. Ibid., 321.

38. Ibid., 322.

39. Ibid.

40. Ibid., 317.

Chapter 2. The Turn to the Subject

1. W. T. Jones, *A History of Western Philosophy*, vol. 3, *Hobbes to Hume*, 2nd ed. (New York: Harcourt, Brace & World, 1969), 77.

2. Ibid., 3:83–85.

3. Ibid., 3:86–87.

4. Ibid., 3:98–99.

5. Alfred North Whitehead, *Science and the Modern World* (New York: Free Press, 1967), 58.

6. James Collins, *A History of Modern European Philosophy* (Milwaukee: Bruce Pub., 1965), 81.

7. Ibid., 87.

8. Ibid., 89–91.

9. Jones, *History of Western Philosophy*, 3:115–17.

10. Ibid., 3:116–17.

11. Thomas Aquinas, *Summa Theologiae*, I, q.2, a.3.

12. *Meditations on First Philosophy*, II, in *The Philosophical Works of Descartes*, 2 vols., trans. Elizabeth S. Haldane and G. R. T. Ross (Cambridge: Cambridge University Press, 1978), 1:150.

13. Descartes, *Meditations on First Philosophy*, III, 1:165–66.

14. Ibid., 160; see also Collins, *History of Modern European Philosophy*, 164.

15. Descartes, *Meditations on First Philosophy*, VI, 1:191–92.

16. Collins, *History of Modern European Philosophy*, 140–43.

17. Jones, *History of Western Philosophy*, 3:160–61.

18. Collins, *History of Modern European Philosophy*, 150. See also Descartes, *Meditations on First Philosophy*, III, 1:160–61.

19. Cf. supra, chap. 1.

20. See, e.g., Descartes, *Discourse on Method*, II, in *Philosophical Works of Descartes*, 1:92, where he sums up his method in four precepts, beginning with "what was presented to my mind so clearly and distinctly that I could have no occasion to doubt it." See also Jones, *History of Western Philosophy*, 3:181.

21. John Locke, *An Essay Concerning Human Understanding*, ed. Peter Nidditch (Oxford: Clarendon Press, 1975), 44. See also Collins, *History of Modern European Philosophy*, 314–15.

22. Locke, *An Essay Concerning Human Understanding*, 538; Collins, *History of Modern European Philosophy*, 316.

23. Locke, *An Essay Concerning Human Understanding*, 8; Collins, *History of Modern European Philosophy*, 315–16.

24. Locke, *An Essay Concerning Human Understanding*, 43–46.

25. Ibid., 48–103.   26. Ibid., 65.

27. Ibid., 105.   28. Ibid., 165–66.

29. Ibid., 134–43.   30. Ibid., 453.

31. Ibid., 95.   32. Ibid., 319.

33. Ibid., 325.   34. Ibid., 538.

35. Ibid., 537–39.   36. Ibid., 539.

37. Aaron, *Theory of Universals*, 37.

38. Locke, *Essay Concerning Human Understanding*, 562.

39. Aaron, *Theory of Universals*, 241.

Chapter 3. What Is Matter and What Is Spirit?

1. George Berkeley, *The Principles of Human Knowledge*, in *The Principles of Human Knowledge and Three Dialogues between Hylas and Philonous* (Gloucester, MA: Peter Smith, 1978), n. 8 (p. 68): "If we look but never so little into our own thoughts, we shall find it impossible for us to conceive a likeness except only between our ideas."

2. Ibid., nn. 9–15 (pp. 68–72).

3. Ibid., n. 26 (p. 77): "there is not corporeal or material substance; it remains therefore that the cause of ideas is an incorporeal active substance or Spirit."

4. Berkeley, *Three Dialogues between Hylas and Philonous* in *The Principles of Human Knowledge and Three Dialogues between Hylas and Philonous* (Gloucester, MA: Peter Smith, 1978), 220: "there is an *omnipresent, eternal Mind*, which knows and comprehends all things, and exhibits them to our view in such a manner, and according to such rules as he himself hath ordained, and are by us termed the *laws of nature*."

5. W. T. Jones, *A History of Western Philosophy*, vol. 3, *Hobbes to Hume*, 2nd ed. (New York: Harcourt, Brace and World, 1969), 289.

6. Ibid., 291. See also Berkeley, *Principles of Human Knowledge*, nn. 146–47 (pp. 139–40).

7. Berkeley, *Three Dialogues between Hylas and Philonous*, 221. See also Jones, *History of Western Philosophy*, 3:293.

8. Berkeley, *Principles of Human Knowledge*, n. 145 (p. 139).

9. Jones, *History of Western Philosophy*, 3:294.

10. Berkeley, *Principles of Human Knowledge*, n. 147 (p. 140); James Collins, *A History of Modern European Philosophy* (Milwaukee: Bruce Pub., 1965), 395.

11. Berkeley, *Principles of Human Knowledge*, nn. 1–3 (pp. 65–66).

12. Ibid., n. 48 (pp. 87–88).

13. Collins, *History of Modern European Philosophy*, 408. See also David Hume, *A Treatise of Human Nature*, ed. L. A. Selby-Bigge (Oxford: Clarendon Press, 1967), xx–xxi.

14. Collins, *History of Modern European Philosophy*, 409. Hume, *Treatise of Human Nature*, xxi.

15. Hume, *Treatise of Human Nature*, 1.

16. Ibid., 8. See also Berkeley, *Principles of Human Knowledge*, Introduction, n. 15 (p. 55).

17. Hume, *Treatise of Human Nature*, 2.

18. Ibid., 22.

19. Ibid., 13.

20. Ibid., 87.

21. Ibid., 88.

22. Ibid., 94. See also Collins, *History of Modern European Philosophy*, 428: "This determination of mind or feeling of a necessity to make the causal inference constitutes the causal belief and is the source of the idea of necessary connection."

23. Collins, *History of Modern European Philosophy*, 422.

24. Hume, *Theory of Human Nature*, 207–8.

25. Ibid., 253.

26. Collins, *History of Modern European Philosophy*, 199.

27. *Spinoza's Ethics and De Intellectus Emendatione*, trans. Andrew Boyle (London: J. M. Dent, 1959), 41 (II, Prop. 7).

28. Ibid., 1 (I, Prop. 3).

29. Collins, *History of Modern European Philosophy*, 224. See also *Spinoza's Ethics*, 38–39 (II, Prop. 1–2).

30. Jones, *History of Western Philosophy*, 3:204.

31. *Spinoza's Ethics*, 23 (I, Prop. 19).

32. Ibid., 11 (I, Prop. 15).

33. Ibid., 1 (I, Def. 1, 3).

34. Alfred North Whitehead, *Process and Reality: Essay in Cosmology*, corrected ed., ed. David Ray Griffin and Donald W. Sherburne (New York: Free Press, 1978), 18–19.

35. Ibid., 244.

36. *Spinoza's Ethics*, 29 (I, Prop. 24).

37. Whitehead, *Process and Reality*, 18.

38. T. S. Gregory, Introduction to *Spinoza's Ethics*, viii.

39. Collins, *History of Modern European Philosophy*, 230–31.

40. Ibid.

41. Ibid., 204: "Employing Cartesian terminology, Spinoza distinguishes between the *formal essence* or actual nature of the thing known and its *objective* or *representational essence*, which is nothing other than the true idea of the thing in the mind of the knower. The mind can possess the objective essence of things and thus have truth and certainty about the things in their formal essence."

42. *Leibniz: Selections*, ed. Philip P. Wiener (New York: Scribner's, 1951): "On Substance as Active Force rather than Mere Extension" (Letter of Leibniz to De Volder, March 24/April 3, 1699), 156–62. See also Jones, *History of Western Philosophy*, 3:222–24.

43. Leibniz, *Principles of Nature and of Grace*, in *Selections*, n. 1 (p. 522).

44. Leibniz, *The Monadology*, in *Selections*, n. 7 (p. 534).

45. Leibniz, *Principles of Nature and of Grace*, n. 1 (p. 522).

46. Collins, *History of Modern European Philosophy*, 282.

47. Leibniz, *Monadology*, nn. 47–48, 78 (pp. 542, 549).

48. Ibid., n. 45 (pp. 541–42).

49. Ibid., n. 38 (p. 540).

50. Collins, *History of Modern European Philosophy*, 282.

51. Cf. Leibniz, *Principles of Nature and of Grace*, n. 1 (p. 522).

52. Ibid., n. 3 (p. 523).

Chapter 4. Kant's Copernican Revolution

1. Georges Dicker, *Kant's Theory of Knowledge: An Analytical Introduction* (New York: Oxford University Press, 2004), 23.

2. Ibid., 24.

3. "Preface to Second Edition," in *Immanuel Kant's Critique of Pure Reason*, trans. Norman Kemp Smith (New York: St. Martin's Press, 1956), B xvi (p. 22). N.B.: The references to A and B in these notes is to the first and second editions of the *Critique*, respectively.

4. Ibid., B xiii (p. 20).

5. W. T. Jones, *A History of Western Philosophy*, vol. 4, *Kant to Wittgenstein and Sartre*, 2nd ed. (New York: Harcourt, Brace and World, 1969), 32.

6. Kant, *Critique of Pure Reason*, B 14–16 (pp. 52–54).

7. Dicker, *Kant's Theory of Knowledge*, 28–29.

8. Jones, *History of Western Philosophy*, 4:31.

9. Kant, *Critique of Pure Reason*, B 80 (p. 95).

10. Jones, *History of Western Philosophy*, 4:33. See also H. J. Paton, *Kant's*

Metaphysic of Experience, 2 vols. (New York: Humanities Press, 1970), 2:24: "The power of judgement is a power to subsume under rules, that is, to decide whether anything stands under a given rule or not."

11. Kant, *Critique of Pure Reason*, A 70, B 95 (p. 106).

12. *Aristotle's Metaphysics*, trans. Hippocrates G. Apostle (Grinnell, IA: Peripatetic Press, 1979), 1017a (p. 82).

13. See Dicker, *Kant's Theory of Knowledge*, 57–59.

14. Kant, *Critique of Pure Reason*, A 93, B 126 (p. 126).

15. Ibid., B 132 (p. 153).

16. Ibid., B 151–52 (p. 165).

17. Ibid., B 152 (p. 165); likewise, A 138, B 177 (p. 181). See also Paton, *Kant's Metaphysic of Experience*, 2:31.

18. Kant, *Critique of Pure Reason*, B 152 (p. 165).

19. Ibid., B 158–59 (p. 169).

20. Ibid., A 141, B 180 (pp. 182–83). See also Paton, *Kant's Metaphysic of Experience*, 2:37–41, esp. the summary paragraph on 39.

21. Kant, *Critique of Pure Reason*, A 141, B 180 (pp. 182–83).

22. Ibid., A 162–76, B 202–18 (pp. 197–208).

23. Ibid., B 218 (p. 208).

24. Ibid., A 182, B 224 (p. 212).

25. Ibid., A 182, B 224–25 (pp. 212–13).

26. Ibid., B 225 (p. 213).

27. Ibid., A 186, B 229 (p. 216).

28. See here Paton, *Kant's Metaphysic of Experience*, 2:174: "Kant's view is that objective temporal connexions (which we all claim to experience) are found in experience only because they are imposed by the understanding. More precisely, these connexions are imposed by the transcendental synthesis of imagination which combines given appearances in one time and space in accordance with the categories of the understanding."

29. Kant, *Critique of Pure Reason*, A 182, B 224 (p. 213).

30. Ibid., A 189, B 233 (p. 218).

31. Ibid. See also Paton, *Kant's Metaphysic of Experience*, 2:240–41.

32. Kant, *Critique of Pure Reason*, A 192, B 237 (p. 221).

33. Ibid., A 191, B 236 (p. 220).

34. Ibid.

35. Jones, *History of Western Philosophy*, 4:49.

36. Kant, *Critique of Pure Reason*, A 195, B 240 (p. 223).

37. Paton, *Kant's Metaphysic of Experience*, 2:247.

38. Kant, *Critique of Pure Reason*, A 211, B 257 (pp. 233–34).

39. Ibid.

40. Ibid., A 214–15, B 261 (p. 236).

41. Ibid., A 212–13, B 259 (p. 235): "Each substance (inasmuch as only in respect of its determinations can it be an effect) must therefore contain in itself the causality of certain determinations in the other substance, and at the same time the effects of the causality of that other; that is, the substances must stand, immediately or mediately, in dynamical community, if their coexistence is to be known in any possible experience." See also Paton, *Kant's Metaphysic of Experience*, 2:322–23.

42. Kant, *Critique of Pure Reason*, A 219, B 266 (p. 239).

43. Ibid., A 225, B 272 (p. 243).

44. Ibid., A 341–642, B 399–670 (pp. 328–531). See also Jones, *History of Western Philosophy*, 4:51–58.

45. Kant, *Critique of Pure Reason*, A 671, B 699 (p. 550).

46. Ibid.

47. Ibid., A 672, B 700 (p. 551).

48. Ibid.

49. Ibid.

50. Ibid., B 275 (p. 245): "The mere, but empirically determined, consciousness of my own existence proves the existence of objects in space outside me." The key words here, of course, are "empirically determined," since by that fact Kant excludes the possibility of the human subject creating its own objects of experience and thus living in its own self-created world.

Chapter 5. Transcendental Idealism and the Empirical Other

1. James Collins, *A History of Modern European Philosophy* (Milwaukee: Bruce Pub., 1965), 546–47. See also "First Introduction," in *Fichte: Science of Knowledge*, trans. Peter Heath and John Lachs, 3–28 (New York: Appleton-Century-Crofts, 1970).

2. Fichte, "First Introduction," 14: "The dispute between the idealist and the dogmatist is, in reality, about whether the independence of the thing should be sacrificed to the independence of the self or, conversely, the independence of the self to the independence of the thing."

3. Fichte, "Second Introduction," *Science of Knowledge*, 48–52.

4. Collins, *History of Modern European Philosophy*, 544.

5. Ibid., 551. See also Fichte, "Second Introduction," 40. Only the transcendental Ego, of course, realizes that the alleged intellectual intuition is its own spontaneous activity and/or mode of existence.

6. Fichte, "Second Introduction," 38, 45–46. Fichte concedes that Kant and his disciples reject the notion of an intellectual (as opposed to a sensory) intuition but argues that the Categorical Imperative in *Critique of Practical Reason*, can only be understood as an intellectual intuition into the self-legislating activity of the Transcendental Ego.

7. Collins, *History of Modern European Philosophy*, 552.

8. Fichte, *Science of Knowledge*, 97: "The self's own positing of itself is thus its own pure activity. The *self posits itself*, and by virtue of this mere self-assertion it *exists*; and, conversely, the self *exists* and *posits* its own existence by virtue of merely existing. It is at once the agent and the product of action; the active, and what the activity brings about."

9. Ibid., 104: "Nothing is posited to begin with, except the self; and this alone is asserted absolutely. Hence there can be an absolute opposition only to the self. But that which is opposed to the self = the *not-self*."

10. Ibid., 109: "The self is to be equated with, and yet opposed to, itself. But in regard to consciousness it is equal to itself, for consciousness is one: but in this consciousness the absolute self is posited as indivisible; whereas the self to which the non-self is opposed is posited as divisible. Hence, insofar as there is a not-self opposed to it, the self is itself in opposition to the absolute self."

11. Collins, *History of Modern European Philosophy*, 556–57.

12. Ibid., 559. See also Fichte, *Science of Knowledge*, 251–56.

13. Collins, *History of Modern Philosophy*, 562.

14. Ibid., 568. See also Fichte, *Die Anweisung zum seligen Leben, oder auch die Religionslehre, Sämmtliche Werke*, ed. I. H. Fichte, vol. 5 (Berlin: Veit u. Comp., 1845), 406.

15. Collins, *History of Modern European Philosophy*, 607. Also G. W. F. Hegel, *Phänomologie des Geistes*, ed. Johannes Hoffmeister (Berlin: Felix Meiner, 1952), *Vorrede* [Preface], 19.

16. Collins, *History of Modern European Philosophy*, 584–85.

17. See, e.g., Pierre Teilhard de Chardin, *The Phenomenon of Man*, trans. Bernard Wall (New York: Harper and Row, 1959), esp. 53–74.

18. Cf. *Schellings Werke*, vol. 4, ed. Manfred Schröter (Munich: C. H. Beck, 1958), *Philosophie und Religion* (*1–60*), *Philosophische Untersuchungen über das Wesen der menschlichen Freiheit und die damit zusammenhängenden Gegenstände* (223–309). N.B.: Schröter makes reference to the original edition of Schelling's works published by his son, K. F. A. Schelling, in 1860. Since Schröter's edition is preliminary to a critical edition of Schelling's works, I cite the 1860 edition in these endnotes.

19. Collins, *History of Modern European Philosophy*, 585. Cf. also Schelling, *Wesen der menschlichen Freiheit*, in *Schellings Werke*, 7:357–66.

20. Schelling, *Wesen der menschlichen Freiheit*, 7:359. See also Collins, *History of Modern European Philosophy*, 585–86, where he describes Schelling's God-world relationship here as "dynamic pantheism." In my judgment, Collins errs on this point since he fails to distinguish between pantheism and panentheism (everything created being grounded in God but with its own autonomous existence and activity). The latter term more properly corresponds to what Schelling really had in mind.

21. Schelling, *Wesen der menschlichen Freiheit*, 7:364.

22. Ibid., 7:364–66.

23. Ibid., 7:357–58.

24. See, e.g., "A Psychological Approach to the Doctrine of the Trinity," in *The Collected Works of C. G. Jung*, vol. 11, *Psychology and Religion: West and East*, 2nd ed., trans. R. F. C. Hull, 107–200 (Princeton, NJ: Princeton University Press, 1969), esp. 164–87.

25. Collins, *History of Modern European Philosophy*, 589. See also Schelling, *Wesen der menschlichen Freiheit*, 7:373–74, 381–82. What Schelling describes as a free choice made outside of space and time is perhaps better understood as the ongoing interplay of human freedom (or more generally of spontaneity at different levels of existence and activity within Nature) with the determinism proper to strict cause-and-effect relations within Nature. Nature clearly exhibits both types of causality, and to reduce the one to the other (as we shall see below) is to notably oversimplify what is happening within the natural order. On this point, cf. Nicholas Rescher, "Causal Necessitation and Free Will," *Process Studies* 35 (2006): 193–206.

26. Schelling, *Wesen der menschlichen Freiheit*, 7:380. Schelling argues that this is the deeper reason for the Incarnation. Only a divine person can effectively heal human persons by restoring for them the reality of Spirit, the proper balance between the will of the ground and the will of reason within human consciousness.

27. Joseph A. Bracken, *Freiheit und Kausalität bei Schelling* [*Symposion, n. 38*] (Munich: Alber Verlag, 1972).

28. *Die Welalter* in *Schellings Werke*, 8:195–344. See also *Schellings Werke: Nachlassband* (Munich: Biederstein Verlag und Leibniz Verlag, 1946), where Schroeter collected further drafts of the unfinished *Weltalter*.

29. See Bracken, *Freiheit und Kausalität bei Schelling*, 67–89.

30. G. W. F. Hegel, *Phänomenologie des Geistes*, ed. Johannes Hoffmeister (Hamburg: Felix Meiner, 1952), 21.

31. Collins, *History of Modern European Philosophy*, 623–24. See also G. W. F. Hegel, *Wissenschaft der Logik*, 2 vols., ed. Georg Lasson (Hamburg: Felix Meiner, 1963), 2:483–506.

32. Collins, *History of Modern European Philosophy*, 619. See also Hegel, *Wissenschaft der Logik*, 1:36.

33. Collins, *History of Modern European Philosophy*, 614: "The *Phenomenology* is the autobiography of the mind in its itinerary from naive consciousness to absolute knowledge or reflective science."

34. Ibid., 616. See also Hegel, *Phänomenologie des Geistes*, 79–89.

35. Hegel, *Phänomenologie des Geistes*, 87.

36. Collins, *History of Modern European Philosophy*, 618.

37. Hegel, *Phänomenologie des Geistes*, 549–64, esp. 556.

38. Collins, *History of Modern European Philosophy*, 635–36: The Logic is "'the Truth as it is, without husk in and for itself. One may therefore express it thus: that this content shows forth God as he is in his eternal essence before the creation of Nature and of a Finite Spirit.'" Reference is to Hegel, *Wissenschaft der Logik*, 1:31.

39. Hegel, *Wissenschaft der Logik*, 1:66–67.

40. Ibid., 67. See also Collins, *History of Modern European Philosophy*, 369: "Logic and philosophy as a whole begin with the recognition that *pure thought is a dialectical becoming*, and that only in and through this becoming is the concrete universal achieved."

41. Hegel, *Wissenschaft der Logik*, 2:3.

42. Ibid., 2:156.

43. Ibid., 2:504–5.

44. Collins, *History of Modern European Philosophy*, 640. See also G. W. F. Hegel, *Enzyklopädie der Philosophischen Wissenschaften*, ed. Friedhelm Nicolin und Otto Poggeler (Hamburg: Felix Meiner, 1959), n. 247 (p. 200).

45. Hegel, *Enzyklopädie*, n. 381 (p. 313).

46. Ibid., n. 483 (p. 389).

47. Ibid., n. 487 (p. 391).

48. Collins, *History of Modern European Philosophy*, 647. See also Hegel, *Enzyklopädie*, n. 535 (p. 413).

49. Collins, *History of Modern European Philosophy*, 647. As Collins notes, there is an implicit totalitarianism in Hegel's notion of the State. The State enjoys "absolute right over its component members, both as individuals and as groups" (647), ostensibly to guarantee maximum freedom for all citizens, but in point of fact to impose its will as the supreme objective embodiment of Absolute Spirit.

50. Collins, *History of Modern European Philosophy*, 648.

51. Ibid., 653. See also Hegel, *Enzyklopädie*, n. 556 (p. 441), n. 565 (p. 447), n. 573 (p. 451).

52. Collins, *History of Modern European Philosophy*, 593–97.

53. See here Schelling's lectures at the University of Munich in 1827, which were published under the title *Zur Geschichte der neueren Philosophie*, in *Schellings Werke*, 10:1–200, esp. 73ff.

54. Collins, *History of Modern European Philosophy*, 593–94. See also *Einleitung in die Philosophie der Mythologie*, vol. 2, twenty-fourth lecture in *Schellings Werke*, 11:553–72, esp. 566. The self will not rest until it experiences God through an intersubjective encounter as its Lord *(Herr)*.

55. See here Schelling's *Einleitung in der Philosophie der Mythologie*, vol. 2, eleventh lecture, in *Schellings Werke*, 11:255–76, esp. 255. Reason alone cannot produce a philosophically validated religion but only reason reflecting on what history reveals by way of divine revelation.

56. Collins, *History of Modern European Philosophy*, 596.

Chapter 6. The Revolt against Systems Thinking

1. "Kierkegaard's Rhetoric," in *Stanford Encyclopedia*, s.v. "Søren Kierkegaard," http://plato.stanford.edu/entries/kierkegaard: "Kierkegaard's 'method of indirect communication' was designed to sever the reliance of the reader on the authority of the author and on the received wisdom of the community. The reader was to be forced to take individual responsibility for knowing who s/he is and for knowing where s/he stands on the existential, ethical and religious issues raised in the texts."

2. Søren Kierkegaard, *Either/Or: A Fragment of Life*, vol. 1, trans. Howard V. Hong and Edna H. Hong (Princeton, NJ: Princeton University Press, 1987), 301–445.

3. Ibid., 1:307–8.

4. Søren Kierkegaard, *Either/Or*, vol. 2, trans. Howard V. Hong and Edna H. Hong (Princeton, NJ: Princeton University Press, 1987), 94.

5. Ibid., 2:143–46.

6. Ibid., 2:146–48.

7. Ibid., 2:165–69, 176.

8. Ibid., 2:213.

9. Ibid., 2:250–51. N.B.: Since the forthcoming citations from Kierkegaard refer to the generic human being as "he," "his," or "him." I do the same in commenting upon these passages. The continued effort to convert Kierkegaard's usage to gender-neutral language is too cumbersome.

10. Ibid., 2:328.

11. Ibid., 2:329.

12. Ibid., 2:330.

13. Søren Kierkegaard, *Fear and Trembling/Repetition*, trans. Howard V. Hong and Edna H. Hong (Princeton, NJ: Princeton University Press, 1983), 1–123.

14. Ibid., 59–60.   15. Ibid., 57.

16. Ibid., 70.   17. Ibid., 79–80.

18. Ibid., 70.

19. Søren Kierkegaard, *Concluding Unscientific Postscript to Philosophical Fragments*, trans. Howard V. Hong and Edna H. Hong (Princeton, NJ: Princeton University Press, 1992), 2 vols.

20. Ibid., 1:15 (translators' introduction).

21. Ibid., 1:98–99, 105.   22. Ibid., 1:33.

23. Ibid., 1:173–74.   24. Ibid., 1:204.

25. Ibid., 1:200.   26. Ibid., 1:230.

27. Michael Polanyi, *Personal Knowledge: Towards a Post-Critical Philosophy* (New York: Harper Torchbook, 1964), esp. 249–324. See also by the same author *The Tacit Dimension* (Garden City, NJ: Doubleday, 1967).

28. See Kierkegaard, *Concluding Unscientific Postscript*, 1:301–60, where he effectively reduces actuality to individual subjectivity and regards even the actuality of others as simply possibility for the ethical self-realization of the individual.

29. John Wall, "Introduction," in Emmanuel Levinas, *Totality and Infinity: An Essay on Exteriority*, trans. Alphonso Lingis (Pittsburgh, PA: Duquesne University Press, 1969), 13.

30. Emmanuel Levinas, *Otherwise Than Being or Beyond Essence*, trans. Alphonso Lingis (The Hague: Martinus Nijhoff, 1981), 3: "If transcendence has meaning, it can only signify the fact that the *event of being*, the *esse*, the *essence*, passes over to what is other than being. . . . Not *to be otherwise*, but *otherwise than being*. And not to not-be; passing over is not here equivalent to dying. Being and not-being illuminate one another, and unfold a speculative dialectic which is a determination of being."

31. Ibid., 18.

32. Ibid., 114.

33. Levinas, *Totality and Infinity*, 51: "To approach the Other in conversation is to welcome his expression, in which at each instant he overflows the idea a thought would carry away with it. It is therefore to *receive* from the Other beyond the capacity of the I, which means exactly: to have the idea of infinity."

34. Ibid., 39: "The relation between the same and the other, metaphysics, is primordially enacted as conversation [*discours*], where the same, gathered up in its ipseity as an 'I,' as a particular existent unique and autochthonous, leaves itself."

35. See Lingis, "Translator's Introduction," in *Otherwise than Being*: "[Levinas] holds that the sense of infinity has its origin not in a formalization and idealization of the spatial sense of horizontal openness, nor in the absolutization of the idea of truth—as Husserl had said, but in the inapprehendability of alterity and the unsatisfiability of the moral exigency" (xxxii).

36. Levinas, *Totality and Infinity*, 43. 37. Ibid., 53.

38. Ibid., 62. 39. Ibid., 96.

40. Ibid., 69. 41. Ibid., 78.

42. Ibid., 85. 43. Ibid., 87.

44. Ibid., 71.

45. Lingis, "Translator's Introduction," *Otherwise Than Being* xxxv; see also Levinas, *Otherwise Than Being*, 156–62.

46. Levinas, *Totality and Infinity*, 78.

47. Ibid., 67.

48. Ibid., 103.

49. Walter Kaufmann, "Prologue," in Martin Buber, *I and Thou* (New York: Scribner's, 1970), 11.

50. Ibid., 12–13. 51. Ibid., 13.

52. Ibid., 13–14. 53. Ibid., 14.

54. Ibid., 31–33.

55. Ibid., 37. Kaufmann's comments on classical Christology here may be a bit one-sided since they are grounded in the notion of Jesus paying the penalty for our sins (Anselm of Canterbury) rather than in the alternate notion of Jesus as revealing the love of God for humankind and thereby inspiring the rest of us to risk loving God in return (Peter Abelard).

56. Kaufmann, "Prologue," 25–28.

57. Martin Buber, *I and Thou*, trans. Walter Kaufmann (New York: Scribner's, 1970), 54.

58. Ibid. 59. Ibid., 57–58.

60. Ibid., 59. 61. Ibid., 62.

62. Ibid. 63. Ibid., 63.

64. Ibid., 67. 65. Ibid., 68.

66. Ibid., 71–72. 67. Ibid., 74.

68. Ibid., 77–79. 69. Ibid., 82–85.

70. Ibid., 87. 71. Ibid., 93.

72. Ibid., 94.

73. Ibid., 123: "Extended, the lines of relationship intersect in the eternal You. Every single You is a glimpse of that. Through every single You the basic word addresses the eternal You."

74. Ibid., 89.

75. Ibid., 113.

76. Ibid., 123–24.

77. Ibid., 160–62.

78. Ibid., 163.

79. Ibid., 164.

80. Ibid., 129.

81. Ibid., 130.

82. Ibid., 137.

83. See here Thomas Aquinas, *Summa Theologiae*, I, q.29, a.4 , where Aquinas defines the divine persons as "subsistent relations" who as one God share everything except their irreconcilable differences as persons.

84. See Wolfhart Pannenberg, *Systematic Theology*, vol. 1, trans. Geoffrey W. Bromiley (Grand Rapids: Eerdmans, 1991), 370–84.

Chapter 7. Starting with Events Rather Than Things

1. Martin Heidegger, *Being and Time*, trans. John Macquarrie and Edward Robinson (New York: Harper and Row, 1962), 19–35.

2. Martin Heidegger, *Contributions to Philosophy (From Enowning)*, trans. Parvis Emad and Kenneth Maly (Bloomington: Indiana University Press, 1999). See also *Beiträge zur Philosophie (Vom Ereignis)* (Frankfurt am Main: Vittorio Klostermann, 1989).

3. See, e.g., Heidegger, *Contributions to Philosophy*, 286–87; *Beiträge zur Philosophie*, 407–8.

4. Alfred North Whitehead, *Process and Reality*, corrected ed., ed. David Ray Griffin and Donald W. Sherburne (New York: Free Press, 1978), 21.

5. Ibid., 18.

6. Heidegger, *Being and Time*, 279–311.

7. The full intelligibility of an entity, of course, is a combination of what it has in common with other entities of the same class or species or class and what makes it different from those other entities. Cf. on this point Robert Cummings Neville, *Eternity and Time's Flow* (Albany: State University of New York Press, 1993), 71–76, where he distinguishes between essential and conditional features of an individual entity: to be a thing is to be related to other things and thus conditioned by them, but the way in which one chooses to be related to other things is peculiar to oneself and thus essential to what one is here and now. Note how Neville thus inverts the traditional understanding of what is essential and conditional. "Essential" is not what a thing has in common with

other entities of the same class or species but what makes it different from those other entities to which it is related in virtue of its conditional features. "Conditional," on the contrary, is not what is somehow accidental to the identity of an entity but the necessary correlate or co-determinant of the entity's individual identity here and now. People working in the natural and social sciences generally look for the conditional features of the entity under investigation in order to integrate it into a broader causal scheme. Artists and other people in the humanities, by way of contrast, are usually in search of the essential features of their topic of inquiry—what makes it stand out or be different—from its environmental context.

8. Heidegger, *Beiträge zur Philosophie*, 52–53. Cf. *Contributions to Philosophy*, 37.

9. Richard Polt, *The Emergency of Being: On Heidegger's Contributions to Philosophy* (Ithaca, NY: Cornell University Press, 2006).

10. Ibid., 25–27.

11. Ibid., 33–43.

12. Ibid., 35–36.

13. Heidegger, *Being and Time*, 67–273.

14. Ibid., 274–488.

15. Ibid., 312–48; see also Polt, *Emergency of Being*, 37–40.

16. Polt, *Emergency of Being*, 41; Heidegger, *Being and Time*, 228.

17. Heidegger, *Being and Time*, 274–78.

18. Polt, *Emergency of Being*, 45; Heidegger, *Beiträge zur Philosophie*, 189.

19. Polt, *Emergency of Being*, 48; Heidegger, *Beiträge zur Philosophie*, 230–31.

20. Polt, *Emergency of Being*, 51–52; cf. Heidegger, *Beiträge zur Philosophie*, 451–52.

21. Polt, *Emergency of Being*, 53; Heidegger, *Beiträge zur Philosophie*, 256, 260.

22. Whitehead, *Process and Reality*, 21.

23. Ibid., 88.

24. Ibid., 31.

25. Ibid.

26. Cf., e.g., Robert C. Neville, *Creativity and God: A Challenge to Process Theology* (New York: Seabury Press, 1980), 41–43. Neville's own distinction between cosmological creativity, an empirical generalization, and ontological creativity as an activity without a determinate source or as *creatio ex nihilo* is highly original but not widely shared among students of Whitehead's philosophy.

27. Alfred North Whitehead, *Modes of Thought* (New York: Free Press, 1938),

164. N.B.: In *Process and Reality*, Whitehead focused primarily on creativity as a principle of novelty within actual occasions; in his later writings such as *Modes of Thought*, he emphasized creativity as a principle of creative advance or transition.

28. Andre Cloots, "The Metaphysical Significance of Whitehead's Creativity," *Process Studies* 30 (2001): 42.

29. At the same time, one should recognize the difference between creativity for Whitehead and *Seyn* for Whitehead. Creativity is the cosmological principle of novelty and transition for all actual occasions, whether living or nonliving, within Whitehead's metaphysics. *Seyn* in Heidegger's philosophy has a special relation to *Da-sein* as its "site of the moment," the event of the self-giving of *Seyn*. But Heidegger does not specify the relation, if any, of *Seyn*, to human beings apart from this event or, even more, to the vast array of nonhuman entities in this world.

30. Polt, *Emergency of Being*, 182; *Beiträge zur Philosophie*, 183. Heidegger distinguishes in this essay between the "guiding question" (*Leitfrage*) of classical metaphysics which asked about the beingness of beings, that which they all have in common, and the "grounding question (*Grundfrage*) of inceptual thinking which inquires into the happening (*Wesung*) of the truth of be-ing in the reciprocal grounding activity of be-ing and *Da-sein*.

31. See Whitehead, *Process and Reality*, 31, 88.

32. Polt, *Emergency of Being*, 109: "Bethinking is not just *about* be-ing, but *is* be-ing—if this claim is properly understood. Bethinking is a happening that belongs inextricably to the happening of appropriation itself, because bethinking is a crucial instance of the emergence of meaning that the word *appropriation* indicates."

33. Whitehead, *Process and Reality*, 21, 25–26.

34. Ibid., 244. See below, chap. 11 of this volume, for further discussion of the role of "divine initial aims" in God's providence for the world of creation.

35. Polt, *Emergency of Being*, 119.

36. Whitehead, *Process and Reality*, 177–78.

37. Ibid., 109, 162.

38. Polt, *Emergency of Being*, 56–57; see also Heidegger, *Being and Time*, 47–48.

39. Polt, *Emergency of Being*, 59–60; Heidegger, *Beiträge zur Philosophie*, 346–48.

40. Polt, *Emergency of Being*, 140–55; Heidegger, *Beiträge zur Philosophie*, 242–47.

41. Whitehead, *Process and Reality*, 27–28.

42. Polt, *Emergency of Being*, 149; Heidegger, *Beiträge zur Philosophie*, 267. For Heidegger, *das Nichts* is not the opposite of Being, or the absence of Being, but part of the gift of Being to *Dasein* so as to enable *Dasein* to break free of its preoccupation with beings.

43. Polt, *Emergency of Being*, 153–54; Heidegger, *Beiträge zur Philosophie*, 282.

44. Polt, *Emergency of Being*, 156–61; Heidegger, *Beiträge zur Philosophie*, 293.

45. Polt, *Emergency of Being*, 164–70; Heidegger, *Beiträge zur Philosophie*, 87–95.

46. Polt, *Emergency of Being*, 173–74; Heidegger, *Beiträge zur Philosophie*, 319–21.

47. Polt, *Emergency of Being*, 182; see also Heidegger, *Beiträge zur Philosophie*, 379–88, where Heidegger distinguishes between *Grund* (ground) and *Abgrund* (background or implicit context). Both are ultimately derivative from *Urgrund* (*Seyn* in its ongoing self-giving).

48. Whitehead, *Process and Reality*, 66.

49. Polt, *Emergency of Being*, 188; cf. Heidegger, *Beiträge zur Philosophie*, 384.

50. Polt, *Emergency of Being*, 197; Heidegger, *Beiträge zur Philosophie*, 389–90.

51. Polt, *Emergency of Being*, 201; Heidegger, *Beiträge zur Philosophie*, 391.

52. Polt, *Emergency of Being*, 208; Heidegger, *Beiträge zur Philosophie*, 411.

53. Polt, *Emergency of Being*, 210; cf. Heidegger, *Beiträge zur Philosophie*, 411.

54. Whitehead, *Process and Reality*, 340.

55. Ibid., 346.

56. Polt, *Emergency of Being*, 254.

57. Ibid., 248.

Chapter 8. The One, the Three, and the Many

1. Colin E. Gunton, *The One, the Three and the Many: God, Creation and the Culture of Modernity* (Cambridge: Cambridge University Press, 1993), 13–14.

2. Ibid., 17–18.

3. Ibid., 22–27.

4. Ibid., 34.

5. Ibid.

6. Ibid., 48.

7. Ibid., 79. Reference is to Plato's *Timaeus*, n. 37: in *The Dialogues of Plato*, trans. Benjamin Jowett (Oxford: Clarendon Press, 1875), III, 619–20.

8. Gunton, *The One, the Three and the Many*, 117.

9. Ibid., 58, 120–21. See also chap. 1 in this book.

10. Gunton, *The One, the Three and the Many*, 117.

11. Ibid., 149–54.

12. Ibid., 152.

13. See Thomas Aquinas, *Summa Theologiae*, I, q.3, a.7.

14. Gunton, *The One, the Three and the Many*, 166.

15. Ibid., 183.   16. Ibid.

17. Ibid., 190.   18. Ibid., 181.

19. Ibid., 229.   20. Ibid., 225.

21. Ibid., 226.   22. Ibid., 231.

23. Alfred North Whitehead, *Process and Reality*, corrected ed., ed. David Ray Griffin and Donald W. Sherburne (New York: Free Press, 1978), 18.

24. Whitehead, *Adventures of Ideas* (New York: Free Press, 1967), 204.

25. Ibid.

26. Whitehead, *Process and Reality*, 18.

27. See David Ray Griffin, *Two Great Truths: A New Synthesis of Scientific Naturalism and Christian Faith* (Louisville, KY: Westminster John Knox Press, 2004), 78–82. See also Pierfrancesco Basile, "Rethinking Leibniz, Whitehead, Ward, and the Idealistic Legacy," *Process Studies* 35 (2006): 207–29. Basile calls attention to the fact that a predecessor of Whitehead at Cambridge University in England, James Ward, had already adopted and revised the *Monadology* of Leibniz so as to stipulate that the ultimate units of reality are not inert bits of matter but subjects of experience which have causal influence on one another.

28. For that matter, we human beings experience different levels of self-awareness within the course of an ordinary day. We do many things while only half-awake and are fully alert and focused on the matter at hand only at intervals (see Whitehead, *Process and Reality*, 160–62).

29. Ibid., 34–35.

30. Here I presume that the objective unity proper to the society is reflected in the subjective unity of each of its constituent actual occasions rather than that the concrete unity of each of the constituent actual occasions is somehow reflected in the abstract unity of the society. At stake is the difference between a "concrete universal" in the Hegelian sense of the unity of an existential totality rather than the "abstract universal" to be found in formal logic. Whitehead would presumably defend his own position by arguing that unity presumes an antecedent process of unification and that "agency belongs exclusively to actual occasions" (ibid., 31). In the next chapter, I indicate how in terms of my scheme Whiteheadian societies (structured fields of activity) exercise agency of a different kind than what Whitehead had in mind.

31. Ibid., 99, 103.   32. Ibid., 100.

33. Ibid., 31.   34. Ibid., 34.

Chapter 9. Open-Ended Systems

1. Ervin Laszlo, *Introduction to Systems Philosophy: Toward a New Paradigm of Contemporary Thought* (London: Gordon and Breach, 1972), 30.

2. Ibid. Even "artificial" or humanly constructed systems, of course, have components that are themselves natural systems (e.g., wood or metal for a table or chair).

3. Alfred North Whitehead, *Process and Reality*, corrected ed., ed. David Ray Griffin and Donald W. Sherburne (New York: Free Press, 1978), 19–20.

4. Ibid., 18.

5. See Ervin Laszlo, *The Systems View of the World: The Natural Philosophy of the New Developments in the Sciences* (New York: Braziller, 1972), 30–33.

6. Whitehead, *Process and Reality*, 34.

7. Ibid., 99–100.

8. Ibid., 99.

9. See here John B. Cobb Jr., "Ecology, Science, and Religion: Toward a Postmodern Worldview," in *The Reenchantment of Science: Postmodern Proposals*, ed. David Ray Griffin (Albany: State University of New York Press, 1988), 107–8. Cobb argues that molecules are "ecosystems." But how does that correspond to Whitehead's description of an inanimate "structured society"? See also David Ray Griffin, "Of Minds and Molecules: Postmodern Medicine in a Psychosomatic Universe," in *Reenchantment of Science*, 158. Griffin claims that atoms and molecules are themselves subjects of experience rather than composites of lower-order subjects of experience with a "common element of form." So there seems to be no agreement between them about the ontological unity of an inanimate "structured society."

10. Whitehead, *Process and Reality*, 31.

11. Ibid., 214.

12. Ervin Laszlo, *The Connectivity Hypothesis: Foundations of an Integral Science of Quantum, Cosmos, Life, and Consciousness* (Albany: State University of New York Press, 2003), 40–48.

13. Ibid., 41.

14. Joseph A. Bracken, "The Field-Metaphor in Ervin Laszlo's Philosophy and in Neo-Whiteheadian Metaphysics," *Process Studies* 33 (2004): 303–13.

15. Ibid., 305; see also Laszlo, *Connectivity Hypothesis*, 1–2.

16. Stuart Kauffman, *At Home in the Universe: The Search for the Laws of*

Self-Organization and Complexity (New York: Oxford University Press, 1995), vii. In their comprehensive review of the history of Darwinism, David Depew and Bruce Weber conclude that Kauffman with his theory of self-organizing systems stands midway between two rival research traditions in evolutionary biology, namely, developmentalism and standard Darwinism. Developmentalism emphasizes the inner-driven activity of the organism; standard Darwinism, its relatively passive adaptation to changes in the external environment (see David J. Depew and Bruce H. Weber, *Darwinism Evolving: Systems Dynamics and the Genealogy of Natural Selection* [Cambridge, MA: Massachusetts Institute of Technology Press, 1995], 429–30). But for the same reason they argue that Kauffman's approach might well be the way in which Darwinism itself will evolve to explain more complex patterns of adaptation and change in Nature.

17. Kauffman, *At Home in the Universe*, 8.

18. Stuart Kauffman, *Investigations* (New York: Oxford University Press, 2000).

19. Kauffman, *At Home in the Universe*, 47. As others have noted and as Kauffman himself concedes, he has developed this theory for the emergence of life from the self-organization of molecular components not from observation and experimentation in Nature but from Boolean networks and other mathematical models with computer-generated results (see, e.g., Depew and Weber, *Darwinism Evolving*, 431–33; Kauffman, *At Home in the Universe*, 75–86, 99–111). But at this exploratory stage of investigation into the laws of self-organization in Nature, his theories have generated considerable attention and interest among colleagues not only in molecular biology but in other areas of research (e.g., economics and politics) as well.

20. Whitehead, *Process and Reality*, 34.

21. Kauffman, *Investigations,* 3–4, 8, 29, 68–73, 105, 120, 128–29 et al.

22. Whitehead, *Process and Reality*, 103.

23. Ibid., 100.

24. Ibid., 35.

25. Ibid., 18.

26. Kauffman, *At Home in the Universe*, 26. See also Kauffman, *Investigations*, 22: "Communities of agents will coevolve to an 'edge of chaos' between overrigid and overfluid behavior. . . . Moreover, autonomous agents forever push their way into novelty—molecular, morphological, behavioral, organizational." Some of these experiments in novel self-organization work and others fail. Here is where Darwin's theory of natural selection comes into play in the gradual buildup of complexity within Nature.

27. Kauffman, *At Home in the Universe*, 29.

28. Whitehead, *Process and Reality*, 187.

29. Ibid., 103.

30. Kauffman, *At Home in the Universe*, 205; *Investigations*, 240–41: "Laws for any biosphere extend, presumably, to laws for any economy. Nor should that be surprising. The economy is based on advantages of trade. But those advantages accrue no more to humans exchanging apples and oranges than to root nodules and fungi exchanging sugar and fixed nitrogen that both make enhanced livings. Thus, economics must partake of the vast creativity of the universe." See also Rocco Gangle, "Collective Self-Organization in General Biology: Gilles Deleuze, Charles S. Pierce, and Stuart Kauffman," *Zygon* 42 (2007), 238: "Just as the rediscovery of Aristotelian philosophy in late twelfth and early thirteenth-century Europe led to the later reformulation of theological concepts of nature and creation in such thinkers as Thomas Aquinas, the scientific research of Kauffman and others working in a similar vein in various fields today presents a challenge and opportunity to rethink creation and nature for the future."

31. Kauffman, *At Home in the Universe*, 247–71.

32. Ibid., 253.

33. Whitehead, *Process and Reality*, 34 (emphasis added).

34. Kauffman, *At Home in the Universe*, 262. See also *Investigations*, 73–79.

35. Kauffman, *At Home in the Universe*, 267.

36. Ibid., 267–78.

37. Whitehead, *Process and Reality*, 41.

38. Kauffman, *At Home in the Universe*, 188. See also 8: "Laws of complexity spontaneously generate much of the order of the natural world. It is only then that selection comes into play."

39. Alfred North Whitehead, *Science and the Modern World* (New York: Free Press, 1967), 55, 75–94.

40. Whitehead, *Process and Reality*, 18.

41. Alfred North Whitehead, *Modes of Thought* (New York: Free Press, 1968), 127–69.

42. Kauffman, *At Home in the Universe*, 185. See also *Investigations*, 104: "While we have, it seems, adequate concepts of matter, energy, entropy, and information, we lack a coherent concept of organization, its emergence, and self-constructing propagation and self-elaboration."

Chapter 10. Parts and Wholes in Contemporary Natural Science

1. Paul Davies, *The Cosmic Blueprint: New Discoveries in Nature's Creative Ability to Order the Universe* (Philadelphia: Templeton Foundation Press, 2004), 12.

2. Ibid., 105–6.

3. See above, chap. 9 of this book; likewise cf. Philip Clayton, *Mind and Emergence: From Quantum to Consciousness* (New York: Oxford University Press, 2004), vi: "Emergence is the view that new and unpredictable phenomena are naturally produced by interactions in nature; that these new structures, organisms, and ideas are not reducible to the subsystems on which they depend; and that the newly evolved realities in turn exercise a causal influence on the parts out of which they arose."

4. Davies, *Cosmic Blueprint*, 8.

5. Cf. Ilya Prigogine and Isabelle Stengers, *Order Out of Chaos: Man's New Dialogue with Nature* (New York: Bantam Books, 1984), 131–209.

6. Davies, *Cosmic Blueprint*, 104–5.

7. See Rupert Sheldrake, *A New Science of Life: The Hypothesis of Formative Causation* (Los Angeles: J. P. Tarcher, 1981), esp. 33–54.

8. Davies, *Cosmic Blueprint*, 106.

9. Alfred North Whitehead, *Process and Reality*, corrected ed., ed. David Ray Griffin and Donald W. Sherburne (New York: Free Press, 1978), 214–15.

10. Ibid., 34–35. I am, of course, moving beyond Whitehead's own definition of a society in *Process and Reality* with the claim that a society is an ontological reality in its own right and not simply a collection of similarly constituted actual occasions. This has been the work of preceding chapters in this book.

11. The implicit reference here is to the use of these terms in another context by Hegel in *The Phenomenology of Mind*. See above, chap. 5, where I emphasize how for Hegel truth is to be found in the whole as a system of interconnected partial truths rather than in any single one of those partial truths. The whole is thereby the concrete universal; each of its partial truths is an abstract universal.

12. Whitehead, *Process and Reality*, 34 (emphasis added).

13. Davies, *Cosmic Blueprint*, 103.

14. Ibid., 164.

15. Sheldrake, *New Science of Life*, 77.

16. Ibid., 199–208.

17. For a brief overview of the history of the conflict between physical reductionism and vitalism, see Philip Clayton, *Mind and Emergence: From Quantum to Consciousness* (New York: Oxford University Press, 2004), 1–37.

18. Ibid., 60–62. See also Arthur Peacocke, *All That Is: A Naturalistic Faith for the Twenty-First Century*, ed. Philip Clayton (Minneapolis: Fortress, 2007), 12–16. Peacocke also endorses the idea of emergent monism. My objection to the use of this term is that it concedes too much to those natural scientists with

a materialistic mind-set who question the reality of spirit altogether. Furthermore, when Clayton and Peacocke then claim the reality of spiritual agency at the human level, they remain open to the charge that they are no longer emergent monists but covert dualists. In my judgment, their materialistic opponents have the better argument. Either spirit in some form is present in matter from the beginning or it is not there at all.

19. Clayton, *Mind and Emergence*, 128–29.

20. Whitehead, *Process and Reality*, 28.

21. Ibid., 41.

22. Ibid., 29.

23. Clayton, *Mind and Emergence*, 130.

24. Ervin Laszlo, *The Connectivity Hypothesis: Foundations of an Integral Science of Quantum, Cosmos, Life and Consciousness* (Albany, NY: State University of New York Press, 2003), 41. See also above, chap. 9.

25. This is the term used by David Griffin and other Whiteheadians to describe Whitehead's understanding of reality (see, e.g. David Ray Griffin, *Two Great Truths: A New Synthesis of Scientific Naturalism and Christian Faith* [Louisville, KY: Westminster John Knox Press, 2004], 78–82).

26. Whitehead, *Process and Reality*, 21.

27. Clayton, *Mind and Emergence,* 175. In this context, Clayton concedes that "the resources of scientific naturalism are inadequate to conceptualize agents" (175).

28. Ibid., 195.

29. Ibid, 20–22; see also my article "Emergent Monism and Final Causality; A Field-Oriented Approach" in *Tradition and Discovery* 31, no. 2 (2004–5): 18–26, where I defend Polanyi's espousal of morphogenetic fields against the counterarguments of Clayton and other students of Polanyi's thought.

30. Davies, *Cosmic Blueprint*, 166.

31. Ibid., 166–67.

32. Ibid., 168.

33. I have found quite valuable information on these topics in Roland Omnes, *Understanding Quantum Mechanics* (Princeton, NJ: Princeton University Press, 1999), esp. 196–266.

34. See Lewis Ford, "Inclusive Occasions," in *Process in Context: Post-Whiteheadian Perspectives*, ed. Ernst Wolf-Gazo (Bern/ Frankfurt: Peter Lang, 1988), 107–36; David Ray Griffin, "Of Minds and Molecules: Postmodern Medicine in a Psychosomatic Universe," in *The Reenchantment of Science: Postmodern Proposals*, ed. David Ray Griffin (Albany: State University of New York Press, 1988), 158.

35. See Harold Morowitz, *The Emergence of Everything: How the World Became Complex* (New York: Oxford University Press, 2002), for a detailed account of the different kinds of emergence within Nature.

36. Some years ago the celebrated German theologian Wolfhart Pannenberg proposed that the underlying nature of the triune God is a "force-field" that is shared equally by the three divine persons and which likewise serves as the field of activity for the Holy Spirit's work in the world of creation (see Pannenberg, *Systematic Theology*, vol. 1, trans. Geoffrey W. Bromiley [Grand Rapids, MI: Eerdmans, 1991], 382–84; *Systematic Theology*, vol. 2, trans. Geoffrey W. Bromiley [Grand Rapids, MI: Eerdmans, 1994], 79–84). His use of the term "force-field" in this context was sharply criticized by John Polkinghorne and other scientist/theologians as an inappropriate transfer of terms from philosophy/theology to theoretical physics (see John Polkinghorne, *Belief in God: Issues in an Age of Science* [New Haven, CT: Yale University Press, 1998], 82). In defense of Pannenberg's hypothesis, one could argue that he intended the notion of field as a strictly analogical rather than as a univocal concept (somewhat akin to the category of "substance" in classical metaphysics). In any case, as I have already made clear in chap. 9, this has certainly been my own intention in using the term "field" in the present book. As an analogical term always requiring further specification in its various applications, "field" is for me an objective ontological unity emergent out of the ongoing interplay of interrelated parts or members. Applied to the context of theoretical physics, it would refer to the immediate environment for a set of interrelated micro-events (actual occasions). As a necessary conditioning factor in their occurrence, it here and now helps to shape the individual self-constitution of those events even as they in turn by their dynamic interrelation shape the pattern or structure which it will then transmit to the next set of closely related events (actual occasions) within the same overall process.

Chapter 11. Time and Eternity in Religion and Science

1. Russell Stannard, "God in and beyond Space and Time," in *In Whom We Live and Move and Have Our Being*, ed. Philip Clayton and Arthur Peacocke (Grand Rapids: MI: Eerdmans, 2004), 113. See also Stannard, *Science and the Renewal of Belief* (Philadelphia: Templeton Foundation Press, 2004), 143–60.

2. Stannard, "God in and beyond Space and Time," 111.

3. See here Carl S. Helrich, "Is There a Basis for Teleology in Physics," *Zygon* 42 (2007): 97–100. Measurement is, so to speak, the gold standard in physics. What cannot be measured and thus mathematically calculated must be left to philosophy and theology.

4. Stannard, "God in and beyond Space and Time," 111–12.

5. Alfred North Whitehead, *Process and Reality*, corrected ed., ed. David Ray Griffin and Donald W. Sherburne (New York: Free Press, 1978), 73.

6. I have developed this hypothesis in a series of books and article, notably *Society and Spirit: A Trinitarian Cosmology* (Cranbury, NJ: Associated University Presses, 1991), 123–39; *The Divine Matrix: Creativity as Link between East and West* (Maryknoll, NY: Orbis, 1995), 62–65; and *The One in the Many: A Contemporary Reconstruction of the God-World Relationship* (Grand Rapids, MI: Eerdmans, 2001), 109–30.

7. See here Alan Padgett, *God, Eternity, and the Nature of Time* (New York: St. Martin's Press, 2001), 130; see also Padgett, "Eternity and Relative Timelessness," in *God and Time: Four Views*, ed. Gregory E. Ganssle (Downers Grove, IL: InterVarsity Press, 2001), 92–110.

8. See Bracken, *Society and Spirit*, 140–60; *Divine Matrix*, 63–66; *One in the Many*, 131–55.

9. Padgett, *God, Eternity, and the Nature of Time*, 122–26.

10. Ibid., 96–97. The distinction between an "A-series" and a "B-series" approach to time was originally made by John McTaggert in an article entitled "The Unreality of Time," which appeared in the journal *Mind* 17 (1908): 456–73. McTaggert also introduced a "C-series" to the discussion of time which corresponds more closely to what I mean here by a "B-series," namely, "before" and "after" as opposed to "earlier" and "later." Yet a "B-series" for me is unidirectional and thus temporally ordered whereas a "C-series" for McTaggert is bidirectional or strictly timeless.

11. Robert Cummings Neville, *Eternity and Time's Flow* (Albany: State University of New York Press, 1993), 95–120.

12. Ibid., 111.

13. Ibid., 112.

14. Whitehead, *Process and Reality*, 24: "Any condition to be satisfied by one actual entity in its process expresses a fact either about the 'real internal constitutions' of some other actual entities, or about the 'subjective aim' conditioning that process." In other words, an actual entity in its process of concrescence must take account of past actual entities and look to the future in terms of its potential impact on subsequent actual entities through its "subjective aim" here and now.

15. Ibid., 346.

16. Ibid., 348: "God and the World are the contrasted opposites in terms of which Creativity [the principle of becoming within the cosmic process] achieves its supreme task of transforming disjoined multiplicity, with its diver-

sities in opposition, into concrescent unity, with its diversities in contrast." Hence, in Whitehead's metaphysical scheme God and the world codevelop within one and the same temporal process. There is, accordingly, no way for God to transcend the cosmic process so to "prehend" a future event in the world before it actually happens.

17. See here Brian Leftow, *Time and Eternity* (Ithaca, NY: Cornell University Press, 1991), 17–45. Leftow defends a theory of God as absolutely timeless on the grounds of divine immutability and simplicity, but he uses the model of divine and temporal frames of reference in somewhat the same way that I do here. That is, he argues that the temporal order exists in its entirety within God and is sustained therein by God rather than that God somehow exists here and now within the temporal order so as to deal with creaturely events as they happen.

18. Wolfhart Pannenberg, *Systematic Theology*, vol. 1, trans. Geoffrey W. Bromiley (Grand Rapids, MI: Eerdmans, 1991), 401–10; *Systematic Theology*, vol. 3, trans. Geoffrey W. Bromiley (Grand Rapids, MI: Eerdmans, 1998), 595–607.

19. Ibid., 3:586–607, esp. 601.

20. See here Pannenberg, *Systematic Theology*, 1:410–22. Pannenberg's thought on this issue is ambiguous to me. His linkage of the divine attributes of omnipresence and omnipotence might well imply that what God knows God wills and vice versa, so that God unilaterally makes things happen in this world. But in the same discussion he aligns himself with Karl Barth in the claim that divine omnipotence is the power of divine love, namely, that which empowers rather than overpowers the spontaneity/freedom of the creature (ibid., 419, 422).

21. Bracken, *Christianity and Process Thought: Spirituality for a Changing World* (Philadelphia: Templeton Foundation Press, 2006), 83–85.

22. Whitehead, *Process and Reality*, 244.

23. Cf. on this point W. Norris Clarke, *The One and the Many: A Contemporary Thomistic* Metaphysics (Notre Dame, IN: University of Notre Dame Press, 2001), 215–26.

24. Pannenberg, *Systematic Theology*, 3:586–607.

Chapter 12. Conclusions

1. David J. Depew and Bruce H. Weber, *Darwinism Evolving: Systems Dynamics and the Genealogy of Natural Selection* (Cambridge, MA: Massachusetts Institute of Technology Press, 1995), 479–95.

2. Stuart Kauffman, *At Home in the Universe: The Search for the Laws of Self-Organization and Complexity* (New York: Oxford University Press, 1995), 185.

3. Cf. here Bracken, *Christianity and Process Thought: Spirituality for a Changing World* (Philadelphia: Templeton Foundation Press, 2006), 81–82: "Presumably for the three divine persons, eternity is also the togetherness of past, present, and future. But their past necessarily overlaps the past for each of us as individuals, the past of all other human beings, even the past of the entire universe from the Big Bang onwards. The past of the divine persons is the past history of the divine life, which may have included still other universes that in the meantime have come and gone. By the same token, the present for the three divine persons includes not only all the events taking place in our universe but also events possibly taking place in other universes existing simultaneously with ours but with which we have as yet no contact. Finally, the future for the divine persons extends well beyond the time that our universe, at least in its present form, will cease to exist."

4. See here Arthur Peacocke, *All That Is: A Naturalistic Faith for the Twenty-First Century*, ed. Philip Clayton (Minneapolis: Fortress, 2007), 11: "The idea of emergence is becoming central to our understanding of the dynamics and evolution of the natural world, including human beings." This statement is notable in view of the fact that Peacocke, a longtime participant in the religion and science dialogue, wrote these words in the final months of his life while consciously trying to sum up his personal worldview.

INDEX